Lecture Notes in Business Information Processing

524

Series Editors

Wil van der Aalst , *RWTH Aachen University, Aachen, Germany*
Sudha Ram , *University of Arizona, Tucson, AZ, USA*
Michael Rosemann , *Queensland University of Technology, Brisbane, QLD, Australia*
Clemens Szyperski, *Microsoft Research, Redmond, WA, USA*
Giancarlo Guizzardi , *University of Twente, Enschede, The Netherlands*

W0230405

LNBIP reports state-of-the-art results in areas related to business information systems and industrial application software development – timely, at a high level, and in both printed and electronic form.

The type of material published includes

- Proceedings (published in time for the respective event)
- Postproceedings (consisting of thoroughly revised and/or extended final papers)
- Other edited monographs (such as, for example, project reports or invited volumes)
- Tutorials (coherently integrated collections of lectures given at advanced courses, seminars, schools, etc.)
- Award-winning or exceptional theses

LNBIP is abstracted/indexed in DBLP, EI and Scopus. LNBIP volumes are also submitted for the inclusion in ISI Proceedings.

Lodovica Marchesi · Alfredo Goldman ·
Maria Ilaria Lunesu · Adam Przybyłek ·
Ademar Aguiar · Lorraine Morgan ·
Xiaofeng Wang · Andrea Pinna
Editors

Agile Processes in Software Engineering and Extreme Programming – Workshops

XP 2024 Workshops
Bozen-Bolzano, Italy, June 4–7, 2024
Revised Selected Papers

 Springer

Editors

Lodovica Marchesi
University of Cagliari
Cagliari, Italy

Maria Ilaria Lunesu
University of Cagliari
Cagliari, Italy

Ademar Aguiar
University of Porto
Porto, Portugal

Xiaofeng Wang
Free University of Bozen-Bolzano
Bozen-Bolzano, Italy

Alfredo Goldman
Universidade de São Paulo
São Paulo, Brazil

Adam Przybyłek
Gdańsk University of Technology
Gdansk, Poland

Lorraine Morgan
University of Galway
Galway, Ireland

Andrea Pinna
University of Cagliari
Cagliari, Italy

ISSN 1865-1348   ISSN 1865-1356 (electronic)
Lecture Notes in Business Information Processing
ISBN 978-3-031-72780-1   ISBN 978-3-031-72781-8 (eBook)
https://doi.org/10.1007/978-3-031-72781-8

This Springer imprint is published by the registered company Springer Nature Switzerland AG
The registered company address is: Gewerbestrasse 11, 6330 Cham, Switzerland

If disposing of this product, please recycle the paper.

Preface

It is with great pleasure that we introduce this volume of papers from the research workshops, the posters track, the education track, and the PhD Symposium track of XP 2024, the 24th International Conference on Agile Software Development, held on June 4–7, 2024 at the Free University of Bolzano, Italy.

The XP conference is the premier Agile software development conference combining both research and practice. This year we celebrated 25 years of XP with the theme "Reflect, Adapt, Envision," prompting the Agile community to pause, reflect on the progress made, and envision future directions for both research and practice in the field. It is a unique forum where Agile researchers, practitioners, thought leaders, coaches, and trainers get together to present and discuss their most recent innovations and research results.

Research papers from the XP 2024 conference were published in the first conference proceedings, LNBIP volume 512. This companion volume, published after the conference, contains selected revised papers from the workshop, poster, and PhD symposium tracks that took place during the conference event. XP 2024 hosted the following tracks:

- International Workshop on Advances in Software Intensive Startups
- Workshop on AI for Agile Software Engineering (AI4ASE)
- 2nd International Workshop on Global and Hybrid Work in Software Engineering (GoHyb)
- 11th International Workshop on Large-Scale Agile Development
- Workshop on the AI Scrum Master: Incorporating AI Into Your Agile Practices and Processes
- Agile Training and Education Track
- PhD Symposium Track
- Posters Track

The number of submitted research papers to these tracks was 58, out of which 29 were accepted for publication in these post-proceedings. The review cycles used single-blind reviews in EasyChair.

In addition to the workshop papers, these post-conference proceedings include a summary of the 25th Anniversary Track workshop and panel discussion.

We would like to extend our sincere thanks to all the people who contributed to XP 2024: the authors, reviewers, chairs, and volunteers. Finally, we would like to express our gratitude to the XP Conference Steering Committee and the Agile Alliance for their ongoing support.

July 2024

Lodovica Marchesi
Alfredo Goldman
Maria Ilaria Lunesu
Adam Przybyłek
Ademar Aguiar
Lorraine Morgan
Xiaofeng Wang
Andrea Pinna

Organization

Conference Co-chairs

Xiaofeng Wang	Free University of Bozen-Bolzano, Italy
Michele Marchesi	University of Cagliari, Italy

Workshops Program Co-chairs

Lodovica Marchesi	University of Cagliari, Italy
Alfredo Goldman	Universidade de São Paulo, Brazil

PhD Symposium Track Co-chairs

Lorraine Morgan	University of Galway, Ireland
Ademar Aguiar	University of Porto, Portugal

Posters Track Co-chairs

Maria Ilaria Lunesu	University of Cagliari, Italy
Adam Przybyłek	Gdańsk University of Technology, Poland

Agile Training and Education Track Co-chairs

Martin Kropp	University of Applied Sciences and Arts Northwestern Switzerland, Switzerland
Maarit Laanti	WikiAgile, Finland

Publication Co-chairs

Andrea Pinna	University of Cagliari, Italy
Peggy Gregory	University of Glasgow, Scotland

Workshops Organizers

Advances in Software Intensive Startups (AiSIS)

Henry Edison   Blekinge Institute of Technology, Sweden
Nirnaya Tripathi   University of Oulu, Finland

AI for Agile Software Engineering (AI4ASE)

Astri Barbala   SINTEF, Norway
Viktoria Stray   University of Oslo, Norway
Geir Kjetil Hanssen   SINTEF, Norway
Klaas-Jan Stol   Lero, University College Cork, Ireland

The Second International Workshop on Global and Hybrid Work in Software Engineering (GoHyb)

Maria Paasivaara   LUT University, Finland & Aalto University,
                                    Finland
Dron Khanna   Free University of Bozen-Bolzano, Italy

11th International Workshop on Large-Scale Agile Development

Julian Bass   University of Salford, UK
Gloria Iyawa   University of Salford, UK

The AI Scrum Master: Incorporating AI Into Your Agile Practices and Processes

Zorina Alliata   Georgetown University, USA
Lyuba Berzin   Private Sector Group, USA

Program Committee

Abdallah Salemeh   University of Salford, UK
Aleksander Jarzębowicz   Gdańsk University of Technology, Poland
Alena Buchalcevova   Prague University of Economics and Business,
                                    Czechia
Alexander Poth   Volkswagen AG, Germany
Alfredo Goldman   University of São Paolo, Brazil
Anh Nguyen Duc   University College of Southeast Norway, Norway

Arlinta Barus	Del Institute of Technology, Indonesia
Arne Noyer	Ostfalia University of Applied Sciences, Germany
Aurora Vizcaíno	University of Castilla-La Mancha, Spain
Bartosz Marcinkowski	University of Gdańsk, Poland
Beatriz Cabrero-Daniel	University of Gothenburg, Sweden
Carla Silva Rocha Aguiar	University of Brasília, Brazil
Casper Lassenius	Aalto University, Finland
Christof Ebert	Vector Consulting, Germany
Darja Smite	Blekinge Institute of Technology, Sweden
David Redmiles	University of California, Irvine, USA
Dron Khanna	Free University of Bozen-Bolzano, Italy
Elizabeth Bjarnason	Lund University, Sweden
Eric Knauss	Gothenburg University, Sweden
Fernando de Sá	Instituto Tecnológico de Aeronáutica, Brazil
Filippo Lanubile	University of Bari, Italy
George Moschoglou	Georgetown University, USA
Gloria Iyawa	University of Salford, UK
Hannes Salin	Swedish Transport Administration, Sweden
Helena Holmströom Olsson	Malmö University, Sweden
Hina Saeeda	Karlstad University, Sweden
Iflaah Salman	LUT University, Finland
Igor Steinmacher	North Arizona University, USA
Jakub Miler	Gdańsk University of Technology, Poland
Jan Pries-Heje	Roskilde University, Denmark
John Noll	University of Hertfordshire, UK
Jorge Melegati	Free University of Bozen-Bolzano
Joseph Puthenpurackal Chakko	Wells Fargo, India
Jutta Eckstein	IT Communication, Germany
Karen Eilers	Institute for Transformation, Germany
Krzysztof Marek	Warsaw University of Technology, Poland
Leigh Griffin	Red Hat, Ireland
Maarit Laanti	WikiAgile, Finland
Maduka Uwadi	University of Central Lancashire, UK
Maha Youssef	Open Institute of Technology, Germany
Mahum Adil	Free University of Bozen-Bolzano, Italy
Mani V. S.	Siemens Healthcare Pvt. Ltd., India
Manuel Mazzara	Innopolis University, Russia
Maryse Meinen	Practical agile, Netherlands
Michael Neumann	Hochschule Hannover, Germany
Michał Przybyłek	Warsaw University, Poland
Mohammad Alshayeb	King Fahd University of Petroleum & Minerals, Saudi Arabia

Morten Elvang	Accenture, Denmark
Muhammad Ovais Ahmad	Karlstad University, Sweden
Muhammad Usman	Blekinge Institute of Technology
Necmettin Özkan	Gebze Technical University, Turkey
Nils Brede Moe	SINTEF, Norway
Ömer Uludağ	TUM, Germany
Özden Özcan Top	Middle East Technical University, Turkey
Paolo Tell	IT University of Copenhagen, Denmark
Pedro Filipe Soares	University Institute of Lisbon, Portugal
Pertti Seppänen	University of Oulu, Finland
Piotr Trojanowski	Resonate, Poland
Ramesh Lal	Auckland University of Technology, New Zealand
Ricardo Britto	Ericsson/BTH, Sweden
Richard Berntsson Svensson	University of Gothenburg, Sweden
Scarlet Rahy	University of Salford, UK
Sergio Rico	Mid Sweden University, Sweden
Tomas Gustavsson	Karlstads Universitet, Sweden
Tomas Herda	Austrian Post, Austria
Tony Clear	Auckland University of Technology, New Zealand
Torben Worm	University of Southern Denmark, Denmark
Viktoria Stray	University of Oslo, Norway
Włodzimierz Dąbrowski	Warsaw University of Technology, Poland
Woubshet Behutiye	University of Oulu, Finland
Yen Ying Ng	Nicolaus Copernicus University, Poland

Other Reviewers

Aakash Ahmad	Lancaster University Leipzig, Germany
Anastasia Griva	University of Galway, Ireland
Clare Dillon	University of Galway, Ireland
Eriks Klotins	Blekinge Institute of Technology, Sweden
Jingyue Li	Norwegian University of Science and Technology, Norway
Kai-Kristian Kemell	University of Helsinki, Finland
Kari Systa	Tampere University of Technology, Finland
Kieran Conboy	University of Galway, Ireland
Malik Abdul Sami	Tampere University, Finland
Moritz Mock	Free University of Bozen-Bolzano, Italy
Muhammad Waseem	University of Jyväskyla, Finland
Ömer Uludag	TU München, Germany
Pekka Abrahamsson	Tampere University, Finland

Rasmus Ulfsnes   SINTEF, Norway
Shadab Mashuk   University of Salford, UK
Tor Sporsem   SINTEF Digital, Norway
Torgeir Dingsøyr   Norwegian University of Science and Technology,
                                  Norway
Viggo Tellefsen Wivestad   SINTEF, Norway
Zeeshan Rasheed   Tampere University, Finland
Zheying Zhang   Tampere University, Finland
Zorina Alliata   Georgetown University, USA

Steering Committee

Hubert Baumeister   Technical University of Denmark, Denmark
François Coallier   École de Technologie Supérieure, Canada
Jutta Eckstein   IT Communication, Germany
Hendrik Esser   Ericsson, Germany
Teresa Foster   Agile Alliance, USA
Juan Garbajosa   Universidad Politécnica de Madrid, Spain
Peggy Gregory (chair)   University of Glasgow, UK
Wouter Lagerweij   Lagerweij Consultancy, Netherlands
Maria Paasivaara   LUT University & Aalto University, Finland
Viktoria Stray   University of Oslo, Norway
Xiaofeng Wang   Free University of Bozen-Bolzano, Italy

Sponsoring Organization

Agile Alliance, USA   Teresa Foster

Contents

International Workshop on Advances in Software Intensive Startups

Exploring the Potential of Generative AI: Use Cases in Software Startups 3
Mario Simaremare, Triando, and Sergio Rico

AI for Agile Software Engineering

Autonomous Agents in Software Development: A Vision Paper 15
Zeeshan Rasheed, Muhammad Waseem, Malik Abdul Sami,
Kai-Kristian Kemell, Aakash Ahmad, Anh Nguyen Duc, Kari Systä,
and Pekka Abrahamsson

Generative AI for Test Driven Development: Preliminary Results 24
Moritz Mock, Jorge Melegati, and Barbara Russo

Responsible AI in Agile Software Engineering - An Industry Perspective 33
Rasmus Ulfsnes, Nils Brede Moe, Jostein Emmerhoff, Marcin Floryan,
Anastasia Griva, Jan Henrik Gundelsby, Astri Moksnes Barbala,
and Kieran Conboy

A Journey Through SPACE: Unpacking the Perceived Productivity
of GitHub Copilot 42
Viggo Tellefsen Wivestad and Rasmus Ulfsnes

**The 2nd International Workshop on Global and Hybrid Work in
Software Engineering (GoHyb)**

Analyzing the Impact of Constant Feedback on Hybrid Agile Team
Performance: Preliminary Results 53
Wardah Naeem Awan and Iflaah Salman

Dual Effects of Hybrid Working on Performance: More Work Hours
or More Work Time 63
Darja Smite, Anastasiia Tkalich, Nils Brede Moe,
Panagiota Chatzipetrou, Eriks Klotins, and Per Kristian Helland

Hybrid Meetings in Agile Software Development 71
Viktoria Stray, Nils Brede Moe, and Susanne Semsøy

The 11th International Workshop on Large-Scale Agile Development Information on Submission

Agile Approaches in Critical Infrastructures 83
  Geir Kjetil Hanssen and Martin Gilje Jaatun

Social Capital in Software Product Management: A Case Study From
a Large-Scale Agile Context 90
  Astri Barbala, Nils Brede Moe, and Marthe Berntzen

The AI Scrum Master: Incorporating AI Into Your Agile Practices and Processes

ChatGPT for Tailoring Software Documentation for Managers
and Developers 103
  Saimir Bala, Kristina Sahling, Jennifer Haase, and Jan Mendling

The AI Scrum Master: Using Large Language Models (LLMs) to Automate
Agile Project Management Tasks 110
  Zorina Alliata, Tanvi Singhal, and Andreea-Madalina Bozagiu

Copilot's Island of Joy: Balancing Individual Satisfaction with Team
Interaction in Agile Development 123
  Viggo Tellefsen Wivestad, Astri Barbala, and Viktoria Stray

Can ChatGPT Suggest Patterns? An Exploratory Study About Answers
Given by AI-Assisted Tools to Design Problems 130
  *João José Maranhão Junior, Filipe F. Correia,
  and Eduardo Martins Guerra*

Education Track

Towards Improving Behavior-Driven Development and Acceptance
Testing-Driven Development Teaching in a University Project Course 141
  Marina Filipovic and Fabian Gilson

Agile Software Engineering Capstone Courses: Exploring the Impact
of Gender 150
  Gyda Elisa Sæter, Camilla Kielland Lund, and Viktoria Stray

PhD Symposium Track

Towards Continuous Certification of Software Systems for Aerospace 161
  J. Eduardo Ferreira Ribeiro

Shared Leadership for Better Understanding Agile Teams 169
    Jakub Perlak

Design Framework for Software Startups Applying Remote Work 175
    Triando

Bridging Silos: Amplifying InnerSource Adoption Using an Activity
Theory Perspective 181
    Clare Dillon

Posters Track

Where Do Developers Admit their Security-Related Concerns? 189
    Moritz Mock, Thomas Forrer, and Barbara Russo

Digital Twin Adapted Agile Software Development Life Cycle 196
    Mariam Jaber, Abdallah Karakra, Ahmad Alsadeh, and Adel Taweel

Drawing Based Game for Teaching Scrum 203
    Krzysztof Marek and Kamila Martyniuk-Sienkiewicz

Selected Concepts of Leadership in Self-organizing Teams 209
    Jakub Perlak

Towards a Double-Edged Sword: Modelling the Impact in Agile Software
Development 216
    Michael Neumann and Philipp Diebold

An Agile Mindset in a VUCA-World 223
    Carolina Appel Bangshøj, Tanja Elina Havstorm, and Åsa Algulin

The Right Amount of Technical Debt in an Agile Context 229
    *Marcus Ciolkowski, Philipp Diebold, Andrea Janes,
    and Valentina Lenarduzzi*

Stories Vs. User Stories: A Terminological Clarification 236
    *Xavier Franch, Hans-Jörg Steffe, Stan Bühne, Lidia López,
    and Stefan Sturm*

LD@Taiga: An Embedded Learning Dashboard for Agile Project
Management in Student Teams 242
    Carles Farré, Lidia López, Marc Oriol, and Xavier Franch

XP 25th Anniversary Workshop and Panel Report

XP 25th Anniversary Workshop and Panel Report: Innovating Software
Solutions – Past, Present, and Future 251
  Steven D. Fraser and Dennis Mancl

Author Index 259

International Workshop on Advances in Software Intensive Startups

Exploring the Potential of Generative AI: Use Cases in Software Startups

Mario Simaremare[1,2(✉)] ⦿, Triando[3]⦿, and Sergio Rico[4]⦿

[1] Department of Software Engineering, Blekinge Institute of Technology, Karlskrona, Sweden
[2] Faculty of Informatics and Electrical Engineering, Institut Teknologi Del, Sitoluama, Indonesia
mario.simaremare@bth.se
[3] Faculty of Engineering, Free University of Bozen-Bolzano, Bolzano, Italy
[4] Mid Sweden University, Östersund, Sweden

Abstract. *Background and Related Work*: Software startups face unique challenges in product development, including limited resources, the need for rapid innovation, and the constant pressure to adapt to market changes. Generative Artificial Intelligence (GenAI) has recently gained significant attention, offering capabilities to assist creative processes, generate content, and enhance decision-making through data analysis. However, how GenAI can be integrated into agile product development processes in software startups remains an open question. *Objective*: This study aims to identify potential use cases for GenAI in software startups and explore how GenAI can support innovation, overcome development challenges, and integrate with agile practices to improve product quality and development speed. *Method*: We identified a list of GenAI use cases from existing systematic literature reviews and mapped them to engineering process areas in software startups. Following that, we conducted workshops with experts to validate our results. *Results*: The results provide a descriptive overview of GenAI's potential applications in software startup environments. Given the current state of the art, we identified areas that could benefit faster from integrating GenAI. *Conclusions*: The study delineates the prospective impact of GenAI on agile product development in software startups, showcasing areas of immediate applicability.

Keywords: software startups · product development · potential applications · generative ai

1 Introduction

Given their flexibility and agility, software startups have enormous potential to disrupt markets and innovate rapidly [5]. However, they face unique challenges in product development, including limited resources, the need for rapid innovation, and the constant pressure to adapt to market changes [7]. Agile methodologies are widely adopted in software startups to address these challenges, as

L. Marchesi et al. (Eds.): XP 2024 Workshops, LNBIP 524, pp. 3–11, 2025.
https://doi.org/10.1007/978-3-031-72781-8_1

they enable iterative development, continuous feedback, and quick adaptation to evolving requirements [9].

The ongoing revolution in generative artificial intelligence (GenAI) technologies may offer promising features for software startups to enhance their product development processes, accelerate innovation, and improve product quality [6]. As discussed by Tripathi et al. [9], choosing technologies to speed up product development is crucial for software startups.

GenAI refers to technologies that can create content of various forms based on a large-sized trained dataset [1]. These technologies have shown significant potential across various industries, including software development and product innovation [6]. Although the potential of GenAI in software startups is promising, existing research has yet to explore how GenAI can be integrated into engineering processes at startups. Consequently, We developed the following research question to guide us in conducting this study.

What are the potential use cases of GenAI to support software startups in their software engineering practices and challenges?

This study is our first effort to explore and use GenAI in software startups. Specifically, we aimed to identify potential use cases for GenAI capabilities in the product development in software startups. To achieve this goal, we first identified the type of GenAI technologies and their capabilities from the academic literature. Then, we mapped these capabilities with the engineering model for software startups. As a result, we identified use cases for potential uses of GenAI for software startups.

This paper's contributions include a list of potential use cases of GenAI mapped to the engineering process and avenues to continue research with GenAI in software startups. The remainder of this paper is organized as follows. The next section provides an overview of software startups, GenAI technologies, and their potential applications in software startups. Section 3 presents the research methodology used in this study. Section 4 presents the results of our research and the potential use cases for software startups. Section 5 discusses the implications of our findings. Finally, Sect. 6 concludes the paper and summarizes our key findings and avenues for future research.

2   Related Work

2.1   Software Startups

Software startups are newly established companies that develop innovative software products or services under challenging circumstances [10]. The primary goal of startup companies is to craft a scalable and sustainable business [8]. Studies report that software startups often partially adopt unorthodox software development practices during product development due to the influence of diverse factors, including entrepreneurial vision, market needs, and capital constraints [7,9]. This emphasizes the essential role of adaptable methodologies like Lean Startup and Agile, often present in software startups [7].

Klotin et al. [4] identify common goals, practices, and challenges across life-cycle and engineering process areas in the software startup context. The life-cycle consists of four stages: inception, stabilization, growth, and maturity. The inception stage focuses on forming a capable team and developing a minimum viable product (MVP). Stabilization involves refining the product based on customer feedback and preparing for scaling. Growth emphasizes achieving market share, while maturity focuses on optimizing operations and maintaining market position. The engineering areas include team, requirement engineering, value focus, quality goals and testing, architecture and design, and project management. The study outlines several key challenges and practices in software startups. Challenges include forming and managing a skilled team, particularly in the early stages, dealing with dynamic requirements, avoiding feature creep, and maintaining quality assurance while managing technical debt. To address these, startups adopt practices such as using external experts for specialized tasks, relying on iterative and agile development methodologies to adapt to rapid changes, and establishing continuous feedback loops with customers to validate requirements.

2.2 GenAI and Its Potential

GenAI represents a subfield of artificial intelligence focused on synthetic content generation [1]. It employs advanced generative models, large language models (LLMs), trained on vast text, graphics, audio, or video datasets [1]. These models analyze patterns and relationships within the datasets to synthesize novel responses to user prompts [6]. GenAI technologies hold significant promise across various industries, potentially fostering new ideas, automating tasks, enhancing creative exploration, streamlining processes in software engineering, and beyond [2]. These vast potentials of GenAI attract new ventures[1] and projects[2].

A comprehensive study groups more than 350 GenAI applications into 15 use categories, encompassing text, images, video, 3D, code and software, speech, AI understanding, business, gaming, music, biotech, brain, and others, showcasing the technology's versatility [3]. Zhang et al. categorize GenAI by the type of content it generates, such as text, images, video, 3D, and speech, while also exploring the technology's industrial applications [11].

3   Methodology

Our methodology leverages existing systematic literature reviews to explore the application of GenAI in software startups:

1. GenAI Use Cases: We referred to (two) existing systematic literature reviews: one by Zhang et al. [11], which covers various GenAI content generation tasks, and another by Zheng et al. [12], focusing on the application of LLMs in software engineering tasks. These reviews provide a representative snapshot of

---

[1] https://www.ycombinator.com/companies/industry/ai.
[2] https://github.com/filipecalegario/awesome-generative-ai.

advancements and applications in GenAI. We selected these two systematic literature reviews because they cover a broad range of GenAI use cases, offering a clear view of current trends and research focus areas. Given the field's rapid pace, we aim to capture its direction and key topics of interest.

2. Practices and Challenges in Software Startups: We referred to the progression model of software engineering in startups by Klotins et al. [4] to select specific goals, challenges, and practices across startup stages mapped into six engineering process areas.

3. Cross-Referencing and Synthesis: Independently, each author cross-referenced GenAI use cases (step 1) with the startup progression elements (step 2). We then converged to synthesize a collective analysis, addressing contradictions through discussion.

4. Expert Workshop for Validation: We presented our results to two senior researchers twice to validate our synthesis, followed by additional meetings to discuss and refine the analysis. The senior researchers are experts in software engineering in the software startup context.

4   Results

Below we present our results as the *Use cases* (☰), derived by mapping the elements of the progression model (⌁) [4] for software startups to the use cases identified in the literature reviews [11,12]. These results directly answer our research question by showing how the identified use cases align with the six elements of the deployed progression model [4], highlighting the practical applications of GrnAI in addressing software engineering challenges in startups.

⌁ **Team area** refers to forming and managing effective teams [4]. **Goals** include establishing a team with sufficient skills and expertise, recognizing the team as a catalyst for product development, and emphasizing characteristics like cohesion, coordination, leadership, and continuous learning for project success. **Challenges** involve team formation, management, expertise, leadership, coordination, and engineering skills shortages. **Practices** in this area include establishing a feedback loop with customers, documenting feature ideas, and determining the "good-enough" level of quality, all aimed at advancing through the startup life-cycle stages and addressing the difficulties in practicing software engineering.

☰ *Use cases*: In the team area, GenAI can support cross-team communication, such as automatic time zone tracking with multi-lingual translation, generating and managing communication artifacts (e.g., emails), visualizing data and ideas, creating presentations, transcribing, and summarizing discussions. Additionally, trained chatbots can support various engineering activities such as generating source code, developing relevant test cases, and fixing bugs. Moreover, GenAI can also help recruit new team members and communicate with external stakeholders in a personalized way.

⊦• Requirement engineering area focuses on eliciting, analyzing, validating, documenting, and scoping software requirements [4]. This area is crucial for identifying and validating relevant product ideas, which are essential startup activities. The primary **goal** of this area is to identify market opportunities, devise feasible solutions, and prioritize customer feedback to drive product development and innovation. **Challenges** include transitioning from inventing requirements to using customer input as the product matures, managing feature creep, and maintaining domain knowledge through documentation. **Practices** involve collecting input from potential customers early on to identify relevant requirements, analyzing the usefulness of features to customers to prevent feature creep, and documenting requirement ideas to facilitate knowledge sharing and avoid misunderstandings within the team.

⌸ *Use cases*: GenAI can play a role in the requirements engineering area, e.g., acting as a user with specific characteristics (data-driven persona) to generate requirements, refine ideas from various use cases, and identify key features. Furthermore, it can help the team capture, document, analyze, and synthesize immersive feedback given in any language from customers around the globe. A trained GenAI can guide the team to develop meaningful MVPs based on comprehensive feedback, relevant test cases, and documentation.

⊦• Value focus area consists of several **goals** that are related to maintaining a focus on value [4]. These include enhancing the external and customer-perceived value through better functionality and user experience, realizing the internal market potential to capture and expand market share, generating significant financial value through effective revenue management, and establishing internal differentiation value to set the product apart from competitors. There is no specific **challenge** in this area.

⌸ *Use cases*: GenAI can offer tools to enhance user experience and streamline development. By simulating user interactions, GenAI can perform preliminary quality checks, identifying potential issues and areas for improvement before a product reaches its final stages. This capability not only improves the user experience but also accelerates value delivery. Additionally, GenAI-driven chatbots can be instrumental in guiding decision-making processes related to technology selection. These chatbots analyze vast amounts of data and user inputs to tailor recommendations on the most suitable technologies and frameworks.

⊦• Quality goals and testing area consists of goals, challenges, and practices related to quality and testing [4]. The **goals** include ensuring the functionality of the product to meet specific needs, maintaining maintainability for easy updates and repairs, achieving a quick time-to-market to stay competitive, enhancing portability to function across different platforms, and determining a "good-enough" quality level that balances performance with cost-effectiveness. The **challenge** involves manual regression testing, which requires significant effort. **Practices** involve eliciting and validating quality requirements to align product specifications with user needs, conducting informal, manual, exploratory testing to uncover unforeseen issues, and establishing a robust QA process with clearly defined roles for testers.

⋮☰ *Use cases*: GenAI can offer valuable insights into optimal interaction pathways and support usability studies, which is essential for refining user interfaces. It also plays a role in generating test cases and test scenarios, enhancing test automation processes. Additionally, it can provide recommendations for defining the criteria necessary to achieve MVP quality, ensuring that the product meets essential requirements while remaining lean. Moreover, GenAI assists in collecting and analyzing performance metrics, suggesting improvements for software products, and offering code corrections to increase coding quality. Furthermore, chatbots powered by GenAI can be useful in guiding manual testing efforts, and their capabilities extend to automating these tests to reduce the manual work in test execution.

Architecture and design refers to the technical decisions and design choices that shape the product's structure and functionality [4]. Startups prioritize stable technologies over cutting-edge alternatives to minimize risks and accelerate product development. They often adopt open-source and well-established frameworks to avoid reinventing the wheel. **Challenges** are related to managing technical debt, especially as startups scale, with earlier architecture decisions leading to complications. For UI design, startups utilize mockups and design frameworks, continuously improving based on customer interaction data, aiming for usability and usefulness. **Practices** focus on using best practices and avoiding complex, untested solutions, with some mature startups innovating in-house to support product evolution.

⋮☰ *Use cases*: In addressing architecture and design challenges, task-oriented GenAI can help the startup select suitable frameworks and generate architecture diagrams to enhance the development process and stakeholder comprehension. Descriptive image generation enables the creation of user interface mockups directly from textual descriptions, streamlining the design phase. For technical debt mitigation, GenAI for code completion and automated test generation accelerates development and enhances quality and maintainability.

Project Management within software startups involves strategically planning and controlling resources to navigate from inception to maturity [4]. It is crucial for optimizing resource usage and achieving set milestones. **Challenges** include the lack of clear, measurable goals in the early stages and evolving needs for more sophisticated metrics for progress assessment. Resource constraints and the necessity for flexible adjustment to market demands further complicate project management. **Practices** evolve from an informal approach, often based on intuition, to more structured methods using planning and resource management tools as startups mature.

⋮☰ *Use cases*: In project management, GenAI technologies may play a role in enhancing strategic planning and resource control. Task-oriented chatbots support collecting and analyzing metrics, facilitating quick planning adjustments, and aiding in project management activities such as meetings and budgeting. Moreover, using GenAI can schedule resources, prioritize tasks, and predict future needs based on data analysis. These potential uses contribute to startups' transition from intuition-based methods to structured, data-informed strategies, streamlining the process from inception to maturity and addressing challenges and the need for flexible market adjustment.

5   Discussion

Our results show that GenAI can support software startups in various use cases during product development across life-cycle and engineering areas [4]. Most of GenAI's use cases are carried out through interactive conversational chatbots, which allow interaction using various forms of data [6]. Popular use cases include multi-lingual translation, code and test generation, access to expert and knowledge systems, and image generation. These capabilities enable more efficient development, better alignment with customer needs, and continuous process improvement.

However, not all GenAI use cases are equally relevant to software startups. For example, no suitable use cases for features like generating 3D talking characters, complex 3D models, and music generation. Moreover, there is no clear connection between GenAI features and the following product development goals: balancing customer value with time-to-market considerations, internal market potential value, financial value, and revenue generation. We believe these complex goals demand human judgment and domain expertise beyond the current capabilities of GenAI.

We identified various GenAI use cases broadly supporting general work-related tasks. These include capabilities such as summarizing information, generating content, and facilitating communication. We identified tailored use cases related to software tasks that directly contribute to product development, such as generating test cases and providing architectural recommendations. These applications demonstrate how GenAI can enhance efficiency and decision-making within software development processes. However, the overall impact and value of GenAI tools for software startups remain to be thoroughly evaluated. Future studies are necessary to determine how these technologies can best be integrated into the startup ecosystem and to what extent they can replace or augment existing processes.

6   Conclusion

Software startups have unique characteristics, goals, challenges, and engineering practices. On the other hand, the recent advancement of GenAI brings opportunities to help the software industry and beyond. This study aimed to identify potential use cases for GenAI technologies in software startups and explore how these technologies can support innovation and overcome development challenges to improve the product development process [9].

Our mapping shows use cases where GenAI can help software startup during product development spread in six engineering areas. However, several product development goals are not directly addressed using GenAI.

Future research directions will focus on validating our findings through empirical studies. We also aim to develop practical guidelines for startups on effectively integrating GenAI into their product development processes. This will involve simulating scenarios, experimenting with ideas, validating assumptions, etc.

Acknowledgements. This work has been supported by ELLIIT, the Swedish Strategic Research Area in IT and Mobile Communications.

References

1. Banh, L., Strobel, G.: Generative artificial intelligence. Electron. Markets **33**(1) (2023)
2. Cao, Y., et al.: A comprehensive survey of AI-generated content (AIGC): a history of generative AI from GAN to chatGPT. arXiv preprint arXiv:2303.04226 (2023)
3. Gozalo-Brizuela, R., Garrido-Merchán, E.C.: A survey of generative AI applications. arXiv preprint arXiv:2306.02781 (2023)
4. Klotins, E., et al.: A progression model of software engineering goals, challenges, and practices in start-ups. IEEE Trans. Software Eng. **47**(3), 498–521 (2019)
5. Nguyen-Duc, A., Kemell, K.K., Abrahamsson, P.: The entrepreneurial logic of startup software development: a study of 40 software startups. Empir. Softw. Eng. **26**, 1–55 (2021)
6. Ozkaya, I.: The next frontier in software development: Ai-augmented software development processes. IEEE Softw. **40**(4), 4–9 (2023)
7. Paternoster, N., Giardino, C., Unterkalmsteiner, M., Gorschek, T., Abrahamsson, P.: Software development in startup companies: a systematic mapping study. Inf. Softw. Technol. **56**(10), 1200–1218 (2014)
8. Ries, E.: Lean Startup: How Today's Entrepreneurs Use Continous Innovation to Create Radically Successful Businesses. Crown Business, New York (2011)
9. Tripathi, N., Oivo, M., Liukkunen, K., Markkula, J.: Startup ecosystem effect on minimum viable product development in software startups. Inf. Softw. Technol. **114**, 77–91 (2019)
10. Unterkalmsteiner, M., et al.: Software startups-A research agenda. E-Informatica Softw. Eng. J. **10**(1), 89–123 (2016)
11. Zhang, C., et al.: A complete survey on generative AI (AIGC): Is chatGPT from GPT-4 to GPT-5 all you need? arXiv preprint arXiv:2303.11717 (2023)
12. Zheng, Z., et al.: Towards an understanding of large language models in software engineering tasks. arXiv preprint arXiv:2308.11396 (2023)

AI for Agile Software Engineering

Autonomous Agents in Software Development: A Vision Paper

Zeeshan Rasheed[1], Muhammad Waseem[2(✉)], Malik Abdul Sami[3],
Kai-Kristian Kemell[4], Aakash Ahmad[5], Anh Nguyen Duc[1,2,3,4,5],
Kari Systä[1,2,3,4,5], and Pekka Abrahamsson[1,2,3,4,5]

[1] Tampere University, Tampere, Finland
{zeeshan.rasheed,kari.systa,pekka.abrahamsson}@tuni.fi,
Anh.Nguyen.duc@usn.no
[2] University of Jyväskylä, Jyväskylä, Finland
muhammad.m.waseem@jyu.fi
[3] University of Helsinki, Helsinki, Finland
[4] Lancaster University Leipzig, Leipzig, Germany
kai-kristian.kemell@helsinki.fi
[5] University of South Eastern Norway, Notodden, Norway

Abstract. Large Language Models (LLM) are reshaping the field of
Software Engineering (SE). They enable innovative methods for executing many SE tasks, including automation of entire process of Software Development Life Cycle (SDLC). However, only a limited number of existing works have thoroughly explored the potential of LLM based AI agents to automate the entire lifecycle in SE. In this paper, we demonstrate the success of our initial efforts in automating the entire lifecycle autonomously based on given software specification as input, which has shown remarkable efficiency and significantly reduced development time. Our preliminary results suggest that the careful implementation of AI agents can enhance the development lifecycle. We aim to streamline the SDLC by integrating all phases into an AI-driven chat interface, enhancing efficiency and transparency. Furthermore, we seek to enhance collaboration, creating an environment where stakeholders from various backgrounds can contribute, review, and refine ideas and requirements in real-time. This forward-looking direction guarantees to redefine the paradigms of SE and also make software creation more inclusive, collaborative, and efficient.

.

Keywords: OpenAI · AutoGPT · Artificial Intelligence · Natural Language Processing · Generative AI · Software Engineering · Large Language Model

M. Waseem, K.-K. Kemell, A. Ahmad, A. N. Duc, K. Systä and P. Abrahamsson— Contributing authors.

L. Marchesi et al. (Eds.): XP 2024 Workshops, LNBIP 524, pp. 15–23, 2025.
https://doi.org/10.1007/978-3-031-72781-8_2

1 Introduction

AI has reshaped our interaction with machines and impacted many industries. Its most promising use is in Natural Language Processing (NLP), which helps computers understand and interact with human language [1]. Recent advancements in NLP have led to the development of Large Language Models (LLMs) such as the GPT series [2,3]. The interaction between LLMs and the domain of Software Engineering (SE) has led to significant advancements and intriguing possibilities [4]. LLMs have shown their potential to streamline multiple facets of the Software Development Life Cycle (SDLC) [5]. These advanced language models have emerged as a formidable force, utilizing the power of AI to autonomously generate code, offer insights, and assist developers across various stages of the SDLC. However, challenges such as ensuring code correctness, maintenance, and bridging the gap between NLP and programming semantics remain critical considerations in this symbiotic relationship.

In this paper, we demonstrate the success of our initial work in automating the entire SDLC by utilizing AI agents based on LLMs. We utilized 12 AI agents collaboratively functioning to autonomously execute all stages of the SDLC, including project planning, requirements engineering, system design, development, testing, deployment, among others. To assess the capabilities of our proposed model, we implemented software specification of varying sizes as inputs. Initial results suggest that our model reduces the development time, allowing for project completion within five minutes, and also enhances accuracy by delivering precise outcomes. We aim to redefine the frameworks of SE, making software creation a more inclusive, collaborative, and efficient process. With this goal in mind, we plan to extend this work to revolutionize software development through AI-driven chat interfaces, transforming the entire creation lifecycle by integrating all phases of software development into an AI-driven chat interface. Our proposed model will also facilitate a collaborative environment where multiple stakeholders can contribute, review, and refine ideas and requirements in real-time. The AI chat-based environment will include a feedback loop where the system learns from each interaction, refining its support and providing code recommendations over time. Our contribution can be summarized as follow:

- Demonstrate successful automation of the whole process of SDLC with LLM-based AI agents, enhancing efficiency and reducing time.
- Our future goal is to proposed an AI-driven chat interface integrating all development phases to promote real-time stakeholder collaboration and continuous AI learning for improved code recommendations.
- We also aimed to redefine the frameworks of SE to make the process of software creation more inclusive, collaborative, and efficient.

2 Background

2.1 Generative AI

Generative AI refers to a category of AI models and algorithms that are designed to generate new content that is often similar to content created by humans [6].

This type of AI has experienced notable progress in recent times [7]. Nowadays, generative AI has been utilized in various fields, such as NLP, computer vision, and image and video generation [8]. In NLP, generative AI techniques are commonly used for various tasks, including text generation, machine translation, dialog systems, and code generation. LLM is a specific type of generative AI model that excels at generating human-like text due to its architecture, pre-training, and fine-tuning processes [2]. The foundation of the LLM can be traced back to the introduction of the transformer architecture proposed by Vaswani *et al..* [9]. This architectural innovation transformed the field of NLP by introducing the self-attention mechanism, enabling the model to capture contextual connections among words, irrespective of their position within a sequence. In 2018, OpenAI introduced the GPT-1 model to demonstrate the potential of LLMs for text generation tasks [2]. Several researchers and OpenAI have made significant contributions to improving the performance of GPT models by using a variety of techniques and approaches [2,3].

2.2   Large Language Models in SE

LLMs have shown promise in various SE applications [10,11]. LLMs generation capabilities offer valuable assistance and enhancements to SE processes [12–15]. By utilizing the remarkable natural language generation capabilities of GPT models, various SE tasks can now be automated and streamlined, including code generation, error detection, documentation creation, and beyond. Through GPT-powered code completion and generation, developers can swiftly produce high-quality code and even entire programs, significantly expediting the SDLC [16–19]. Several studies (e.g., [20–23]) has explored LLMs in SE. However, much of this research has been limited to case studies, with a focus on user perceptions in coding and writing. To fill this gap, our goal is to leverage multiple LLM based AI agents for autonomy generate the whole process of SDLC based on developer-provided software specification.

3   Research Methodology

In this study, we present an innovative approach to automating the entire SDLC by integrating multiple AI agents inspired by LLMs. This section outlines the methodology employed to design and implement our model. We have formulated the research question (RQ):

> **RQ.** *How do multi-AI agents collaborate with each other to automate the entire lifecycle of software development?*

The main objective of **RQ** is to determine how multiple AI agents work together to automate the entire lifecycle of software development. **RQ** primarily aims to determine the dynamics of how these agents interact, coordinate, and function collectively to automate tasks from requirement engineering to deployment.

3.1   AI Agent Approach for Automating the SDLC (RQ)

As shown in Fig. 1, we utilized 12 LLM-based AI agents that collaborate to achieve the final result. Each agent in the system is a specialized instance of an LLM, trained to handle different aspects of SDLC. Each agent specializing in a distinct aspect of the software development process, collectively contribute to improving efficiency and enhancing the SDLC. Below, we discuss in detail that how AI agents collaborate to autonomously carry out the SDLC.

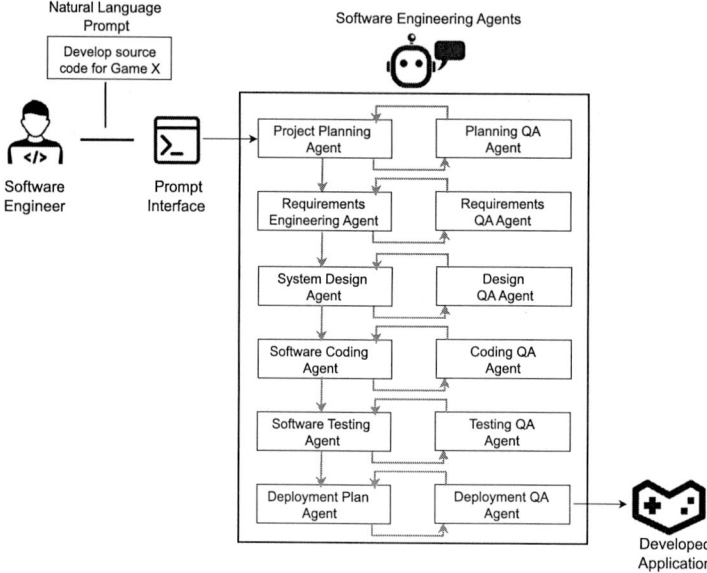

Fig. 1. A schematic representation of an automated software development process using autonomous agents

Agent-01 is crucial for project planning, starting with gathering software specifications and defining the project's scope, goals, and execution plan. Its main role includes outlining steps to achieve these objectives. Agent-2 complements this by evaluating the quality and feasibility of Agent-01's plans against the organization's goals, ensuring the project's plan is comprehensive, feasible, and aligned with overarching objectives, serving as a critical phase in the project lifecycle. Agent 3 moves to requirement engineering as the next phase, showing skill in identifying and understanding high-level requirements. This phase guarantees that all future stages of development are solidly based on a detailed understanding of the project's goals and constraints. Through this process, Agent 3 establishes a clear plan, which acts as the foundation for all upcoming project development efforts, closely matching the project's specified goals and the limits within which it must work. Collaborating with Agent-3, Agent-4's primary role is to assess the quality and precision of the project requirements. Early results show significant improvements in the quality and consistency of requirements documentation, highlighting Agent-4's essential contribution to defining clear requirements. This leads to smoother development phases and enhances the project's overall success and efficiency. Agent-5 is pivotal in converting high-level requirements into detailed system designs, accelerating the design phase and ensuring compliance with project specifications, laying a foundation for development with clear technical directions. Agent-6 enhances this by analyzing design quality and identifying system architecture flaws early, boosting efficiency by saving time and resources. Agent-07 streamlines software testing and defect detection through automation, facilitating continuous testing, speeding up development, and improving quality with less manual effort. Working in tandem, Agent-8 assesses the effectiveness of these automated tests, leading to better bug detection and resolution, underlining the importance of comprehensive testing in achieving high-quality software and efficient resource utilization. Agent-9 plays a important role in translating high-level design specifications into executable code. Early analysis of performance metrics suggests a significant reduction in development time. This efficiency accelerates the software development process and also ensures that the final product meets the expected performance and reliability criteria, showcasing the agent's pivotal role in streamlining software creation. Agent-10 is tasked with code quality analysis, focusing on ensuring that the generated code follows established coding standards and best practices. Initial findings highlight its success in promoting the development of clean, maintainable code. This reinforces the agent's role in enhancing software maintainability and reliability through rigorous quality assessments. Agent-11 is instrumental in managing the deployment phase of software projects, focusing on the systematic coordination and execution of steps essential for launching the software in a production environment or to its end-users. This phase is crucial for the seamless transition of software from development to actual use, ensuring that all components are correctly configured, integrated, and ready for operation in their intended settings. Agent-12's responsibility is to carefully review, assess, and refine the deployment plan formulated by Agent-11, aiming to guarantee a seamless and robust deployment process. This involves ensuring that the plan follows high standards of quality, anticipating potential challenges, and incorporating measures for a smooth transition to the production environment or end-user delivery.

4   Preliminary Empirical Results

In this section, we present preliminary results from our developed novel LLM based model. To evaluate capability of our model, we prompted 10 projects and as the outcome of the autonomous development process, the agents produced a requirements engineering specification, a software design plan, commented software code, a test and deployment plans. To offer a clear understanding of the model's outcome, we have provided Table 1 to show the results generated by our proposed model. However, below we only explain the outcomes of three projects due to page limitations.

Initially, the agents were prompted to "develop a snake game with GUI". As output the agents perform the whole SDLC process. The amount of documentation including review rounds is 6216 words. This is about 13 pages of single-spaced text. Requirements specification agent produced 7 Functional Requirements (FR), 7 Non-Functional Requirements (NFR) and 4 constraints. 11 were fully met, 2 partially, 4 not verified and 4 were not met. There was no restart-option, the code was not commented according to the standard PEP 257 and object-oriented programming principles were not implemented. The code did not include test-cases. The actual generated software code was 115 Lines of Code (LOC) and the whole project took less than 4 min to complete. Game required human debugging to make it run.

The second experiment was "Build a chat based application". The amount of documentation including review rounds is 7685 words. Requirements specification agent produced 9 FR and 9 NFR and 0 constraints. 14 were fully met and 4 were not met. The actual generated software code was 175 lines and the whole project took less than 7 min to complete.

Preliminary results highlight our multi-agent framework's potential to automate and optimize the software development process. Key focuses include scaling autonomous capabilities, defining limits, and extending this work to integrate all phases into an AI-driven chat interface for improved efficiency and transparency. Additionally, we aim to enhance collaboration by enabling stakeholders from diverse backgrounds to contribute and refine ideas in real time.

5   Future Work

Our future work aims to innovate the software development through AI-driven chat interfaces. This initiative aims to transform the SDLC, making it more inclusive, efficient, and collaborative through the innovative application. Our future goal is to utilize advanced AI functionalities to support deeper multi-user collaboration, enabling the AI to understand and adapt to the context of discussions. The result of this effort will be continuous integration of these AI capabilities with project management tools, transforming discussions into actionable items without manual intervention. For instance, when a team discusses a new feature, the AI would automatically prioritize this in the project's backlog, generate relevant user stories, and even suggest test cases based on the discussion's content. Moreover, to ensure that the AI remains effective over time and adapts to the evolving landscape of software development, we plan to incorporate a continuous learning mechanism. This system will refine the AI's recommendations and decision-making processes based on feedback and enable it to learn from the collective intelligence of its user base.

Accessibility will also be a key focus, with efforts aimed at making the collaborative workspace inclusive for global teams through real-time transcription and translation capabilities. This will break down language barriers and faster a more diverse and inclusive environment for software development. Finally, the implementation phase and iterative refinement of the AI system based on user

Table 1. Result produced by LLM based AI agent model

S.No	Input	Words	FR	NFR	Const.	LOC	Mins	Output
01	Develop a snake game with GUI	6216	7	7	4	115	4	Snake game with restart button
02	Build a chat based application	7685	9	9	0	175	7	Messaging chat based app
03	Create a tic-tac-toe game	5366	9	6	3	94	4	Tic tac toe game with GUI
04	Build a real-time weather app	6189	8	6	2	119	5	Real-time weater forecasting app
05	Create a fitness tracker app	4890	6	5	2	107	4	Real-time tracker app
06	Develop a virtual reality tour app	7112	7	9	5	189	9	Developed virtual app
07	Create a blog platform with user authentication	6788	7	9	3	149	6	Blog platform
08	Develop a personal finance tracker app	5312	6	3	2	134	5	Finanace app
09	Develop a short e-commerce website	5982	8	9	4	151	8	Small E-commerce Website
10	Create a recipe finder app	4112	5	4	2	133	4	Recipe search app

feedback and performance metrics will be critical. This approach will ensure that the system meets the initial goals and evolves in response to real-world use and feedback, Therefore Continuously enhancing the efficiency and innovation within software development processes.

6 Conclusions

This paper proposes to explore how LLM based AI agents can autonomously perform various SE tasks. Through initial experiments, we have shown some interesting results which may have significant consequences. We demonstrate that our method significantly reduces development time and advances code generation methodologies, reinforcing the potential of AI-driven practices in the SE domain. With this goal in mind, we aim to extend our work to study how far we can scale these methods and where do really need human developers to be involved in. Experimenting using our proposed framework, we can gain many insights on how AI technology can fundamentally change how software is developed. The various SE roles and activities are designed based on human nature, capabilities and limitations in knowledge, skills and communication. AI agents may not have these limits. Then a follow up question to ask is, do we still need the same activities and life cycles as we did in the past 50 to 60 years of software engineering?

Acknowledgment. We express our sincere gratitude to Business Finland for their generous support and funding of our project. Their commitment to fostering innovation and supporting research initiatives has been instrumental in the success of our work.

References

1. Chowdhary, K., Chowdhary, K.: Natural language processing. Fundam. Artif. Intell. 603–649 (2020)
2. Radford, A., Narasimhan, K., Salimans, T., Sutskever, I., et al.: Improving language understanding by generative pre-training (2018)
3. Radford, A., et al.: Language models are unsupervised multitask learners. OpenAI blog **1**(8), 9 (2019)
4. Rasheed, Z., Waseem, M., Systä, K., Abrahamsson, P.: Large language model evaluation via multi AI agents: preliminary results. In: ICLR 2024 Workshop on Large Language Model (LLM) Agents (2024)
5. Khan, J.Y., Uddin, G.: Automatic code documentation generation using GPT-3. In: Proceedings of the 37th IEEE/ACM International Conference on Automated Software Engineering, pp. 1–6 (2022)
6. Baidoo-Anu, D., Owusu Ansah, L.: Education in the era of generative artificial intelligence (AI): understanding the potential benefits of chatGPT in promoting teaching and learning. Available at SSRN 4337484 (2023)
7. Cao, Y., et al.: A comprehensive survey of AI-generated content (AIGC): a history of generative AI from GAN to chatGPT. arXiv preprint arXiv:2303.04226 (2023)
8. Hacker, P., Engel, A., Mauer, M.: Regulating chatGPT and other large generative AI models. In: Proceedings of the 2023 ACM Conference on Fairness, Accountability, and Transparency, pp. 1112–1123 (2023)
9. Vaswani, A., et al.: Attention is all you need. In: Advances in Neural Information Processing Systems, vol. 30 (2017)
10. Feng, Y., Vanam, S., Cherukupally, M., Zheng, W., Qiu, M., Chen, H.: Investigating code generation performance of chat-GPT with crowdsourcing social data. In: Proceedings of the 47th IEEE Computer Software and Applications Conference, pp. 1–10 (2023)
11. Waseem, M., Das, T., Ahmad, A., Fehmideh, M., Liang, P., Mikkonen, T.: Using chatGPT throughout the software development life cycle by novice developers. arXiv preprint arXiv:2310.13648 (2023)
12. Thiergart, J., Huber, S., Übellacker, T.: Understanding emails and drafting responses–an approach using GPT-3. arXiv preprint arXiv:2102.03062 (2021)
13. Sami, A.M., et al.: System for systematic literature review using multiple AI agents: concept and an empirical evaluation. arXiv preprint arXiv:2403.08399 (2024)
14. Rasheed, Z., et al.: Can large language models serve as data analysts? A multi-agent assisted approach for qualitative data analysis. arXiv preprint arXiv:2402.01386 (2024)

15. Waseem, M., et al.: Artificial intelligence procurement assistant: enhancing bid evaluation. In: International Conference on Software Business, pp. 108–114. Springer, Cham (2023)
16. Dong, Y., Jiang, X., Jin, Z., Li, G.: Self-collaboration code generation via chatGPT. arXiv preprint arXiv:2304.07590 (2023)
17. Rasheed, Z., et al.: Autonomous agents in software development: a vision paper. arXiv preprint arXiv:2311.18440 (2023)
18. Waseem, M., Ahmad, A., Liang, P., Fehmideh, M., Abrahamsson, P., Mikkonen, T.: Conducting systematic literature reviews with chatGPT (2023)
19. Rasheed, Z., Waseem, M., Saari, M., Systä, K., Abrahamsson, P.: CodePori: large scale model for autonomous software development by using multi-agents. arXiv preprint arXiv:2402.01411 (2024)
20. Ahmad, A., Waseem, M., Liang, P., Fahmideh, M., Aktar, M.S., Mikkonen, T.: Towards human-bot collaborative software architecting with chatGPT. In: Proceedings of the 27th International Conference on Evaluation and Assessment in Software Engineering, pp. 279–285 (2023)
21. Barke, S., James, M.B., Polikarpova, N.: Grounded copilot: How programmers interact with code-generating models. In: Proceedings of the ACM on Programming Languages, vol. 7, no. OOPSLA1, pp. 85–111 (2023)
22. Vaithilingam, P., Zhang, T., Glassman, E.L.: Expectation vs. experience: evaluating the usability of code generation tools powered by large language models. In: CHI Conference on Human Factors in Computing Systems Extended Abstracts, pp. 1–7 (2022)
23. Ma, W., et al.: The scope of chatGPT in software engineering: a thorough investigation. arXiv preprint arXiv:2305.12138 (2023)

Generative AI for Test Driven Development: Preliminary Results

Moritz Mock[(✉)][iD], Jorge Melegati[iD], and Barbara Russo[iD]

Free University of Bozen-Bolzano, 39100 Bolzano, Italy
{momock,jorge.melegati,brusso}@unibz.it

Abstract. Test Driven Development (TDD) is one of the major practices of Extreme Programming for which incremental testing and refactoring trigger the code development. TDD has limited adoption in the industry, as it requires more code to be developed and experienced developers. Generative AI (GenAI) may reduce the extra effort imposed by TDD. In this work, we introduce an approach to automatize TDD by embracing GenAI either in a collaborative interaction pattern in which developers create tests and supervise the AI generation during each iteration or a fully-automated pattern in which developers only supervise the AI generation at the end of the iterations. We run an exploratory experiment with ChatGPT in which the interaction patterns are compared with the non-AI TDD regarding test and code quality and development speed. Overall, we found that, for our experiment and settings, GenAI can be efficiently used in TDD, but it requires supervision of the quality of the produced code. In some cases, it can even mislead non-expert developers and propose solutions just for the sake of the query.

Keywords: AI4SE · Test Driven Development · Generative AI

1 Introduction

Test-driven development (TDD) is one of the major practices in Extreme Programming (XP) [1]. Nevertheless, its effectiveness is still controversial [7,9]. The major strength of TDD lies in its ability to deliver high-quality code through the granularity and uniformity of development [6]. To be effective, TDD developers must have a strong command of the practice and experience in development [3]. To facilitate its adoption, automation can be an option, and generative artificial intelligence (GenAI) tools, such as GitHub's Copilot[1] and OpenAI's ChatGPT[2], can be helpful [5]. In particular, recent literature has shown promising results in software testing. For instance, Piya and Sullivan [13] proposed an approach in which a test suite is fed to ChatGPT, and prompts are generated accordingly upon test failures. Liang *et al.* [11] have further shown that the use of GenAI

---

[1] https://copilot.microsoft.com.
[2] https://chat.openai.com.

© The Author(s) 2025
L. Marchesi et al. (Eds.): XP 2024 Workshops, LNBIP 524, pp. 24–32, 2025.
https://doi.org/10.1007/978-3-031-72781-8_3

can speed up testing. However, the quality of the generated tests and code and the role of the developers are still under discussion [11].

In this work, we explore the use of GenAI in automating TDD and reflect on the role of the developer. We then perform an exploratory experiment with five developers to assess the effectiveness of our method and compare it with non-AI TDD.

2   Methodology

Our goal is to automatize the TDD process with GenAI, exploring which minimal knowledge is needed in each iteration and which kind of role AIs and developers may have. To this aim, we developed a threefold methodology: first, we defined a workflow to automate the TDD process with GenAI, then we identified interaction patterns between developers and GenAIs supporting different types of automation activities of the workflow. Finally, we implemented a tool automatizing the workflow according to the interaction patterns and then performed an experiment to compare them. To design the workflow, we first identified the type of information that is handled in an iteration of a TDD process. The information includes the context, the feature to be developed, the test and production code, and the execution log that was eventually output in the previous iteration. To obtain coherent answers, we queried ChatGPT a few times with different types of prompts. The major challenge here is to obtain an incremental output. We do not want ChatGPT to generate the code for the feature in one shot as we are not implementing Test First [1]. Thus, we first automated the query process by implementing a Python script that leverages OpenAI's API to use ChatGPT as GenAI. We employed the model *gpt-3.5-turbo-16k*, which can have as context up to 16k tokens. We have also explored different ways of querying the ChatGPT: (i) not mentioning the testing task at all and retrieving each message as a stand-alone, (ii) including the output of the previous query as input for the next query, or (iii) querying with all data in (i) and (ii). Based on our observation, scenario (ii), in which we send the result of the last output, is the best one. In scenario (i), ChatGPT struggled to grasp the task, and in scenario (iii), it got confused. In the first attempts to query ChatGPT, we also observed that it had the tendency to produce the complete solution instead of performing incremental steps. To prevent from doing so, we added the sentence *"stub and drivers to develop the first barely minimal test and production code"*. From the second iteration onwards, the additional phrase *"Keep the existing tests"* at the beginning needed to be added so that the existing tests were not lost. In the end, we were able to formulate the following prompts:

– First iteration: Use the Assertion First pattern in TDD and stubs and drivers to develop the first barely minimal test and production code for the feature ⟨*feature description*⟩ with input ⟨*names*⟩ and ⟨*values*⟩ and expected output ⟨*values*⟩
– Intermediate iteration: Keep the existing tests and run the next iteration of TDD to develop the barely minimal test and production code

– Final iteration: Refactor the code.

A second step in our methodology consists of defining the role of the developers in the TDD process automated with GenAIs. To this aim, we defined three collaboration patterns: collaborative, fully-automated, and non-automated. In the *collaborative pattern*, we introduce an interaction between the human developer and the AI, in which the developer is in charge of writing the test code and modifying any test or production code generated by the AI before passing it again to the AI. Then, the AI generates the production code. The *fully-automated pattern* automates both steps. The developer only verifies the quality of the produced code at refactoring. The *non-automated pattern* does not involve any AI. Finally, we evaluated and compared the patterns with five practitioners who had experience with Python and TDD: three used the collaborative pattern, and two used the non-automated one. All have received the same initial exercise:

The goal of this experiment is to develop in Python the following feature: Develop a class TextFormatter that takes arbitrary words and horizontally center them into a line. The class TextFormatter shall have three functions. The first is called setLineWidth and sets the length of the line. The second function receives a single word and returns the word in the center of the line. The third function receives two words and centers the two words in the line. To develop it you will use Test Driven Development and, in particular, assertion first.

All participants were allowed to consult any source they liked. We recorded the screen while the participants performed their exercise. At the end of the task, they filled out a brief questionnaire. We compared the results in terms of the number of test functions, number of assertions, test LOC, code LOC, and time to complete the task. We also inspected their test, code, and logs (in case of automation) and qualitatively evaluated the quality of what has been produced. We further collected feedback from the participants. The code produced in the experiment can be found at https://github.com/moritzmock/AI4TDD.

3   Results

RQ1. Can generative AI be used to automate TDD? To answer this question, we designed two workflows, one implementing the collaborative pattern and the other fully-automated. We further implemented Python scripts that actuate them. Figure 1 illustrates the workflow for the fully-automated pattern: the activities with the AI symbol are performed by the AI model, and the execution of each activity in the workflow is automated by our scripts. The note boxes show the input needed for the next action: the prompts as described in Sect. 2 and the type of data to pass to the next activity. From the response of the AI, the production code is automatically integrated, and the test suite is launched. If the AI is not able to write code that fulfils the test case(s), the prompt is resent up to five times. In the collaborative pattern, the workflow is the same but different in its execution. Firstly, activities ① and ② are executed by the developer. Secondly, the developer can modify the input passed to the AI in activity ③. The red text in the note boxes indicates the part of the output of the previous activity that the developer can modify. The rest is the same as in the fully-automated pattern.

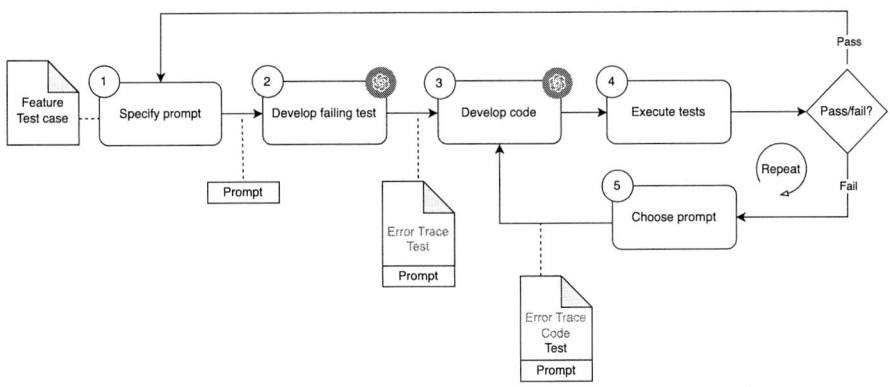

Fig. 1. Fully-automated pattern

In our experiment, we executed the two interaction patterns with five developers, whereas the authors launched the fully-automated pattern. In all cases, the experiment's task was successfully completed. The final test and production code, the process log, the screen recording, and a short feedback from the participants were collected.

RQ2. What kind of interaction model between generative AI and human developers is more promising? For our exploratory experiment, we selected five developers located in two different countries with some knowledge of the programming language and experience with TDD, as shown in Table 1.

Table 1. Demographics of the developers

	TDD Experience	Python Experience	Role	Interaction Scenario
P1	>3 years	<1 year	Software developer	collaborative
P2	1–3 years	>3 years	Data scientist	collaborative
P3	1–3 years	>3 years	Software developer	non-automated
P4	<1 year	<1 years	Software engineering student	collaborative
P5	1–3 years	<1 years	Software developer	non-automated

Three followed the collaborative pattern, and two followed the non-automated one. We compared the results of the experiment in terms of the metrics defined in Sect. 2. Table 2 reports the results for the five participants P1–P5 and the fully-automated pattern, F1. For F1, the authors launched the task a few times. The first times were used to learn the type of prompts needed to automate TDD iteratively, and the last one was executed to compare the results of the fully-automated with the ones of the other patterns. Table 2 reports the value for the last run. It is worth noticing that the AI acts as a tester and developer, so we are able to log the activities of both. In some iterations, the developer implemented the code with no interaction with a tester, as may happen in real cases.

Table 2. Evaluation of the results for the participants P1, P2, and P3 and the fully-automated one F1. # of LOC does not contain blank lines.

	# test functions	# assertions	test LOC	code LOC	Time to complete	# iterations
P1	7	7	34	25	30 min	32
P2	3	9	19	19	30 min	49
P3	11	17	69	31	35 min	NA
P4	4	4	16	12	40 min	44
P5	3	3	16	14	40 min	NA
F1	1	3	14	17	12 min	8

Test Coverage and Code Inspection. All participants managed to complete the tasks within the time limit of 40 min. They created different sets of tests and considered different edge cases. P1 did not develop tests for all the valid inputs but implemented the edge cases where words are larger than the line width or empty and a new functionality that cuts the word if its length is larger than the line. P2 did not create a class but three individual functions instead. In this case, our script was not able to parse the messages received from ChatGPT and extract the generated code. Thus, P2 had to struggle a bit until he was able to understand the automation. The final code was clean, with only assertions per test function, but it contained one redundant assertion per function and no edge cases. P3 implemented the largest number of test cases, including all valid and invalid cases and specific exceptions: *InvalidLineWidthException, CenteringNotPossibleError,* and *SpreadNotPossibleError.* The final code is not completely clean, though, as it includes repeated assertions for one method and more than one test method for the same function to test. P4 implemented all test cases for all functions, but no edge cases and the final code is not correct (see Log inspection, next paragraph). P5 worked with no assistance from the AI and implemented only one test case per function, with valid input and no edge cases. F1 produced one test function with three assertions, each testing a valid input. One valid case was missing and no edge case or invalid value was tested. F1 was the fastest to complete the task.

Log and Screen Inspection. For all developers who collaborated with the AI, we logged the interactions and watched the screens' recordings. The last column of Table 2 reports the number of interactions. At each interaction, we logged the test and production code, the execution trace, and the changes made by the developer to fix the AI output and make the test pass. All the changes have finally produced a correct code except in the case of P4. ChatGPT recommended these changes at the final interaction:

```
Changes made to the code:
1. In the `test_TwoWordSpreadEven` test, the `TextFormatter`
   variable was mistakenly assigned instead of `textFormatter`.
2. In the `test_TwoWordSpreadOdd` test, the `TextFormatter`
   variable was mistakenly assigned instead of `textFormatter`.
3. In the `test_WordCenterOdd` test, the expected result was
   corrected by removing the extra spaces.
```

However, the proposed changes do not fix the bug but simply avoid the execution of the code revealing the bug. For F1, no test failed, suggesting that the AI was more concerned with not failing the test than with developing a high-quality solution.

Analysing Feedback. We finally asked the participants about their experience with AI. The answers are reported in Table 3. The positive feeling described by P1 is related to the compatibility of the tool with the way P1 works. This feeling of comfort is known to be a key determinant for acceptance and adoption of new technologies and methodologies in software engineering [14]. This aspect will also be important for the adoption of AI-based tools and, as such, should be considered in the development of this new generation of tools. P2, who created a set of functions rather than a class, got frustrated when the GenAI tool did not work as expected. Apparently, the same frustration has also been observed in students in a study on using GenAI tools for teaching software engineering [4].

Table 3. Feedback

	Perceived difficulty	Feedback
P1	Easy	To be honest, the "presence" of the AI made me a little unsure in the beginning, because I was concerned about its behavior and if I should adapt to fit its need. Once I realized the AI would adapt to my needs (in particular my dev-flow), I think the experience went way more smoothly
P2	Easy	The tool did not work as expected. It seemed kinda buggy, as it did not add any code to the existing file. I was expecting more from an AI tool as normally ChatGPT is able to complete such trivial tasks
P3	Easy	It was fun, the requirements are very broad, so maybe the assumptions can vary a bit from person to person
P4	Fine	NA
P5	Hard	NA

In this case, though, it was not the GenAI that did not process the query as expected but rather our script, which was not designed to extract functions from the messages of ChatGPT. Of course, the developer could not distinguish the difference. Clearly, P2 did not read the task's description, which required developing a class, but this gave us the hint to refactor our tool so that it is now also capable of extracting functions from ChatGPT messages. Also P3 had a positive experience in performing the task autonomously and even suggested the authors some refinement of the experiment. Being expert in both TDD and Python the task was not hard, and the resulting code was the most creative. No feedback was obtained from P4 and P5. Overall, we found that ChatGPT can meet the expectations of the developers in assisting in their job, but without replacing developers in terms of creativity and quality of the code. To obtain satisfactory collaboration with developers, AI should be well integrated into the automation of development activities. The solutions generated may be incomplete or buggy, and non-expert developers may not notice this and trust the AI straight away.

4   Related Work

In this section, we present research works on GenAI for software testing and TDD, in particular. Bird *et al.* [2] analyzed forum discussions from early GitHub's Copilot users, collected their impressions on the tool usage, and observed that support in writing unit tests was one of the major benefits. Producing test cases quickly was the major result of a large survey on the usability of AI programming assistants of Liang *et al.* [11]. They reported that finding edge cases in testing was among the major reasons for using AI. On the other hand, verifying AI answers (e.g., to meet software requirements) was the major reason for not using them. Guilherme and Vincenzi [8] used OpenAI API to generate unit tests and concluded that the tool has a good performance in terms of mutation score and code coverage. GPTDroid [12] uses ChatGPT for GUI testing of mobile apps as a Q&A task and was able to achieve higher coverage and greater efficiency in finding bugs. Lahiri *et al.* [10] propose ITDCG, a workflow with Open AI's Codex for interactive test-driven code generation. Tests and code are generated simultaneously, not incrementally and iteratively, as in TDD. No particular mention is made of how to query the AI or the role of the developer. Tian and Chen [15] introduce Test-case-driven Chain of Thought (TCoT), an approach for improving code generation by using the description of the tests in natural language. The results are promising; however, they did not focus on TDD or any iterative testing process. Piya and Sullivan [13] introduced the LLM4TDD framework to incorporate GenAI into TDD. A developer develops within a coding environment that interacts with a GenAI. The developer manually copies, if needed, code and tests and whether the latter ones fail. An evaluation of the framework reached a success rate of 88.5%. The authors also identified best practices to ensure that ChatGPT solves the correct problem and to reduce the effort. Our work follows these recommendations but also provides 1) different ways of interactions between humans and AI, 2) a structure for the input with predefined prompts to avoid generating unwanted code, 3) a control layer for the collaborative pattern in which the quality of the code is iteratively verified by the developer. The experiment with real developers helped to understand the issue of such collaboration at a fine granularity level.

5   Conclusions

In this work, we defined interaction patterns between developers and GenAIs for the automation of TDD. We conducted an exploratory experiment with practitioners to evaluate the feasibility of our automation and the quality of the produced solutions. Overall, we found that for our experiment and settings, GenAI can be efficiently used in TDD, but it requires supervision on the quality of the code produced. In some cases, it can mislead non-expert developers and propose solutions that change tests rather than the production code, which may remain buggy, to make tests pass. In future work, we will extend our methodology to incorporate other interaction patterns (e.g., the developer can choose freely how to query the GenAI), different automation and GenAI, and involve a larger number of practitioners both in the experiment and in the feedback.

Acknowledgments. We thank the practitioners who participated in the study for their valuable contribution. Moritz Mock is partially funded by the National Recovery and Resilience Plan (Piano Nazionale di Ripresa e Resilienza, PNRR - DM 117/2023).

References

1. Beck, K.: Test Driven Development: By Example. Addison-Wesley (2022)
2. Bird, C., et al.: Taking flight with copilot. Queue **20**(6), 35–57 (2022)
3. Causevic, A., et al.: Factors limiting industrial adoption of test driven development: a systematic review. In: Fourth IEEE International Conference on Software Testing, Verification and Validation, pp. 337–346 (2011)
4. Choudhuri, R., et al.: How far are we? The triumphs and trials of generative ai in learning software engineering. In: ICSE (2024)
5. Ernst, N.A., Bavota, G.: Ai-driven development is here: should you worry? IEEE Softw. **39**(02), 106–110 (2022)
6. Fucci, D., et al.: A dissection of the test-driven development process: does it really matter to test-first or to test-last? IEEE Trans. Softw. Eng. **43**(7), 597–614 (2017)
7. Ghafari, M., et al.: Why research on test-driven development is inconclusive? In: ESEM, pp. 1–10. ACM, New York (2020)
8. Guilherme, V., Vincenzi, A.: An initial investigation of ChatGPT unit test generation capability, pp. 15–24. SAST, New York (2023)
9. Karac, I., Turhan, B.: What do we (really) know about test-driven development? IEEE Softw. **35**(4), 81–85 (2018)
10. Lahiri, S.K., et al.: Interactive code generation via test-driven user-intent formalization (2023)
11. Liang, J.T., Yang, C., Myers, B.A.: A large-scale survey on the usability of AI programming assistants: successes and challenges. In: ICSE, pp. 605–617 (2024)

12. Liu, Z., et al.: Make LLM a testing expert: bringing human-like interaction to mobile GUI testing via functionality-aware decisions. In: ICSE (2024)
13. Piya, S., Sullivan, A.: LLM4TDD: best practices for test driven development using large language models (2023). https://doi.org/10.48550/arXiv.2312.04687
14. Riemenschneider, C.K., Hardgrave, B.C., Davis, F.D.: Explaining software developer acceptance of methodologies: a comparison of five theoretical models. IEEE Trans. Softw. Eng. **28**(12), 1135–1145 (2002)
15. Tian, Z., Chen, J.: Test-case-driven programming understanding in large language models for better code generation (2023). https://doi.org/10.48550/arXiv.2309.16120

Responsible AI in Agile Software Engineering - An Industry Perspective

Rasmus Ulfsnes[1,7(✉)] ⓘ, Nils Brede Moe[1] ⓘ, Jostein Emmerhoff[2],
Marcin Floryan[3], Anastasia Griva[4] ⓘ, Jan Henrik Gundelsby[5] ⓘ,
Astri Moksnes Barbala[1] ⓘ, and Kieran Conboy[1,6] ⓘ

[1] SINTEF, 7034 Trondheim, Norway
Rasmus.Ulfsnes@sintef.no
[2] Schibsted Nordic Marketplace, Oslo, Norway
[3] Spotify, Stockholm, Sweden
[4] Bespot, Athens, Greece
[5] Knowit Solutions AS, Oslo, Norway
[6] University of Galway, Galway, Ireland
[7] NTNU, Trondheim, Norway

Abstract. There is a rapid emergence of tools, methods, and guidance
for the use of AI across all parts of the software development process,
from requirements gathering to code generation to testing and user feedback. However, AI raises many concerns regarding responsible use, and
there is a need to understand and develop principles for what responsible
software development entails in practice in an agile context, as well as
carefully evaluate the incorporation of AI tools and methods in software
engineering. We draw on experience from Bespot, Knowit, Schibsted, and
Spotify to identify challenges faced by companies pioneering the use of
AI in their software development efforts and start charting a roadmap
for responsible AI in software engineering.

Keywords: GenAI · Responsible AI · Agile Software Engineering ·
Challenges · Responsible AI · Software Engineering · Industry
Perspective

1 Introduction

The landscape of business is rapidly evolving with the integration of artificial
intelligence, particularly in the realm of software development. The rise of Generative AI (GenAI) has been remarkable, offering transformative capabilities
that enhance various segments of the development lifecycle–from requirements
management [4] to code generation [7] and security testing [6]. The primary
focus of these advancements has been to drive efficiency, automate routine tasks,
and increase productivity [15]. Nonetheless, there is an increasing imperative to
address the ethical dimensions of AI deployment. To date, however the literature on what constitutes responsibility within the software engineering field has

© The Author(s) 2025
L. Marchesi et al. (Eds.): XP 2024 Workshops, LNBIP 524, pp. 33–41, 2025.
https://doi.org/10.1007/978-3-031-72781-8_4

largely been discussed in a separate body of literature to the literature on AI tools in software engineering, and very few studies in either camp are built on empirical data. This paper aims to bring the two communities together, shedding light on which challenges software organizations face in terms of leveraging AI responsibly and outlining a way forward in solving these. Given the recent and rapid emergence of this area, we asked four key experts with extensive industry experience in large-scale agile organizations to provide written statements about challenges associated with responsible AI in their organizational context with regard to software engineering. Our selection was based on software-intensive companies impacted by and in the process of using AI in their engineering processes.

2   Background

In looking into what responsibility means in software engineering by reviewing the current understanding of ethical principles in the field, Ina Schieferdecker [12] asserts that software trustworthiness today hinges more on acceptance than technical quality, emphasizing that software and its features must be comprehensible and explainable. Software and its applications can only succeed if they garner public trust, Schieferdecker notes, which is tied to users' belief that products have been developed according to responsible principles.

Otherwise, literature on the topic in the software engineering field has largely focused on literature reviews. One such study, a rapid review study focusing on what responsible AI means in software engineering, was conducted by Barletta et al. [1]. They investigated frameworks that provide principles, guidelines, and tools designed to aid practitioners in the development and implementation of responsible AI applications. In analyzing each framework in relation to the various phases of the Software Development Life Cycle (SDLC), Barletta et al. found that the majority of these frameworks are focused primarily on the Requirements Elicitation phase, with minimal coverage of other phases. Barletta et al.'s findings thus indicate the absence of a comprehensive "catch-all" framework that effectively supports both technical and non-technical stakeholders in the execution of real-world projects. Similarly, Lu et al. [9] conducted a systematic literature review on responsible AI for software engineering to summarize the current state and identify critical research challenges. They present a research road map on software engineering to operationalize responsible AI. Some of the findings are proposed as tools, such as ethical risk assessments, or as product features embedded within AI systems to mitigate ethical risks and enhance trust in markets where it is currently lacking, for instance, an ethical black box.

In regard to the literature on responsible AI technologies, a multitude of factors are prominent, covering both human, social, and organizational factors. For instance, Mikalef et al. [11] point to 8 dimensions for responsible AI. However, there are different approaches to achieving responsible AI, and one venue is the concept of explainable AI [10], wherein efforts are being made to outline how and at what level different stakeholders need and understand the outputs of AI.

Another venue is that of domain expertise [14] where the argument for bridging the experts of AI, with the experts of whatever domain the technology would assist. Collaborating with the AI-systems developers, however, is not that easy when you are purchasing off-the-shelf AI technology, e.g., Copilot or ChatGPT for software engineers, to assist in their programming tasks (see [13]).

3   Approach

As AI in software engineering is a novel phenomenon, and there are studies and research on the topic, we argue that utilizing a Delphi-type approach is appropriate [8]. The Delphi method can be used both quantitatively and qualitatively. We sourced four experts from different software organizations to elicit their take on responsible AI and how it affects their organization. To guide our inquiry, we utilize the eight dimensions proposed by Mikalef et al. [11]: *Fairness, Transparency, Accountability, Robustness and safety, Data governance, Laws and regulations, Human oversight* and *Societal and environmental well-being*. After eliciting the information, we analyzed the challenges the different organizations experienced in terms of grappling with responsible AI.

All four industry examples adhere to the key principles of Agile, which include incrementally developing the software in iterative cycles, implementing regular ceremonies to review and refine both the product and development methods, collaboratively responding to changes, and consistently engaging with users. Additionally, the software teams within these organizations are organized in a manner typical of agile teams.

4   Industry Perspectives on Responsible AI in Software Engineering

4.1   Bespot - Recruiting Skilled Expertise

In recent years, a significant challenge we've encountered is related to the hiring process for software developers and AI experts. Traditionally, companies have relied on assessing candidates' experience by reviewing their profiles on web-based platforms like GitHub and StackOverflow. This approach allowed us to initially assess their coding abilities, problem-solving skills, and overall expertise. However, with the rise of GenAI we have begun to question the efficacy of using developers' profiles on such platforms as part of our talent screening process.

One issue we identified is the potential for inaccuracies in candidates' profiles, which may not truly reflect their coding skills or contributions to the community. Some discrepancies are apparent upon closer scrutiny of platform data, such as sudden improvements in ratings, reputation, or badges. Still, efforts from the companies' side are required to detect such profiles. Also, it is difficult to figure out whether something is GenAI written in other cases. This situation seems to result in inequalities in evaluating and hiring talents.

While web-based platforms like GitHub and StackOverflow remain valuable resources for assessing candidates, of course software development companies do not only use these. There might also be internal coding tests/challenges, etc., as part of the hiring process. Still, even in such cases, GenAI was detected to be used profoundly or not, affecting hiring once again. This increasing prevalence of GenAI has prompted internal debates among companies regarding its responsible use in hiring practices.

On the one hand, some state that using GenAI to generate code is acceptable, and achieving an optimal equilibrium between automated processes and human intuition is essential in coding. This is reinforced by trends in certificates such as prompt engineering for GenAI. However, detractors caution against relying on AI as a collaborator, citing concerns about perpetuating inequalities and potential risks to the company's integrity. The latter can happen since we are not certain about where the data are stored, who has access, etc.

For example, our company, Bespot, develops location fraud detection and validation software solutions. The company has developed an AI solution utilizing tracking technologies (e.g., WiFi, GPS, cellular) to detect user locations with near-centimeter precision accurately. However, protecting our competitive advantages is crucial since these algorithms are proprietary and treated as black boxes. Consequently, hiring individuals who may inadvertently expose sensitive algorithms to GenAI collaboration poses a significant risk, particularly for companies operating in sectors requiring stringent data protection measures.

In conclusion, navigating the intersection of GenAI and hiring practices presents challenges for companies seeking to maintain a balance between human-GenAI collaboration and responsibility. While leveraging AI technologies offers potential benefits, careful consideration of ethical implications, data security concerns, and competitive interests is important in ensuring responsible decision-making within the hiring process.

4.2 Knowit - Security, Sustainability, and GenAI's Mental Models

While the potential of Generative AI is undeniable, its integration into practical, real-world applications comes with significant challenges. Knowit is a large consultancy firm focused on digital transformation. It combines IT, design, and management with an emphasis on security, cloud, and AI services. At Knowit, we are committed to sustainable practices and human rights. Despite over a year of democratized access to GenAI, our clients are still primarily in the exploration phase, hesitant to fully embrace its potential. We believe this hesitation stems from several fundamental issues, including concerns about security, transformative use of technology, and environmental and economic sustainability.

The main challenge is related to security, uncertainty of regulations, privacy concerns, and a large unknown attack surface through a plethora of chatbots. All this makes it difficult and too risky for our customers to put the technology to production use. Additionally, 'hallucinations'-incorrect or nonsensical information generated by these systems-pose another significant challenge. Our mental models of computer technology usually let us think about data as a fact or something that is deterministic, predictable, and reliable. However, GenAI operates differently; it is based on statistics and probabilities. This unpredictability requires us to rethink the way we understand and use this technology in our systems and daily work. For instance, while tools like GitHub Copilot offer coding assistance, concerns about energy consumption, code quality, and socio-technical impacts on team collaboration continue to raise doubts about their long-term productivity benefits. Another major sustainability challenge is the substantial energy consumption associated with GenAI. For example, a single Chat GPT query consumes fifteen times more energy than a standard Google search, highlighting the environmental impact of this technology. Additionally, the lack of clear revenue generation from GenAI investments raises concerns about its long-term economic sustainability. For instance, the venture capital firm Sequoia estimated that the AI industry spent $50 billion on Nvidia chips to train advanced AI models last year but generated only $3 billion in revenue. Knowit recognizes GenAI's transformative potential but also acknowledges the significant challenges associated with its adoption in real-world applications and the sustainability challenges it brings. Addressing these issues is essential for leveraging GenAI effectively and responsibly, ensuring both environmental and economic viability.

4.3   Spotify on Algorithmic Responsibility

Every new technology should be approached with a healthy dose of skepticism. This becomes harder when you see everyone around you jumping on the bandwagon. Fortunately, at Spotify, we have over a decade of experience using machine learning and artificial intelligence to enhance our products, especially in the recommendation space. As a result, Spotify has been exposed to some of the challenges inherent in using this technology, specifically in terms of algorithmic bias. For example, we want to avoid recommendations that skew towards the artist's gender or towards more popular songs from certain artists. As part of acting responsibly in this space, we have invested to avoid unintended algorithmic harm. Our research into algorithmic responsibility is helping us to avoid the challenges. As AI tools become more popular and start powering more features such as AI DJ or the AI Playlist Generation, we work to ensure that we build a fair product, respects inclusion and diversity, and does not lead to discriminatory outcomes. Another aspect relevant for Spotify, in the area of responsible use of AI, is to consider the environmental impact, especially in the view of our climate action and responsibility towards the climate crisis. This applies both to Spotify using AI as part of our product portfolio and our use of tools such as Large Language Models that help with the day to day tasks of our employees.

4.4   Schibsted Nordic Marketplaces on Governance and Learning

Schibsted Nordic Marketplaces (NMP) offers digital marketplaces for real estate, job listings, mobility services, and classified ads. It is the leading company in the Nordics, with significant market shares in Norway, Finland, Sweden, and

Denmark. We see AI as fundamental in two aspects. 1) The use of AI services will be incorporated in new products based on our large data sets, and 2) AI tools will also be integrated into the company's development practices through the likes of Copilot and other GenAI tools. Just as Apple revolutionized digital marketplaces with the iPhone, AI technologies can bring about similar significant changes to our products and the way we deliver the products. The new technology will change how we operate and affect the daily lives of employees. NMP needs to develop insights and knowledge about how to use commercial GenAI models and deploy AI solutions responsibly.

In practice, "Responsible AI" involves establishing guidelines, processes, and mechanisms to ensure that AI technology is available, easy to use, and implemented in line with the organization's values and goals while adhering to regulations and ethical perspectives for fairness and sustainability. This can be seen as a lesson learned from the move to cloud services, which do not work without a defined governance structure. As with cloud services, this means taking responsibility seriously in the procurement process and will influence the vendors we choose for such products. This will pose a challenge for our software development teams with a high degree of autonomy regarding technology choice and how they work.

AI tools can influence collaboration and knowledge sharing within the organization. For example, internal communication and coordination within teams may change, so governance structures are needed to support collaboration and knowledge sharing. A key aspect will be investing in raising employees' competencies to leverage AI effectively. It's not enough for individuals to learn, as learning together is necessary to develop new practices for the use of technology in a responsible way. And without knowledge of the technology and how to use it responsibly, you won't be able to do your work well.

5   Discussion and Future Research

Based on the industry experts' statements, we have identified several challenges related to responsible AI in agile software engineering. The most prominent are:

Finding a Balance Between Human and AI. As of now, the impact of GenAI, e.g. ChatGPT, is not understood in terms of its long-term effects on software engineering practices and the social processes involved in these practices. This raises concerns for our industry partners, already from before the engineers are hired, raising questions about the eligibility of the candidates and how to manage this from a recruiting standpoint. This might affect the fairness of the hiring processes [11] as new hires are no longer selected on equal terms. However, there is also a need to utilize AI's positive effects, e.g., productivity [7], and finding this balance while remaining responsible is challenging.

Unclear Effects on Communication and Collaboration. While balancing human and AI automation is challenging, some effects go outside the individual use of AI tools. One notable concern is how this will affect teams and organizations and how they deal with learning [13]. This is particularly concerning as large-scale agile organizations are dependent on the communication, collaboration, and knowledge sharing that occurs in and between teams. One approach here is to use governance that limits and sets boundaries on tools and practices for using AI, but this has a cost in terms of reduced autonomy in large-scale agile contexts [2].

Managing Data Governance and Hallucinations. Data governance and privacy issues do not just create challenges regarding AI, but the interest and accessibility of the tools are making it particularly challenging to leverage the technology. Individual developers must manage the data governance themselves [13], which can be challenging for the developers [4]. Additionally, the uncertainty of regulatory bodies makes it difficult for organizations to make good decisions. Moreover, the data that comes out might be the effects of hallucinations, which require developers to learn how to deal with bad code suggestions [7] and advice [13]. Nevertheless, there are also positive effects of using AI, in achieving greater security posture of the software developed [6].

Managing Responsible AI in Software Products. Managing and dealing with the practical issues of using various AI tools are quite challenging. Companies also want to embed these technologies into their products, providing new interactive interfaces or recommendations. This means making development processes that especially consider the potential of algorithmic harm to ensure fairness, transparency, and accountability [11]. While the companies aim to avoid these issues, there is a lack of frameworks and processes for managing this in the software development life cycle [1].

6   Conclusions and Future Work

Organizations are being met with ever-increasing pressure to allow individuals to use GenAI for their activities while also wanting to exploit and explore the potential of both GenAI and AI in their products and services.

According to our findings, organizations need to deal with challenges on different organizational levels: 1) Organization, 2) Team, and 3) Individual, as these challenges are interrelated between the different parts of an organization and need to be managed simultaneously.

What remains, however, is a clear approach to dealing with human-AI collaboration for agile organizations. There are five different ways to look at human-AI collaboration in the organization according to KolbjÃ¿rnson [5]: 1) Individuals working without AI, 2) Collective, multiple people working together, 3) Automated, when work is done without human interference, 4) Augmented individuals, doing work together with AI, and 5) Augmented teams, when multiple people collaborate with AI.

What recent studies have shown, both experimental [3] and real-life settings [13], is that the exploration and subsequent use of GenAI is largely done by individuals and organizations seem to have a goal of automating work, and thus becoming more efficient.

As more and more organizations race towards more automated work, and thus becoming more efficient, there is a risk that we lose out on the decades of research on agile in organizations, putting a focus on collaboration and coordination. We, therefore argue that organizations and researchers should look into how collectives, such as agile teams, and organizations together can collaborate with Artificial Intelligence, be it generative or otherwise.

References

1. Barletta, V.S., Caivano, D., Gigante, D., Ragone, A.: A rapid review of responsible AI frameworks: how to guide the development of ethical AI. In: Proceedings of the 27th International Conference on Evaluation and Assessment in Software Engineering, pp. 358–367 (2023)
2. Bass, J.M., Haxby, A.: Tailoring product ownership in large-scale agile projects: managing scale, distance, and governance. IEEE Softw. **36**(2), 58–63 (2019). https://doi.org/10.1109/MS.2018.2885524, https://ieeexplore.ieee.org/abstract/document/8648277?casa_token=QQesxZ-4c_4AAAAA:F80w6k0IDwalLeXRO2QnHGnIMb4oZQV7JDkwH-pyenQR3DdZwtwmnxgF8XnHHZtEzfRVE-9c9ng
3. Bubeck, S., et al.: Sparks of artificial general intelligence: early experiments with GPT-4. arXiv:2303.12712 [cs] (2023)
4. Ebert, C., Louridas, P.: Generative AI for software practitioners. IEEE Softw. **40**(4), 30–38 (2023). https://doi.org/10.1109/MS.2023.3265877, https://ieeexplore.ieee.org/abstract/document/10176168
5. Kolbjørnsrud, V.: Designing the intelligent organization: six principles for human-AI collaboration. Calif. Manage. Rev. **66**(2), 44–64 (2024). https://doi.org/10.1177/00081256231211020, http://journals.sagepub.com/doi/10.1177/00081256231211020
6. Li, J., Meland, P.H., Notland, J.S., Storhaug, A., Tysse, J.H.: Evaluating the impact of ChatGPT on exercises of a software security course. In: 2023 ACM/IEEE International Symposium on Empirical Software Engineering and Measurement (ESEM), pp. 1–6. IEEE (2023). https://ieeexplore.ieee.org/abstract/document/10304857/
7. Liang, J.T., Yang, C., Myers, B.A.: A large-scale survey on the usability of AI programming assistants: successes and challenges. In: Proceedings of the IEEE/ACM 46th International Conference on Software Engineering, ICSE 2024, pp. 1–13. Association for Computing Machinery, New York (2024). https://doi.org/10.1145/3597503.3608128, https://dl.acm.org/doi/10.1145/3597503.3608128
8. Lilja, K.K., Laakso, K., Palomäki, J.: Using the Delphi method. In: 2011 Proceedings of PICMET 2011: Technology Management in the Energy Smart World (PICMET), pp. 1–10 (2011). https://ieeexplore.ieee.org/abstract/document/6017716. iSSN 2159-5100
9. Lu, Q., Zhu, L., Xu, X., Whittle, J., Xing, Z.: Towards a roadmap on software engineering for responsible AI. In: Proceedings of the 1st International Conference on AI Engineering: Software Engineering for AI, pp. 101–112 (2022)
10. McDermid, J.A., Jia, Y., Porter, Z., Habli, I.: Artificial intelligence explainability: the technical and ethical dimensions. Philos. Trans. Roy. Soc. A: Math. Phys. Eng. Sci. **379**(2207), 20200363 (2021). https://doi.org/10.1098/rsta.2020.0363, https://royalsocietypublishing.org/doi/full/10.1098/rsta.2020.0363

11. Mikalef, P., Conboy, K., Lundström, J.E., Popovič, A.: Thinking responsibly about responsible AI and 'the dark side' of AI. Eur. J. Inf. Syst. **31**(3), 257–268 (2022)
12. Schieferdecker, I.: Responsible software engineering. Future Softw. Qual. Assur. 137–146 (2020)
13. Ulfsnes, R., Moe, N.B., Stray, V., Skarpen, M.: Transforming software development with generative AI: empirical insights on collaboration and workflow. In: Nguyen-Duc, A., Abrahamsson, P., Khomh, F. (eds.) Generative AI for Effective Software Development, pp. 219–234. Springer, Cham (2024). https://doi.org/10.1007/978-3-031-55642-5_10
14. Waardenburg, L., Huysman, M.: From coexistence to co-creation: blurring boundaries in the age of AI. Inf. Organ. **32**(4), 100432 (2022)
15. Ziegler, A., et al.: Productivity assessment of neural code completion. In: Proceedings of the 6th ACM SIGPLAN International Symposium on Machine Programming, MAPS 2022, pp. 21–29. Association for Computing Machinery, New York (2022).https://doi.org/10.1145/3520312.3534864, https://dl.acm.org/doi/10.1145/3520312.3534864

A Journey Through SPACE
Unpacking the Perceived Productivity of GitHub Copilot

Viggo Tellefsen Wivestad[1]([✉]) [iD] and Rasmus Ulfsnes[1,2] [iD]

[1] SINTEF Digital, 7034 Trondheim, Norway
viggo.wivestad@sintef.no
[2] Norwegian University of Science and Technology, 7491 Trondheim, Norway

Abstract. This study examines the influence of perceived changes in productivity in the context of introducing AI Coding Assistants, specifically GitHub Copilot, within two large-scale agile organizations. Using a cross-sectional survey, we measured self-reported changes in productivity using the SPACE framework. Our comparative analysis suggests several perceived benefits of AI Code Assistant adoption, though with a more conservative impact than previously reported. Further, a correlational analysis employing Kendall's tau and PLSR with 10-fold cross-validation suggests that perceived changes to productivity are moderately associated only with four of the nine features tested, namely job satisfaction, flow, task completion speed, and ability to focus on satisfying work. However, the SPACE framework's ability to fully capture perceived productivity was further challenged, indicating discrepancies in its dimensions of "Performance" and "Communication and collaboration".

Keywords: Developer Productivity · AI Code Assistants · SPACE · GitHub Copilot

1 Introduction

In the evolving landscape of software development, Artificial Intelligence (AI) tools are becoming increasingly prevalent. GitHub Copilot, an AI Coding Assistant, has emerged as a notable example of this trend [9], aiding developers with coding tasks in real-time [14].

Recent studies have looked at the effects of using generative AI in software development practices [18]. One notable study was released by GitHub Research, where participants were asked to self-report various perceived benefits using a 5-point Likert agreement scale. This large-scale survey indicated a solid increase in the perceived productivity by users of Copilot [7]. However, an agreement scale is susceptible to overestimating the agreement ratio [10], which motivated this study to replicate their findings instead of measuring *perceived change* rather than agreement toward statements.

While productivity itself and its driving factors are studied and disputed concepts in software development [2,5,13,19], the SPACE framework represents

© The Author(s) 2025
L. Marchesi et al. (Eds.): XP 2024 Workshops, LNBIP 524, pp. 42–50, 2025.
https://doi.org/10.1007/978-3-031-72781-8_5

one attempt to unpack this using five so-called dimensions. This framework is already being used in research, with one notable example being Ziegler et al., who explored whether measuring developers' interactions with GitHub Copilot could predict their self-reported productivity according to SPACE [21]. However, SPACE itself lacks empirical support, and the assumption that it provides a good proxy for productivity is still an open question.

We therefore set out to answer the following two research questions:

1. *Are the perceived benefits of adopting GitHub Copilot altered by transforming the Likert scales from an agreement scale to a change scale?*
2. *Which factors of SPACE influence perceived changes in productivity when adopting an AI Coding Assistant?*

To answer these and address the lack of empirical data on potential productivity gains from adopting AI Coding Assistants, we employed a cross-sectional survey involving two large-scale agile organizations. The survey extends the survey framework developed by GitHub Research [7].

2   Background

Developers and agile organizations have long been interested in how different modes of organizations, teams, and technology can boost developer productivity. In the new age of AI Coding Assistants, some studies proclaim multiple benefits for adopting such technology, [7], while others find that the main difference between users and non-users is mainly related to work satisfaction dependence on colleagues, not productivity [20].

Multiple attempts have been made to develop frameworks for measuring productivity [19], with an ongoing debate related to how to best measure it, using either objective measurements (e.g. lines of code or time spent writing code [2]) or subjective measurements (e.g. self-ratings or peer evaluations) [13]. To consolidate these perspectives, Forsgren et al. proposed the SPACE framework [5], which attempts to describe productivity holistically using five distinct dimensions of the developer's work life.

GitHub Research used this framework to guide their study when assessing potential productivity gains for their own product, GitHub Copilot [7]. SPACE itself is an acronym for its five dimensions: *Satisfaction and well-being* refers to the developer's satisfaction with work, work-life balance, and general happiness. Studies on hackathons have e.g. shown that having fun at work can influence productivity [12]. Emotional states in general are also shown to affect the perceived productivity of the developers [6]. *Performance* relates to outcomes of a system or process, mainly focusing on quality and impact. *Activity* typically consists of more objective measures, like lines-of-code, number of completed actions or outputs during work, *Communication and collaboration* covers communication, coordination, and collaboration within and between teams. Such characteristics are recognized as particularly important for large-scale inter-team coordination. [3,17], especially in the post-pandemic world, with hybrid teams becoming being normalized [16]. The last dimension, *Efficiency and Flow*, focuses on the ability to work focused and uninterrupted. This resonates with previous findings where unplanned meetings and interruptions were found to be the main detriments to unproductive work [11].

3   Method and Study Design

Our research design consisted of a cross-sectional survey, with a target population consisting of software developers with access to GitHub Copilot. Participants were selected from two companies, NAV IT and MarComp (pseudonym). While both are large-scale agile software organizations, NAV IT is a national organization belonging to the public sector in Norway and employs around 500 developers, while MarComp is an international company with developers in Norway, Poland, and India, with a developer headcount of around 80.

We collected a total of 120 responses (70 from NAV IT, 50 from MarComp), consisting of 84% males, 13% females, and 4% who did not wish to reply. 73% of the developers were in-house, and 27% were external consultants. The complete survey instrument is available online at: https://doi.org/10.5281/zenodo.10987170.

The survey instrument extends a subset of GitHub Research's survey [7, 22], which utilizes the SPACE framework [5] to assess perceived productivity. However, the original questionnaire utilized a 5-point Likert agreement scale, which is susceptible to overestimating the agreement ratio [10]. Several questions also posed analytical challenges, with statements like "I am more productive when using Copilot" being somewhat ambiguous to interpret (does "strongly disagree" indicate an explicit reduction in productivity, or no change, i.e. disagreeing with the statement that productivity has increased?). To combat this, we transformed the survey items into a 5-point bidirectional Likert evaluation scale which we call a "change scale", ranging from "Major increase" to "Major decrease", with "No change" being a neutral center point. This transformation required slight modifications to survey item formulations, e.g. "Since getting access to Copilot, have you noticed a change in the following: Your own productivity?".

The final questionnaire consisted of 57 questions, with 10 questions utilizing the transformed change scale. For this study, we are focusing on the questions intersecting GitHub Research's survey. The survey items and their mapping to the SPACE framework can be found in Table 1.

3.1   Comparing Likert Scales Results

In our study, we employed a Top 2-Box (T2B) analysis to compare the outcomes from GitHub Research's study [7] with our survey results. This method concentrates on the proportion of a subset of the Likert scale, e.g. agreement ("strongly agree" + "agree") from GitHub Research's study and increase ("major increase" + "minor increase") from our survey. While this approach omits parts of the response distribution and thus provides an incomplete view of the data, it is recognized for its utility in highlighting areas of interest within data sets [15]. Finally, since this was the only data provided by [7], it was our only choice for comparison.

To examine potential relationships between perceived productivity and the SPACE-based variables, and compensate for the incomplete view given by the Top 2-Box analysis, we employed a bivariate histogram to inspect the distribution between pairs of independent variables and the dependent variable. To test our hypotheses that there exist relationships between the SPACE-based variables and perceived productivity, Kendall's τ coefficient was utilized to examine both strength and relational direction. This non-parametric method is suitable for ordinal data, which is inherent in Likert scale responses. To correct for multiple hypothesis testing, our threshold for statistical significance was reduced using Bonferroni correction.

Finally, to explain the independent variables' impact on perceived productivity, we treated the data as interval scales and employed Partial Least Squares Regression (PLSR) with 10-fold cross-validation. The model's robustness and predictive capabilities were validated using the coefficient of determination (R^2) and Root Mean Squared Error (RMSE) metrics. The aggregated Variable Importance in Projection (VIP) scores statistics quantifies the contribution of each independent variable, with scores above 1 generally indicating a significant influence. Uncertainty is reported using standard deviation.

4   Results

Our study surveyed 120 GitHub Copilot users about their perceived change in productivity, using a survey instrument where one item directly measured perceived productivity and nine items assessed changes according to SPACE.

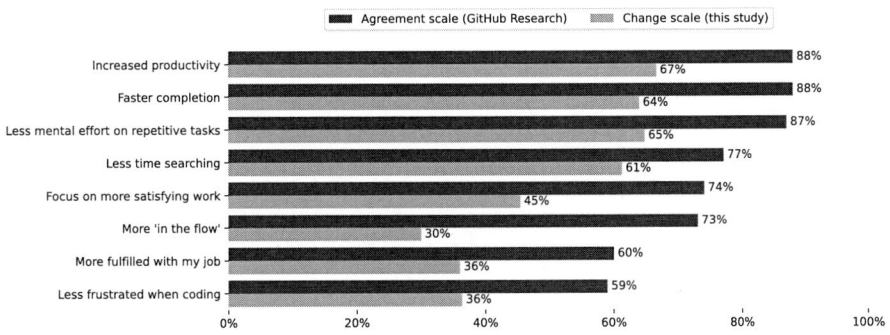

Fig. 1. Top 2-Box plot comparing the proportion of positive agreeement vs. increased change related to various attitudes among Copilot-users (the word "less" indicates that the bars focus on disagreement/decrease rather than agreement/increase)

Comparative Analysis (Agreement vs. Change Scale): Figure 1 compares our change scale results with GitHub Research's agreement scale findings.

Table 1. Results from testing associations between SPACE-based variables and 'perceived productivity'. Independent correlations are tested using Kendall's τ rank correlation with associated P-values for significance with a Bonferroni threshold of $\alpha = 0.0056$.

SPACE Dimensions	Survey Items ("Change in...")	τ	P-value	Accept H_A
Satisfaction and well-being	Job satisfaction	0.468	<0.001	✓
	Focus on satisfying work	0.453	<0.001	✓
	Frustration boring tasks	−0.221	0.014	
Performance	Code quality	0.256	0.005	
Efficiency and flow	Task completion speed	0.598	<0.001	✓
	Flow	0.452	<0.001	✓
	Searching for information	−0.256	0.003	
	Mental work	−0.377	<0.001	
Communication and collaboration	Dependence on colleagues	−0.279	0.002	

Although both scales recorded positive impacts, the change scale showed significantly more conservative outcomes, most notably for the ability to stay in the "flow", where less than a third (30%) of our respondents reported an increase, compared to nearly three-quarters (73%) in GitHub research's study. Our results further showed that about two-thirds of the users reported increased productivity (67%) and completion speed (64%), and decreased mental effort spent on repetitive tasks (65%) and time spent searching for information (61%). However, only about one-third report being more in the flow (30%), feeling more fulfilled with their job (36%), and feeling less frustrated when coding (36%). About half of the users experienced an increase in their ability to focus on satisfying work (45%).

Distribution and Correlation Analysis: Figure 2 presents the distribution of responses for all survey items, visualizing the relationships between perceived changes in productivity and the SPACE variables. We only accept the alternative hypothesis (H_A: there is a correlation) for cases that show *both* a significant correlation towards perceived productivity after Bonferroni correction, and show at least moderate correlation levels ($|\tau| \geq 0.4$) using Dancey and Reidy's thresholds [1,4]. As detailed in Table 1, we were able to accept the alternative hypothesis, and thereby confirm a moderate correlation towards perceived productivity, in four instances: (1) **task completion speed**, (2) **ability to stay in the flow**, (3) **job satisfaction** and (4) **the ability to focus on satisfying work**.

PLSR Model Performance and Feature Importance: The PLSR model, evaluated using 10-fold cross-validation, demonstrated modest predictive capability, with an R^2 of 0.214 ± 0.244, indicating that the model explains 21.4% of the variance on average. An RMSE of 0.616 ± 0.070 suggests moderate predictive errors, with low RMSE scores normally indicating better predictive accuracy. However, the high standard deviation suggests substantial variability in R^2, hinting at potential model instability. Nevertheless, the VIP scores in Fig. 3 align with the Kendall τ results, identifying the same four dimensions as the most influential predictors of perceived changes in productivity, supporting their relevance in the SPACE framework.

5   Discussion and Implications

Our findings show that developers who adopt an AI Coding Assistant report notable increases in productivity, both when asked directly, and indirectly using SPACE variables. This resonates with the findings of GitHub Research [7], and other studies on Generative AI where developers report spending less time searching for information and being blocked by repetitive and boring tasks [18].

Using our proposed change scale, the proportion of users reporting increased benefits declined significantly across all aspects when compared to GitHub Research's findings [7]. This result was expected, as the change scale was designed to counteract potential false inflation of agreement. Most notable was the big drop in users who reported increased "flow", which resonates with other work that found little difference in perceived "flow" when comparing users to non-users of GitHub Copilot [20]. It should be noted that these two Likert scales

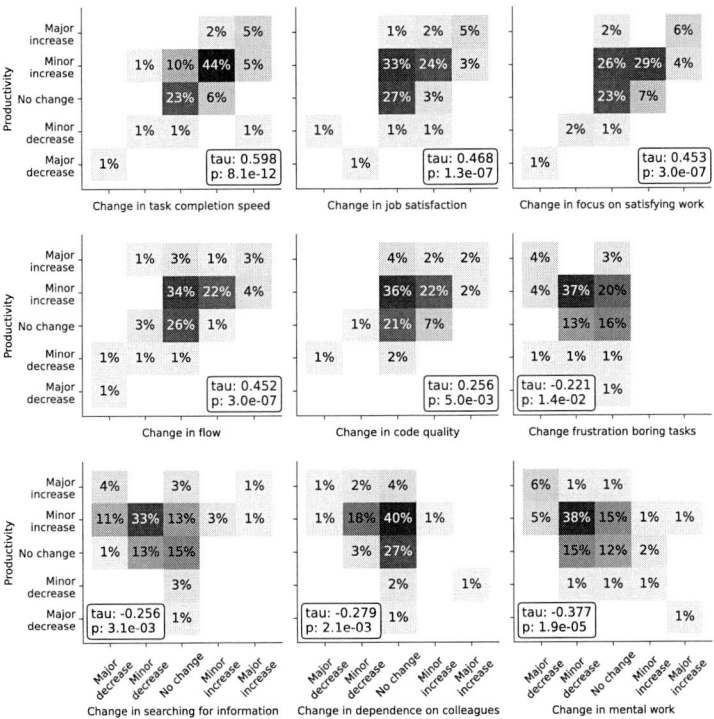

Fig. 2. Bivariate histograms showing the joint distribution of perceived change in productivity and the SPACE-based variables. Kenball's τ (**tau**) measures correlation, while P-value (**p**) measures statistical significance.

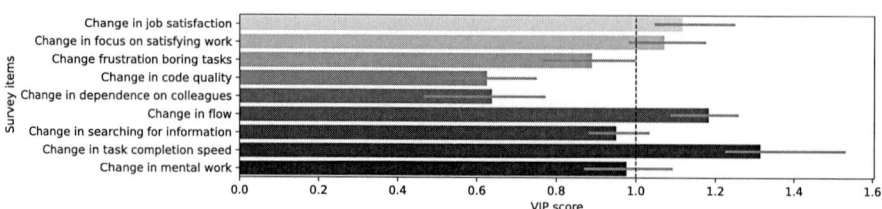

Fig. 3. VIP scores showing the contributions from each variable on the perceived change in productivity. The dotted vertical line marks the significance threshold at 1.0, and error bars show the min/max values from the 10-fold cross-validation

measure slightly different concepts and are not directly comparable, providing only an imprecise comparison. Furthermore, our target population is limited, and our findings might therefore not generalize to a global population.

When looking closer at which factors influence perceived changes in productivity, our study reveals both correlations and discrepancies between developers' perceived productivity and the SPACE dimensions. Both "Satisfaction and well-being" and "Efficiency and flow" contained facets that showed moderate, positive correlation and impact towards perceived productivity. These results confirm previous findings on how different states of mind and contexts might affect perceived productivity [2,8,11]. The dimensions "Performance" and "Communication and collaboration" were not found to be important, though it should be noted that "Performance" was measured with only a single variable.

Overall, our findings suggest that the dimensions of SPACE either do not fully describe productivity, or that productivity, as defined by SPACE, does not align with developers' definition of productivity. This echoes similar discrepancies found by Beller et al., which indicates that perceived productivity does not always align with the type of productivity managers are interested in [2].

Our study provides the following implications for practice

1. Utilizing AI Coding Assistants is associated with perceived benefits, most notably increased levels of productivity, efficiency and flow, and satisfaction and well-being, though more conservative than those proclaimed by GitHub Research.
2. Some dimensions of SPACE seem more influential in changing perceived productivity. Facilitating "Efficiency and flow" and "Satisfaction and well-being" therefore seems more impactful than "Performance" and "Communication and collaboration", if the goal is to increase perceived productivity.

As for research implication, our results indicate that the SPACE framework might be incomplete, misaligned, or inappropriate in terms of capturing perceived productivity, with two of the SPACE dimensions showing little correlation with how developers define productivity. To extend this study, future work should aim for greater coverage of each SPACE dimension, with a special focus on including the "Activity" dimension, when assessing their influence on productivity.

References

1. Akoglu, H.: User's guide to correlation coefficients. Turk. J. Emerg. Med. **18**(3), 91 (2018). https://doi.org/10.1016/j.tjem.2018.08.001, https://www.ncbi.nlm.nih.gov/pmc/articles/PMC6107969/
2. Beller, M., Orgovan, V., Buja, S., Zimmermann, T.: Mind the gap: on the relationship between automatically measured and self-reported productivity. IEEE Software **38**(5), 24–31 (Sep 2021). https://doi.org/10.1109/MS.2020.3048200, https://ieeexplore.ieee.org/abstract/document/9311217/references#references
3. Berntzen, M., Hoda, R., Moe, N.B., Stray, V.: A taxonomy of inter-team coordination mechanisms in large-scale agile. IEEE Trans. Softw. Eng. **49**(2), 699–718 (2022). https://ieeexplore.ieee.org/abstract/document/9739868/
4. Dancey, C.P., Reidy, J.: Statistics Without Maths for Psychology: Using SPSS for Windows, 3rd edn. Pearson Prentice Hall, Harlow, Munich (2006). [repr.] edn
5. Forsgren, N., Storey, M.A., Maddila, C., Zimmermann, T., Houck, B., Butler, J.: The SPACE of developer productivity. Queue **19**(1), 20–48 (2021). https://doi.org/10.1145/3454122.3454124
6. Girardi, D., Lanubile, F., Novielli, N., Serebrenik, A.: Emotions and perceived productivity of software developers at the workplace. IEEE Trans. Softw. Eng. **48**(9), 3326–3341 (2022). https://doi.org/10.1109/TSE.2021.3087906, https://ieeexplore.ieee.org/abstract/document/9449979
7. Kalliamvakou, E.: Research: quantifying GitHub Copilot's impact on developer productivity and happiness (2022). https://github.blog/2022-09-07-research-quantifying-github-copilots-impact-on-developer-productivity-and-happiness/
8. Kim, Y.H., Choe, E.K., Lee, B., Seo, J.: Understanding personal productivity: how knowledge workers define, evaluate, and reflect on their productivity. In: Proceedings of the 2019 CHI Conference on Human Factors in Computing Systems, pp. 1–12. ACM, Glasgow (2019). https://doi.org/10.1145/3290605.3300845, https://dl.acm.org/doi/10.1145/3290605.3300845
9. Liang, J.T., Yang, C., Myers, B.A.: A large-scale survey on the usability of AI programming assistants: successes and challenges. In: Proceedings of the IEEE/ACM 46th International Conference on Software Engineering, pp. 1–13. ICSE 2024. Association for Computing Machinery, New York (2024). https://doi.org/10.1145/3597503.3608128, https://dl.acm.org/doi/10.1145/3597503.3608128
10. Lohr, S.L.: Sampling: Design and Analysis. Chapman & Hall/CRC Texts in Statistical Science, 3rd edn. CRC Press, Taylor & Francis Group, Boca Raton London New York (2022)
11. Meyer, A.N., Barr, E.T., Bird, C., Zimmermann, T.: Today was a good day: the daily life of software developers. IEEE Trans. Softw. Eng. **47**(5), 863–880 (2019)
12. Moe, N.B., Ulfsnes, R., Stray, V., Smite, D.: Improving productivity through corporate hackathons: a multiple case study of two large-scale agile organizations. In: Proceedings of the 55th Annual Hawaii International Conference on System Sciences (HICSS) (2021)
13. Murphy-Hill, E., ct al.: What predicts software developers' productivity? IEEE Trans. Softw. Eng. **47**(3), 582–594 (2021). https://doi.org/10.1109/TSE.2019.2900308, https://ieeexplore.ieee.org/abstract/document/8643844
14. Ross, S.I., Martinez, F., Houde, S., Muller, M., Weisz, J.D.: The programmer's assistant: conversational interaction with a large language model for software development. In: Proceedings of the 28th International Conference on Intelligent User Interfaces, pp. 491–514. ACM, Sydney (2023). https://doi.org/10.1145/3581641.3584037, https://dl.acm.org/doi/10.1145/3581641.3584037

15. Shull, F., Singer, J., Sjøberg, D.I.K. (eds.): Guide to advanced empirical software engineering. Springer, London (2008). https://doi.org/10.1007/978-1-84800-044-5
16. Smite, D., Moe, N.B., Hildrum, J., Huerta, J.G., Mendez, D.: Work-from-home is here to stay: call for flexibility in post-pandemic work policies. J. Syst. Softw. **195**, 111552 (2023). https://doi.org/10.1016/j.jss.2022.111552
17. Ulfsnes, R., Berntzen, M., Moe, N.B., Sporsem, T., Stray, V.: Exploring the organizational models for data science in agile software development: challenges and strategies from a multi-case study. In: Proceeding of the 57th Hawaii International Conference on System Sciences (HICSS 2024) (2024)
18. Ulfsnes, R., Moe, N.B., Stray, V., Skarpen, M.: Transforming software development with generative AI: empirical insights on collaboration and workflow, pp. 219–234. Springer, Cham (2024). https://doi.org/10.1007/978-3-031-55642-5_10
19. Wagner, S., Deissenboeck, F.: Defining productivity in software engineering. In: Sadowski, C., Zimmermann, T. (eds.) Rethinking Productivity in Software Engineering, pp. 29–38. Apress, Berkeley (2019). https://doi.org/10.1007/978-1-4842-4221-6_4
20. Wivestad, V., Barbala, A., Stray, V.: Copilot's island of joy: balancing individual satisfaction with team interaction in agile development. In: Agile Processes in Software Engineering and Extreme Programming - Workshops. 25th International Conference on Agile Software Development, XP 2024, Bolzano, Italy, 4–7 June 2024, p. 7. Springer, Cham (2024)
21. Ziegler, A., et al.: Productivity assessment of neural code completion. In: Proceedings of the 6th ACM SIGPLAN International Symposium on Machine Programming, MAPS 2022, pp. 21–29. Association for Computing Machinery, New York (2022). https://doi.org/10.1145/3520312.3534864, https://dl.acm.org/doi/10.1145/3520312.3534864
22. Ziegler, A., et al.: Measuring GitHub copilot's impact on productivity. Commun. ACM **67**(3), 54–63 (2024). https://doi.org/10.1145/3633453, https://dl.acm.org/doi/10.1145/3633453

The 2nd International Workshop on Global and Hybrid Work in Software Engineering (GoHyb)

Analyzing the Impact of Constant Feedback on Hybrid Agile Team Performance: Preliminary Results

Wardah Naeem Awan$^{(\boxtimes)}$ (ID) and Iflaah Salman (ID)

School of Engineering Science, Lappeenranta-Lahti University of Technology,
Mukkulankatu 19, 15210 Lahti, Finland
Wardah.awan@lut.fi

Abstract. This study investigates the impact of constant feedback in enhancing hybrid scrum team performance from a case study conducted with 24 undergraduate students organized in three teams. This research uses self-perceived performance surveys to identify factors that affect team performance. The objective is to enhance team performance by providing timely feedback for reflection and improvement based on identified challenges. Preliminary findings revealed that constant feedback, facilitated by self-perceived performance surveys after each sprint cycle, enables teams to address identified challenges and enhance performance progressively. This highlights the significance of timely feedback in enhancing team performance and productivity. Future work involves leveraging AI tools to analyze communication data collected throughout the study to understand well-being factors and their influence on a team's performance and productivity.

Keywords: Agile software development · hybrid work · constant feedback · team performance

1   Introduction

Software engineering is a socially interactive activity where developers collaborate and work together to develop and maintain software products [1]. Communication and collaboration among developers have a substantial impact on the success of software projects. In Agile software development communication and teamwork are considered as the key elements for successful software development [2]. Teamwork is crucial for effective team performance, as it determines how tasks and goals are accomplished in a team context and the effectiveness of teamwork directly influences the overall project performance [3].

Many software companies are striving to enhance the performance and productivity of their teams [4]. Enhancing developer's productivity can lead to faster development, enhanced code quality, and increased developer satisfaction which ultimately enhance overall performance. [4,5]. Feedback plays a vital role in

© The Author(s) 2025
L. Marchesi et al. (Eds.): XP 2024 Workshops, LNBIP 524, pp. 53–62, 2025.
https://doi.org/10.1007/978-3-031-72781-8_6

performance improvement [6]. It provides individuals with valuable information about their behavior and performance, enabling them to adjust their behaviors accordingly [7]. Feedback, whether positive or negative is closely linked with affective states(emotions, moods, feelings). These emotions such as happiness, satisfaction, anger, or frustration, are influenced by feedback and, in turn, can impact motivation and engagement with tasks [8]. Effective feedback mechanisms within teams promote better communication, collaboration, and relationships with team members and promote constant learning that ultimately leads to improved performance [9].

This study aims to offer preliminary findings regarding the impact of feedback on the team's performance. The impact of feedback is investigated in the hybrid agile-scrum development context by employing a constant feedback mechanism. We answer the following research question:

RQ: How does the implementation of a constant feedback mechanism impact the performance of hybrid software development teams?

This study and its findings contribute to an ongoing project that aims to assess and enhance hybrid working agile development teams' performance and well-being. The well-being of employees significantly contributes to their productivity leading to the overall enhancement in teams' performance [10–12]. However, the identification of well-being within the hybrid team collaboration remains challenging [13]. Additionally, existing assessment tools for individual well-being often rely on time-consuming surveys and questionnaires, limiting the capacity to offer immediate feedback. The project achieves these objectives by employing constant feedback consistent with the agile-scrum project sprints. The feedback is based on constant: 1) emotional and well-being assessment via AI-powered tools (of verbal, non-verbal and textual data), 2) self-performance assessment on individual and team levels, and 3) team performance assessment by product owners (PO).

To answer the RQ, we conduct a sprint performance survey to collect students' perceived personal and their teams' performance after each sprint. This provided insight into the perceived performance of the individual (team member) and their team for the respective sprint. Based on the survey responses, we provided feedback to the teams regarding the identified challenges. Thus, enabling them to address and improve their performance. The continuous assessment and constant feedback distinguish our approach from traditional feedback methods, where feedback is typically less frequent and not tied to individual performance assessments for each sprint cycle [7].

2   Study Design

This section describes the study design with details on the participants and data collection.

2.1   Participants

We applied convenience sampling to recruit participants. The participants were undergraduate students enrolled in the capstone project course of the international BSc. degree program offered at the Lahti campus of the Lappeenranta-Lahti University of Technology, Finland. We pitched our research work to the students enrolled in the course in the introductory lecture after they were done with forming teams with each other. This was to motivate their voluntary participation in the research study.

A total of 48 students enrolled in the course, organized into six teams, each comprising 7–9 members. Out of the six teams, only three agreed to participate in our research; each team consisted of 8 members. Participants signed the consent forms that complied with the university's rules. The data privacy notice was also shared with them to ensure the protection of their sensitive data. The demographic details of the participants are presented in Sect. 2.3.

2.2   The Steup

The 14-week capstone project began with an introductory lecture on Scrum, followed by six diverse team formations. Each team has eight members representing at least three nationalities including Scrum Master. Each team decided on their own Scrum Master. The students who took on the Scrum Master role attended a two-day certified Scrum Master training and passed the certification test to ensure they have the basic knowledge to serve as Scrum Masters. Project proposals from Finnish companies were presented to students, who then matched with companies via interviews. Each team has a PO from the company and a professional agile coach for guidance. A scrum LEGO simulation was organized for all teams to practice scrum under the guidance of their agile coach. Following the Scrum simulation, teams started their first sprint by holding a sprint planning meeting with the PO to create and prioritize the product backlog. Figure 1

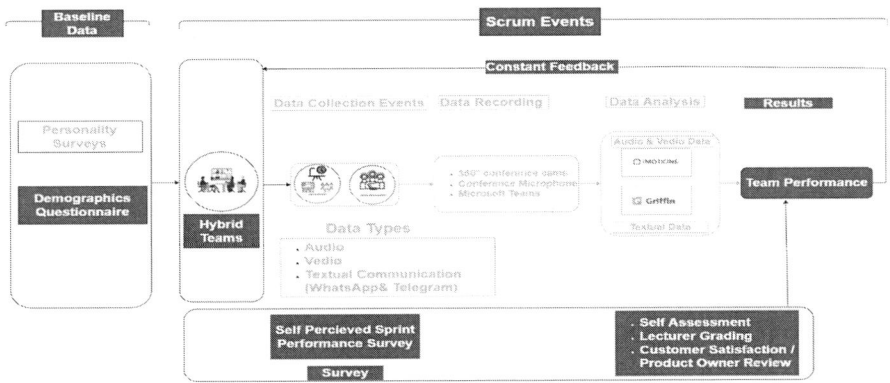

Fig. 1. Study design and overview

shows the design and overview of our study. The green highlights represent the focus of this study.

To accommodate our participants' preferred working styles (described in the demographics in Sect. 2.3), we provided teams with 360-degree cameras and conference microphones for hybrid setups. Team members who opt to meet in person use a provided meeting link to connect with virtual team members and utilize a 360-degree camera so that all the members and the PO joining the meeting online can see and interact with the members meeting in person. This setup enables effective engagement and collaboration for all participants in a hybrid mode.

Table 1 shows the meeting set-up details of teams in the first four sprints. The numbers in parentheses denote participants attending in person or online. T1 usually prefers online meetings, while T2 and T3 prefer a hybrid format, particularly for review and retrospective meetings, incorporating both in-person and online attendance.

Table 1. Meeting set-up detail of teams; T = team

Sprint No	Sprint Events	Meeting mode		Hybrid	
		In-person	Online	In-person	Online
1	Sprint Planning	T3	T1, T2		
	Sprint Review & Retro		T1, T2	T3 (6)	T3(2)
2	Sprint Planning	T1	T2, T3		
	Sprint Review & Retro		T1, T2, T3		
3	Sprint Planning		T1, T2, T3		
	Sprint Review & Retro		T1,T2	T3 (4)	T3 (4)
4	Sprint Planning		T1, T2	T3 (4)	T3 (4)
	Sprint Review & Retro	T1		T2 (6), T3	T2 (2)

2.3   Data Collection

This section presents the details of data collection methods.

Demographics Questionnaire. All the participants were required to fill out a demographics form as the first step of data collection. The demographic survey included questions that asked students about their academic year of study, gender, nationality, working experience, knowledge of scrum, and their preferred and typical mode of working. Table 2 shows the demographic details of participants.

Table 2 suggests that 14 out of 24 participants are experienced; they are either currently working or have previously worked in the industry. Ten are

Table 2. Demographic profile of respondents

Variable	Category	N = 24	% of Respondents
Academic Year	2nd Year	4	17%
	3rd Year	20	83%
Gender	Male	15	63%
	Female	9	37%
Experience	Experienced	14	58%
	Inexperienced	10	42%
Preferred working mode	In-person	7	29%
	Virtual	6	25.0%
	Hybrid	11	46%
Region[a]	Asia	16	66%
	Central Europe	1	4%
	North Europe	3	13%
	East Europe	3	13%
	United States	1	4%

[a] We did not scope in analysing this factor in this study. Yet, we report this because it is a factor that may relate to the facial expressions of participants belonging to different regions [14]

inexperienced. Regarding their preferred working mode, 11 participants prefer a hybrid mode (half in-person, half online), 7 prefer in-person collaboration with their team, and 6 prefer working virtually.

Sprint Performance Survey. In this study, we focus on implementing a constant feedback mechanism to improve team performance through a self-perceived performance survey. To achieve this, we conduct a sprint performance survey after each sprint cycle, gathering data from students about their perceived self-performance and their team's performance. The survey examines several key areas of team dynamics and performance, including self-performance assessment, team collaboration, challenges in teamwork, communication effectiveness, and communication issues. It also addresses team conflicts, individual contributions to team goals, overall team performance, adherence to the Scrum framework, and satisfaction with process improvements and product progress. For the survey's reliability, it was piloted to ensure its comprehensibility and assessment of the intended topics.

The survey uses both qualitative and quantitative measures to assess performance. All questions collected quantitative and qualitative data. For quantitative data, we use a 5-point Likert scale. The qualitative data collection was through an answer field (text box) provided against each Likert scale option to facilitate open responses regarding potential challenges or issues respective to the chosen value. This qualitative response allows us to dig deeper into the possible issues faced by the teams, offering valuable context to complement the quantitative data. Through this combined approach, we gain a comprehensive understanding of the factors influencing sprint performance and identify areas for potential improvement to enhance team effectiveness and productivity. We provide teams with feedback based on responses, highlighting challenges identified by their members.

It is to be noted that the data collection for this research is still in progress because the capstone course is not complete yet.

3   Data Analysis

The data from the first four sprints is analyzed for this study because teams are currently in their fifth sprint. Once all participants responded to the survey, we analyzed both quantitative and qualitative data. For quantitative analysis, we calculated the mean value of all responses after each sprint to track the team's performance improvements across four sprints. In qualitative data analysis of open-ended survey responses(collected from text box incorporated against each Likert scale option), we employed a top-down coding method to identify the challenges encountered by teams. We use the factors outlined in the sprint performance survey as the baseline for coding the qualitative data.

Conducting the same survey after each sprint enables us to examine the trajectory of improvement and observe how the team's performance evolves. Following the analysis of each sprint, a feedback document was shared with scrum masters. Additionally, one-on-one meetings were arranged with each scrum master to discuss the possible solutions to mitigate the identified challenges. The scrum masters were responsible for discussing the feedback with their teams during their next team meetings.

4   Results and Discussion

In this section, we answer our research question: *"How does the implementation of a constant feedback mechanism impact the performance of hybrid software development teams?"*

Figure 2 illustrates the performance improvements achieved by the team across four sprints based on the results of quantitative data. The y-axis represents values from a 5-point Likert scale. The x-axis represents the factors assessed in the survey. We observed a progressive enhancement in team performance over four sprints, accompanied by a reduction in challenges related to communication, collaboration, and team conflict.

From qualitative data analysis of the first sprint survey, we identified that the language barrier is the most significant challenge reported by all teams due to the diverse nationalities within the team. This challenge results in communication and collaboration issues. For example, in response to the question related to communication issues, P1 from T2 reported that *"language barrier -can not express ourselves as freely, lack of communication - even when asking something*

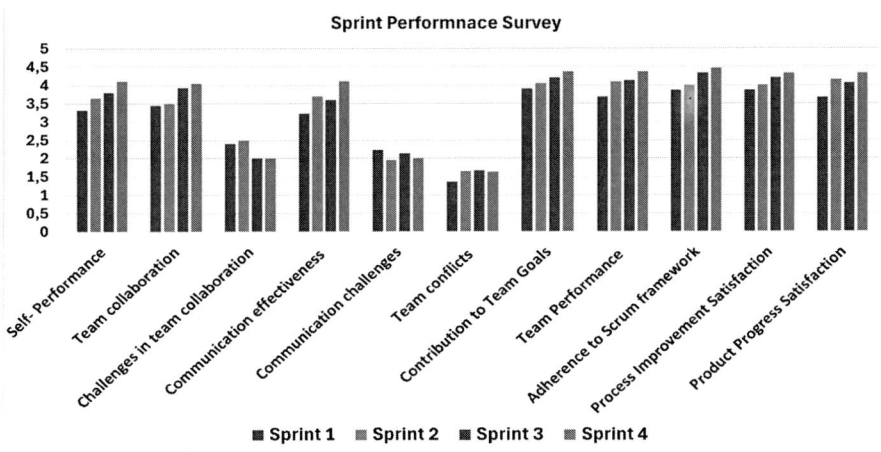

Fig. 2. Comparison of sprint performance survey results across four sprints

some would just keep quiet" and P7 from T3 reported *"despite encouraging active discussion, most members either don't participate in the discussion or find that the topic does not require their input"*. About collaboration effectiveness, P8 from T1 reported *"The team is great and does good work, however, I find that most of the team has a hard time focusing on meetings/are hesitant to actively participate in the discussion and in case most cases the meeting takes excessive effort to carry out"* and P1 from T2 reported that *"Not enough positive feedback between team members"*. Other reported challenges include scheduling the meeting due to conflicting timings, unclear requirements, task division, fewer meetings, technical conflicts, and deviation from agreed working styles. All were reported in the context of the factors that negatively impact team progress and performance.

Following the second sprint, similar challenges persisted. Hence, during feedback sessions, we encouraged Scrum masters to organize team-building activities and implement weekly in-person meetings to enhance team relationships and minimize misunderstandings. To avoid meeting scheduling issues, scrum masters were advised to schedule the next sprint events (planning, review, and retrospective) towards the end of every sprint meeting. They were also advised to consider the availability of their PO along with the team members. We recommended having fixed days with adjustable timings to accommodate team members' schedules for daily meetings.

In the third sprint, teams followed the recommended practices and showed improvements regarding team collaboration, communication effectiveness and overall collaboration. In the fourth sprint, we observed further enhancements in overall performance, as shown in Fig. 2. Teams progressively developed skills and gained experience and constant feedback enabled them to timely reflect on identified factors, enhancing overall performance. In the fourth sprint survey, responding to the same question regarding communication issues participant P1 from T2 reported that *"Communication was much better, even if the language barrier was still there it was well managed"* and P8 from T1 reported *"Communication during the meetings could be more active, but otherwise, the communication was smooth, and in-person meetings especially were quite good for communication"*. In Fig. 3, the left panel shows communication improvements among team members across four sprints. In response to collaboration effectiveness, participant P4 from T3 reported that *"We started having face-to-face meetings which made everything easier"* and P1 from T2 reported *"More feedback has been given since previous Sprints. The team feels more comfortable talking to each other"*. In Fig. 3, the right panel shows collaboration improvement among team members across four sprints.

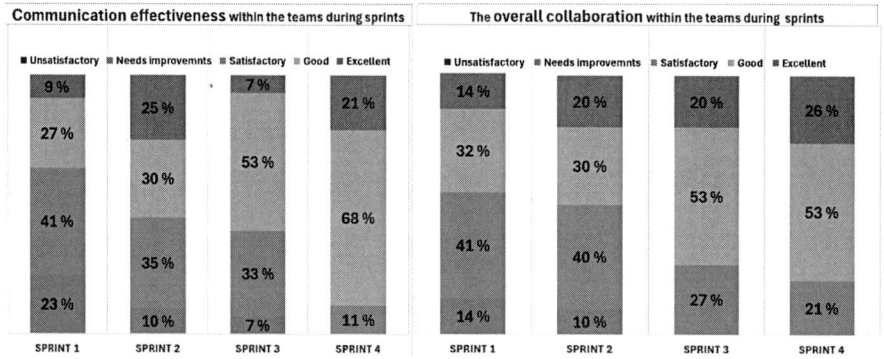

Fig. 3. Communication effectiveness and overall collaboration across four sprints

5   Conclusion and Future Work

In this paper, we discuss the preliminary results on the impact of constant feedback mechanisms in enhancing hybrid scrum team performance from a case study conducted with undergraduate students enrolled in a capstone course. The findings revealed that constant feedback mechanism, facilitated by self-perceived performance surveys after each sprint cycle, significantly contributed to enhancing team performance. This was achieved by providing teams with timely feedback and opportunities for reflection and improvement.

The next phase of our study involves analyzing verbal, non-verbal, and textual communication data collected throughout the course. We'll utilize AI tools to determine the factors influencing individual well-being within teams and assess how these factors impact overall team performance. We also plan to conduct a multiple case study with professionals to assess the effectiveness of the employed approaches in the industrial agile hybrid work context. This step would also leverage the generalizability of our findings.

References

1. Giuffrida, R., Dittrich, Y.: A conceptual framework to study the role of communication through social software for coordination in globally-distributed software teams. Inf. Softw. Technol. **63**, 11–30 (2015)
2. Qureshi, R., Basheri, M., Alzahrani, A.A.: Novel framework to improve communication and coordination among distributed agile teams. Int. J. Inf. Eng. Electron. Bus. **10**(4), 16–24 (2018)
3. Quek, S.W.D., et al.: Improving teamwork in software engineering projects in higher education. In: Proceedings - Frontiers in Education Conference, FIE, Institute of Electrical and Electronics Engineers Inc. (2023)
4. Graziotin, D., Wang, X., Abrahamsson, P.: Do feelings matter? On the correlation of affects and the self-assessed productivity in software engineering. J. Softw.: Evol. Process **27**, 467–487 (2015)
5. Ford, D., et al.: A tale of two cities: software developers working from home during the COVID-19 pandemic (2020)
6. Lind, G., Mishchenko, M.: Positive feedback. In: Radical Therapy for Software Development Teams, pp. 135–141. Apress, Berkeley (2024)
7. Huang, V.W., Krueger, K., Cohen, T., Hilton, M.: Improving software engineering teamwork with structured feedback. In: Proceedings of the 55th ACM Technical Symposium on Computer Science Education, New York, NY, USA, vol. 1, pp. 1414–1420. ACM (2024)
8. Sharp, H., Baddoo, N., Beecham, S., Hall, T., Robinson, H.: Models of motivation in software engineering. Inf. Softw. Technol. **51**, 219–233 (2009)
9. Kluger, A.N., Denisi, A.: The effects of feedback interventions on performance: a historical review, a meta-analysis, and a preliminary feedback intervention theory we argue that a considerable body of evidence suggesting that feedback intervention (FI) effects on performance are quite vari. Technical report, vol. 2 (1996)
10. Laanti, M.: Agile and wellbeing - stress, empowerment, and performance in Scrum and Kanban teams. In: Proceedings of the Annual Hawaii International Conference on System Sciences, pp. 4761–4770 (2013)
11. Ralph, P., et al.: Pandemic programming: how COVID-19 affects software developers and how their organizations can help. Empir. Softw. Eng. **25**, 4927–4961 (2020)
12. Russo, D., Hanel, P.H., Altnickel, S., van Berkel, N.: Predictors of well-being and productivity among software professionals during the COVID-19 pandemic - a longitudinal study. Empir. Softw. Eng. **26**, 7 (2021)
13. Wright, T.A., Bonett, D.G.: Job satisfaction and psychological well-being as non-additive predictors of workplace turnove. J. Manage. **33**, 141–160 (2007)
14. Gendron, M., Roberson, D., van der Vyver, J.M., Barrett, L.F.: Perceptions of emotion from facial expressions are not culturally universal: evidence from a remote culture. Emotion **14**(2), 251–262 (2014)

Dual Effects of Hybrid Working
on Performance: More Work Hours
or More Work Time

Darja Smite[1,2(✉)], Anastasiia Tkalich[1], Nils Brede Moe[1,2],
Panagiota Chatzipetrou[3], Eriks Klotins[2], and Per Kristian Helland[4]

[1] SINTEF, 7034 Trondheim, Norway
`darja.smite@bth.se`
[2] Blekinge Institute of Technology, 371 79 Karlskrona, Sweden
[3] Örebro University, Örebro, Sweden
[4] Storebrand, Oslo, Norway

Abstract. Work in software development companies has become increasingly hybrid with employees altering days of working in the office with days of working remotely from home. Yet, little is know about the efficiency of such way of working because the current scale of remote working is unprecedented. In this paper, we present our findings from a company-wide survey at Storebrand - a large-scale Norwegian fintech company, focusing on perceived performance. Our analysis of 192 responses shows that most employees report being able to perform the planned tasks. Further, half of respondents perceive to have increased work hours. Through qualitative analysis of open-ended commentaries of respondents we learned that remote working has dual effects on the perceived work hours - some employees report working longer hours and others report having more work time due to efficient use of the time throughout the day. Finally, we recommend managers to discuss and address the concerning habits of employees caused by increased connectivity and inability to stop working, before these lead to burnout and disturbances in the work/life balance.

Keywords: Hybrid · Flexible · Remote · Performance · Work hours

1 Introduction and Related Work

Many software development companies today have become places of hybrid working with polices that institutionalize remote-first culture with little onsite presence, hybrid work culture often with rather flexible onsite presence, and office-first culture with frequent office presence yet some flexibility for working remotely [10]. As a result, individuals can choose, at least to some degree, when to work remotely and when to have office-based work [3,7,10,13].

Hybrid working, that is, alternating between working at the office and working remotely, is said to bring the best of the two worlds: remote and onsite working. The documented benefits of remote working include reduced commute time,

L. Marchesi et al. (Eds.): XP 2024 Workshops, LNBIP 524, pp. 63–70, 2025.
https://doi.org/10.1007/978-3-031-72781-8_7

better conditions for focused work, a more comfortable work environment, and better work-life balance [12,13]. In turn, office working provides the opportunities to socialise face-to-face, facilitate efficient brainstorming and problem-solving sessions, provide help and onboard team members, have spontaneous interactions, and strengthen team cohesion and psychological safety, all the aspects that are reported to be missing in fully remote work rhythm [15]. Yet, the ability to tap into these benefits is conditioned by the level of co-presence. Individual office presence, does not guarantee that people meet and interact, if office days are not synchronized [8]. Even when the majority of team members opt for office-based work, many teams maintain a hybrid structure to accommodate those who prefer arrangements that are more remote in nature [13].

The lack of co-presence significantly affects communication, as well as the effectiveness of the regular coordination mechanisms when used in a computer-mediated fashion [5,14]. When some people are working from home and others are working from the office, conducting spontaneous discussions is difficult and sub-groups emerge within the team [15]. Hybrid teams are found to have an increased need for coordination which shifted from informal, spontaneous face-to-face coordination towards more formal, consistent, technology-mediated synchronous (i.e. meetings) and asynchronous (e.g. shared documents; Slack messages) communication [14]. Further, agile ways of working and rituals that heavily rely on co-presence intend to facilitate collaboration and enable individual performance. Early studies of hybrid agile teams show that many agile practices held remotely are compromised [14]. The effects of hybrid work on performance is thus to be understood.

The key questions for leaders today center around the ways to find a balance between individual, team, and organizational needs. In particular, many companies try to understand the value and benefits of office presence vs remote working, and how much office presence or co-presence in work groups is sufficient to maintain performance, and keep employees satisfied.

Motivated by the above-mentioned challenges we seek to answer the following research question: *How is perceived performance affected by hybrid working?* To address our research question, we conducted a case study in a large-scale Norwegian fintech company.

2   Research Methodology

Empirical Background: In this workshop paper, we report our findings based on the data collected at Storebrand, a Norwegian financial services company that offers pension, savings, insurance, and banking products to both the private and the business markets. Based on a strategic work launched at the start of the COVID-19 pandemic, Storebrand committed to changing the corporate work policy to explicitly permit flexible working. Storebrand had used agile methods for over a decade and can be understood as a mature agile organization.

Hybrid strategy at Storebrand is based on a belief that a one-size-fits-all solution does not exist and even one lasting solution for the same team can be utopic. Therefore, the company intentionally fosters team-based discussions over rules to build lasting habits around sound reasoning and cooperation rather than strict policies. Despite a very flexible policy, Storebrand management does believe in the importance of an attractive office and office-based working [9]. However, instead of asking how to attract people to the office, Storebrand defines three core questions to guide their hybrid strategy:

- How can we organize our work as efficiently as possible to create the products and services that our customers need?
- How can we create the most engaging and inclusive workplace possible?
- How can we ensure that all employees experience mastery and development?

Data Collection and Analysis: We collected the data through an online survey. The survey was open during June 12–23, 2023, for all 2,166 employees and gathered 1072 responses (over 50% response rate). Here, we report the analysis of a subset of data from the software engineering department at Storebrand.

The software development department employed 399 software engineers and business people who are involved in developing digital financial products and work according to agile methods - large-scale Scrum and ScrumBan. Employees are situated both in Norway and Sweden. Our sample includes 192 responses (48% response rate). We focus on questions related to individual work rhythm, perceived task performance, and perceived changes in work hours. The responses were collected on a 5-point scale, including the response alternatives on a range between "Not at all" to "Completely", "Very dissatisfied" to "Very satisfied", "To a very small extent" to "To a very large extent". The subset of survey questions relevant for this paper is included in the Appendix.

Stratified analysis was performed for varying degrees of office presence. Responses to open-ended questions were analyzed qualitatively using thematic coding and generated themes that help explain the quantitative results.

3   Results

In the following, we present the results from surveying employees in the software engineering department of Storebrand about their perceived performance. In Fig. 1, we start with the details about the survey respondents and their demographic information, followed by their hybrid work rhythm in Fig. 2. We then, in Fig. 3, present the distribution of responses to the performance question. This is, to the employees' ability to complete their tasks, stratified by the hybrid work rhythm (proportion of the office presence vs remote working). We then seek explanation for our results through the combined analysis of both quantitative and qualitative responses to related questions.

Our survey represents experiences from predominantly Norwegian employees from the software engineering department at Storebrand. 1/3 of the respondents are female, and 2/3 are male respondents. The sample has a good representation of employees in different age groups. With respect to commute time, the majority

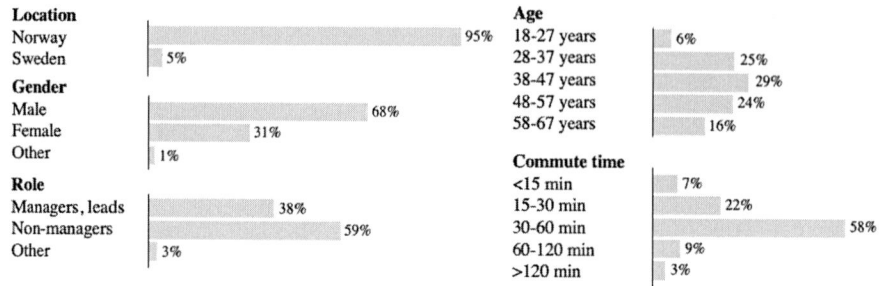

Fig. 1. Overview of the respondents

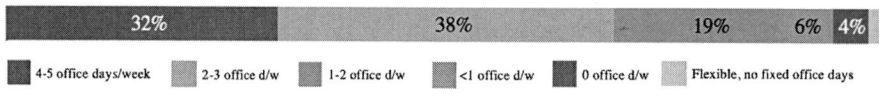

Fig. 2. Hybrid work rhythms

of respondents need 30–60 min to reach the office and roughly 1/3 lives within 30 min commute distance.

One of the interesting findings in the survey is related to the hybrid work rhythms (See Fig. 2). Despite Storebrand's flexible work policy, we found that 70% of respondents are working in the office half of the time or more. Only 10% do not visit the office regularly every week, four of which are working fully remotely.

In Fig. 3, we illustrate the respondents' ability to complete planned tasks. We see that the majority of respondents are able to accomplish their tasks to a large or very large extent. This means that hybrid working does not hinder performance. Although employees with fully flexible and fully remote work rhythms report higher performance scores, this result shall be taken with a grain of salt because there are just a few respondents in these categories. The scores in the categories with higher number of respondents are quite similar, with slightly better scores in the category of employees having one to two days per week working in the office.

To better understand the variance in perceived performance, we asked the respondents about the changes in their work hours due to hybrid work, which directly affect the ability to accomplish the planned work tasks. Further, we explored the free-text responses related to performance questions and identified further impact factors inherent in the hybrid ways of working.

The survey results suggest that half of respondents (50%) do not perceive any change in the work hours and a marginal share of respondents feel that the number of hours has slightly decreased (1%), as shown in Fig. 4. Yet, the other half of respondents (49%) report an increase in work hours (29% responded that work hours Slightly increased and 20% that work hours Increased, see Fig. 4).

Performance: To what extent were you able to perform all your tasks in the past month?

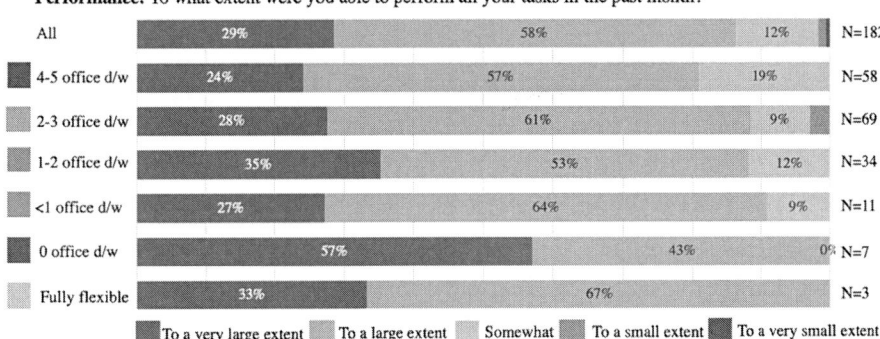

Fig. 3. Ability to complete tasks

Changes in work hours: How do you perceive this aspect have changed due to hybrid work?

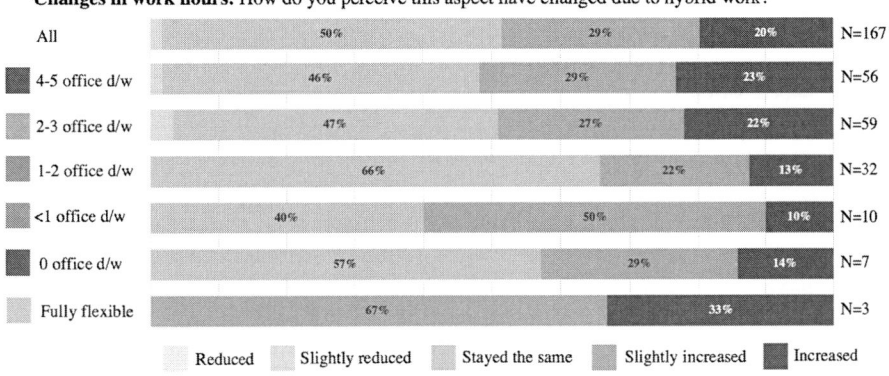

Fig. 4. Changes in work hours and factors explaining these changes

This can also explain our findings with respect to positive performance scores as more can be done when working longer hours. Detailed analysis shows that the lowest number of respondents with increased work hours appear in the category working 1–2 days in the office. Additional commentaries regarding the work hours (from 26 respondents) pointed towards the different aspects of working remotely (See Fig. 4). Among these, we found, for example, positive effects, such as the lack of commute time that led to having more work time. However, the most frequent reason contributing to having more or longer work hours was increased connectivity, which related to higher mobilisation and lower threshold for contacting the colleagues but also a more blurry boundaries between work and private life. Descriptions in this category were sometimes alarming, indicating that people sacrifice their free time and privacy for performing the work. Yet, a fully onsite work is not an escape from increased work hours either. In the category reporting 4–5 days weekly office presence, 52% report having increased work hours.

4   Concluding Discussion

In this paper, we presented our findings from studying hybrid work rhythms and individual performance. We found that a company with flexible work policy had, what one could judge as an unexpectedly high office presence. We also found that the alternation of office presence and remote work results in most employees (87%) reporting being able to perform their tasks to a large or very large extent. This is in line with many other studies that report positive impacts of remote working on productivity due to schedule flexibility, freedom from interruptions, and time saved on commuting [4,7,12,13,16]. Some studies that try to understand why higher productivity occurs, point out that the increased outputs can be attributed to employees working longer hours, suggesting that productivity increases might be illusive [1,2,13,14]. In our case, we found that high performance can be indeed explained by the changes in the work hours - 52% of respondents report an increase in work hours. Similarly, de Souza Santos et al. found in their survey study that half of respondents acknowledged working overtime, with some (3%) even exceeding five extra hours per week [13]. The reasons for increased work hours in our study echo the findings by de Souza Santos et al.. We found increased work hours to be associated with a more efficient use of time (contributing to having more work time), but also due to the negative impacts of increased connectivity and not having a strict work/life separation (contributing to longer work hours). Along with concerns about the tendency to work longer hours, some researchers warn about the threats to work/life balance [6,11,13].

At the same time, our results show that an increase in work hours is not caused by increased remote working, as even respondents with the highest office presence reported negative changes in work hours. Further, we discovered that the lowest increase in work hours was reported by those only in the office 1–2 days a week. This may be due to having more control over work schedule, and fewer interruptions when performing individual tasks. Since there is no clear link between work arrangement and longer hours, we conclude that these concern job pressure and individual habits related to increased connectivity. One recommendation to address the emergent habits for those working from home is to implement a "hard stop" practice-a preset time for logging off or turning off the computer-which we found effective in our earlier study [11]. For those working in the office, the availability of focused work places might be a solution.

In our future work, we will continue monitoring the changes in the work hours and focus on understanding the work/life balance. While this study reports findings on an individual level, further work shall also focus on understanding the impact of remote and hybrid working on teams.

Acknowledgments. We would like to thank the studied company for their engagement in our research. The work was partially supported by the Research Council of Norway through the projects 10xTeams (grant 309344) and Transformit (grant 321477), and by the Swedish Knowledge Foundation through the KK-Hög project WorkFlex (grant 2022/0047).

A   Appendix: Survey Questions

In the following, we provide the subset of survey questions used in the analysis.

Location: Which country do you primarily work from? (Norway/Sweden/Other countries)

Gender: Your gender (Female/Male/Other/Prefer not to disclose)

Role: Do you have responsibility for other's work? (Yes, I have personnel responsibility for 1+ persons/Yes, I have managerial responsibility without personnel responsibility/No/Not sure)

Age: How old are you? (18–27 years/28–37 years/38–47 years/48–57 years/58–67 years/Older than 67 years)

Commute: How much time do you spend commuting to the office (one way)? (Less than 15 min/Between 15 and 30 min/Between 30 min and 1 h/Between 1 and 2 h/More than 2 h/Not relevant)

Work rhythm: How often do you work in the office during a typical week? (I never or almost never work in the office/Less than one day a week/1–2 days a week/2–3 days a week/4–5 days a week/I don't have fixed days I work in the office)

Performance: To what extent were you able to perform all your tasks in the past month? (To a very small extent/To a small extent/Somewhat/To a large extent/To a very large extent)

Changes in work hours: How do you perceive these aspects have changed due to hybrid work - Number of hours you work? (Have been reduced/Slightly reduced/Remained the same/Slightly increased/Have increased/Not relevant)

Explanation: If you experienced any changes, what is the reason for it?

References

1. Bloom, N., Liang, J., Roberts, J., Ying, Z.J.: Does working from home work? Evidence from a Chinese experiment. Q. J. Econ. **130**(1), 165–218 (2015)
2. Chesley, N.: Technology use and employee assessments of work effectiveness, workload, and pace of life. Inf. Commun. Soc. **13**(4), 485–514 (2010)
3. Conboy, K., Moe, N.B., Stray, V., Gundelsby, J.H.: The future of hybrid software development: challenging current assumptions. IEEE Softw. **40**(02), 26–33 (2023)

4. Conradie, W.J., De Klerk, J.J.: To flex or not to flex? Flexible work arrangements amongst software developers in an emerging economy. SA J. Hum. Resour. Manag. **17**(1), 1–12 (2019)
5. Espinosa, J.A., Carmel, E.: The impact of time separation on coordination in global software teams: a conceptual foundation. Softw. Process: Improve. Pract. **8**(4), 249–266 (2003)
6. Gorjifard, R., Crawford, J.: Working from home: impact on wellbeing and work-life balance. N. Z. J. Employ. Relat. **46**(2), 64–78 (2021)
7. Malhotra, A.: The postpandemic future of work (2021)
8. Moe, N.B., Ulsaker, S., Hildrum, J.M., Smite, D., Ay, F.C.: Understanding the difference between office presence and co-presence in team member interactions. In: Proceeding of the 57th Hawaii International Conference on System Sciences (HICSS 2024). AIS Electronic Library (2024)
9. Smite, D., Klotins, E., Moe, N.B.: What attracts employees to work onsite in times of increased remote working? IEEE Softw. 1–5 (2024). https://doi.org/10.1109/MS.2024.3375964
10. Smite, D., Moe, N.B., Hildrum, J., Gonzalez-Huerta, J., Mendez, D.: Work-from-home is here to stay: call for flexibility in post-pandemic work policies. J. Syst. Softw. **195**, 111552 (2023)
11. Smite, D., Moe, N.B., Klotins, E., Gonzalez-Huerta, J.: From forced working-from-home to voluntary working-from-anywhere: two revolutions in telework. J. Syst. Softw. **195**, 111509 (2023)
12. Smite, D., Tkalich, A., Moe, N.B., Papatheocharous, E., Klotins, E., Buvik, M.P.: Changes in perceived productivity of software engineers during COVID-19 pandemic: the voice of evidence. J. Syst. Softw. **186**, 111197 (2022)
13. de Souza Santos, R., Grillo, W., Cabral, D., de Castro, C., Albuquerque, N., França, C.: Post-pandemic hybrid work in software companies: findings from an industrial case study. arXiv e-prints, pp. arXiv–2401 (2024)
14. de Souza Santos, R.E., Ralph, P.: A grounded theory of coordination in remote-first and hybrid software teams. In: Proceedings of the 44th International Conference on Software Engineering, pp. 25–35 (2022)
15. Tkalich, A., Šmite, D., Andersen, N.H., Moe, N.B.: What happens to psychological safety when going remote? IEEE Softw. (2022)
16. Vargas Llave, O., et al.: The rise in telework: impact on working conditions and regulations (2022)

Hybrid Meetings in Agile Software Development

Viktoria Stray[1,2(✉)] ⓘ, Nils Brede Moe[2] ⓘ, and Susanne Semsøy[1]

[1] University of Oslo, 0373 Oslo, Norway
stray@ifi.uio.no
[2] SINTEF, Trondheim, Norway

Abstract. Hybrid meetings, which combine in-person and virtual participants, are becoming increasingly common in modern agile workplaces. Despite their prevalence, these meetings often lead to asymmetric participation. In this study, we explored the nature of participation asymmetries in hybrid meetings and identified the technical and social factors contributing to these disparities. We analyzed anonymized access card data, observed hybrid meetings, and conducted interviews with employees in a large-scale Norwegian software development organization. Our findings reveal that the employees preferred to go to the office on Tuesdays and Wednesdays. In hybrid meetings, we found reduced engagement from virtual participants compared to those co-located at the office, especially in the absence of a clear speaking order. Social-driven asymmetries included difficulties in entering conversations, missing remarks and non-verbal cues, and being left out of pre- and post-meeting discussions. Physical presence in meetings was found to be crucial for newly onboarded team members. Future research should investigate what fosters inclusive meeting practices to improve engagement and collaboration in hybrid work environments.

Keywords: Collaboration · Coordination · Alignment · Hybrid work · Remote participation · Teamwork · Large-scale agile development

1 Introduction

Agile ways of working are changing because hybrid work is becoming the new norm [8]. Agile teams and team members have the flexibility to choose, at least to some degree, between remote and office-based work [3]. Smite et al. [17] surveyed 20 companies and found that preferences for the proportion of time spent in the office versus at home vary both across and within companies. Moe et al. [11] explored the co-presence patterns of 17 agile teams in a company whose employees work partly from home. They found significant variation in co-presence practices. Some teams exhibited a coordinated approach, ensuring team members were simultaneously present at the office. However, other teams demonstrated fragmented co-presence, with only small subgroups of members

© The Author(s) 2025
L. Marchesi et al. (Eds.): XP 2024 Workshops, LNBIP 524, pp. 71–80, 2025.
https://doi.org/10.1007/978-3-031-72781-8_8

meeting in person and the remainder rarely interacting with their team members face-to-face. Agile teams spend a substantial amount of time in meetings, which are crucial venues for coordination, communication, and decision-making [21]. Developers report satisfaction when they invest their time in constructive meetings; however, long or unconstructive meetings are perceived as a waste of time and trigger negative emotions [5,20]. Excessive time in meetings can limit developers' sense of autonomy and reduce their productivity [6]. Scheduled meetings, while necessary for maintaining alignment across multiple teams, are often seen as disruptions to the developers' workflow. Forced participation in meetings, especially those deemed irrelevant to immediate tasks, contributes to a sense of dissatisfaction [6,20]. Additionally, unconstructive meetings result in time away from primary tasks, increasing employee stress and reducing job satisfaction [14]. Hybrid agile meetings are now common, offering both benefits and challenges. Positively, these meetings provide increased flexibility in scheduling and adding participants, save travel time, reduce environmental impact, and improve efficiency [12,19]. Negatively, they can cause videoconference fatigue, with participants feeling physically and mentally drained after attending a meeting virtually [2]. Additionally, remote participation demands more structure, often resulting in remote participants remaining in a listening mode [22].

Hybrid meetings are becoming more common but remain challenging to conduct and can reduce job satisfaction, underscoring the need for more studies on how to manage them effectively. Our objective, therefore, is to answer the following research question: *RQ: How can organizations manage hybrid meetings?* To address our research question, we conducted a case study in a large-scale Norwegian Fintech company called BankDev (a pseudonym).

2 Context and Methodology

BankDev develops software for a group of Norwegian banks. The organization employs roughly 650 people in 24 teams, including both in-house employees and consultants, and caters to both the consumer and professional market [10]. We collected and analyzed anonymized access card data, and found the most popular office days to be Tuesdays and Wednesdays (see Fig. 1). We conducted interviews and observations in two teams: Team Fixed and Team Flex. Team Fixed had virtual days on Monday, where all team members should work from home by default. Tuesday and Wednesday were office days, while the team members could choose on Thursdays and Fridays where to work from. In contrast to Team Fixed, Team Flex offered complete flexibility, allowing individuals to choose their work location on any day without predetermined office or work-from-home days.

In total, 23 meetings were observed in the period October 2021 to March 2022. Three of them can be described as fully virtual, and 20 of them were hybrid. We observed 16 of the meetings physically co-located and 7 virtually using Microsoft Teams. We observed ten different types of meetings: sync meetings (5), retrospectives (4), Friday-wins (3), delivery meetings (2), show-and-tell meetings (2), team meetings/check-ins (2), presentations (2), stand-up in subteam (1), post mortem meeting (1), and team lead hybrid-workshop (1).

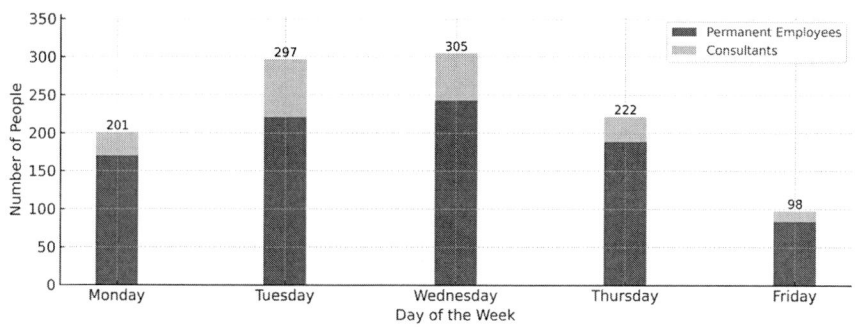

Fig. 1. Office presence of one typical week in BankDev in March 2022.

Table 1. Overview of interviewees

Team	Informant ID	Role	Experience in years	Total commute times
Fixed	1	Team lead	Over 10 years	1 h 20 min
Fixed	2	Developer	Over 10 years	3 h
Fixed	3	Developer	Under 2 years	30 min
Fixed	4	Developer	2–5 years	2 h
Fixed	5	Tester	5–10 years	2 h
Flex	6	Team lead	Over 10 years	1 h 40 min
Flex	7	Developer	Under 2 years	1 h
Flex	8	Developer	5–10 years	1 h 30 min
Flex	9	Developer	Under 2 years	30 min

The company uses Slack, a well-known collaborating tool that allows chatting and video calls. Slack is the main tool for facilitating communication within the organization, especially within and between teams. On one occasion, Slack was described as a business-critical system because the platform facilitates a large amount of internal communication. To gain access, we had to be declared trustworthy by the department handling privacy and security concerns. This process took about two weeks.

The interviews were conducted between January 2022 and March 2022, and aimed to provide further insights into what was found during the observations. All interviews were recorded and transcribed. Table 1 shows an overview of the interviewees' roles, the level of experience each had in their role, and the total daily commute time to the office. Commute time is included because travel time to the office impacts the interviewees' perspectives on hybrid work and its effects on their daily routines. Semi-structured interviews with open-ended questions were chosen in order to cover certain predefined topics, but also allow for exploration of topics as they emerged. In total, nine interviews were conducted split between the two research teams. The interviews lasted between 35 min to 86 min.

3   Results

The interviewees said that working hybrid allowed them more flexibility, which was reported to promote improved work-life balance and well-being. This finding was more likely to apply if the individuals had families with young children.

However, the fact that many in BankDev decided to work several days from home meant that many meetings were hybrid. Hybrid meetings consist of two distinct groups: those attending from a co-located space, typically together in a meeting room, and those participating remotely via digital conference tools. Whereas interviewees could effortlessly name several benefits of co-located and virtual meetings, all interviewees struggled to name benefits of hybrid meetings.

We found that hybrid meetings repeatedly seemed to include some degree of asymmetric participation. These asymmetries never seemed intentional; they occurred unconsciously due to the nature of hybrid meetings. We found that the ones attending virtually consistently contributed and engaged less. Next, we will report on the tech-driven and social-driven asymmetries we found and the factors contributing to these asymmetries.

3.1   Tech-Driven Asymmetries

Tech-driven asymmetries consist of situations where there is a technical issue or suboptimal solution, which causes a significant disadvantage for one group or person. The most obvious example of this was when those co-located in the meeting room had problems connecting to the virtual meeting. This created situations where the meeting could last several minutes before those attending virtually were finally connected. The co-located group would give a short summary of what had been discussed, which seemed to help the situation. Still, having to provide summaries caused disruptions to the meeting. The most prolonged delay we observed was eight minutes. Eight minutes was described as feeling like a long time for virtual participants sitting alone just waiting. Another challenge was related to the sound quality. Interviewee 7 said:

> Conversations where there are many on the same microphone ... it doesn't work that well. [...] For example, if there are discussions and many people are talking over each other, then it becomes impossible to separate what is said and by whom. [...] But when you are in the meeting room, your ears are kind of able to do it.

Similarly, it was typical for noises like coffee mugs being placed on tables, rustling with paper, or coughs and sneezes to override the microphone. Participants attending virtually could, therefore, miss a lot of the conversations, varying from a couple of seconds here and there to not being able to properly hear what was being said for minutes. In addition, several informants explained that since those in the meeting room did not experience the same issues, it was difficult for them to be aware of and mitigate the problem. Those attending virtually sometimes notified those co-located about the challenges. However, the threshold of doing so was perceived as relatively high.

3.2 Social-Driven Asymmetries

Reduced Engagement from Virtual Attendees. When observing hybrid meetings, it became apparent that the participants attending virtually generally engaged and contributed considerably less than those being co-located. We found that it happened consistently regardless of team, sub-team, or who was attending virtually that specific day. Our most extreme observation was a meeting where six were co-located, and two were attending virtually. The meeting lasted just over one hour, and 56 min passed before one of those attending virtually spoke up. The other was muted during the entire meeting. It was generally not uncommon for virtual participants to wait until everyone from the meeting room had said something before eventually engaging themselves. We recorded the time from the start of the meeting to when the first virtual participant spoke in four other meetings; on average, it took about eight minutes. Often, periods of silence almost even seemed like a prerequisite for the virtual participants to engage.

When sitting in the same meeting room, participants would often casually add small comments when others were speaking. These small comments served as transitions in the conversation, allowing new participants to take the word easily or comment on other comments. They also frequently used body language to engage in the conversation. This resulted in conversations that flowed organically. Active participation was more frequent, and the word was more often passed between the co-located participants. This lively interaction in the meeting room, however, created a higher barrier for virtual participants to join in, as the flow of conversation and frequent use of body language among co-located participants made it more challenging for those attending remotely to find opportunities to speak. A developer, Interviewee 9, illustrated this point:

> *I think if there is a critical mass in the office, and you are sitting at home, then it kind of feels like stepping onto a stage when you want to say something. Because they have such a good flow in the conversation, and suddenly you interrupt them from [Microsoft] Teams. You get scared that you might ruin that flow.*

Interviewee 7 noted:

> *[When co-located] adding a quick comment doesn't interrupt anyone. Virtually it can and that's a really nasty feeling if you suddenly interrupt someone's flow just because you wanted to add a little comment. There's less natural flow. You have to wait for one person to finish and the next and the next. You really have to wait for your turn.*

As a result, several informants reported only speaking up when they felt it was imperative and warranted what they saw as an interruption. The characteristics of hybrid meetings create a barrier between the co-located and the remote participants.

Virtual Attendees Missing Out on Side Conversations and Remarks.
Co-located participants sometimes turned to the person sitting close to them
and initiated small conversations. Not only were the virtual participants unable
to hear these conversations, but people ended up facing away from the meeting
room camera. This example also contributed to establishing an invisible barrier
between the two groups. At times, the rest of the co-located participants over-
heard these conversations and further commented on them, especially if it was
a question. As a result, the meeting could change topics without virtual participants hearing the initial trigger. If no one repeated the question to the virtual
participants, we found that they engaged considerably less while discussing that
particular topic. This asymmetry was especially apparent when funny remarks or
jokes were whispered between co-located participants. The whole meeting room
could start laughing, while the virtual participants often looked quite confused.

**Virtual Attendees Missing Out on Talk Before and After the Meet-
ings.** Virtual participants were excluded from the talk before and especially
after the meetings, e.g., when walking back to the desks. Although these conversations and feedback statements were not necessarily critical, they often served
as a positive and uplifting end to the meetings. Also, there were occasions where
these after-meeting talks were essentially a continuation of the meeting, with
exclusively the co-located group present. Unofficial sessions like these could last
several minutes. It never seemed like this was intentional, but rather sponta-
neously happened. On a few occasions, co-located participants sat down at their
desks and further discussed the topics of the meeting. Whenever this happened,
the discussions usually lasted between 5–15 min.

We also noticed that recently onboarded team members tended to stay in the
meeting room after the meetings to ask clarifying questions. We informally asked
an individual about this during observation, to which the person answered:

> "When joining via Microsoft Teams, I usually have just as many questions,
> but I don't really want to spam my colleagues with messages. But when
> we're in the same room, I can ask these questions while finishing our coffee
> after the meeting."

3.3   Factors Contributing to Asymmetries

The number of participants and the type of meeting were important factors
influencing the degree of asymmetric participation. The types of meetings that
included discussion or did not have a clear agenda or speaking order performed
the worst in a hybrid meeting setting. Examples are different types of workshops
and planning meetings. When observing, we found that a lack of a clear speaking order resulted in the co-located participants speaking up significantly more
frequently than virtual participants. If all participants were free to take the word
when they wished, the balance dramatically shifted towards those attending co-
located.

One of the most apparent examples of this pattern was in a Friday Wins meeting where each team member could highlight what they had achieved that week. They would also praise others for their wins. The conversation was exclusively dominated by co-located participants for roughly ten minutes. When most of the co-located participants had said something, the first virtual participant spoke up. Of the five attending the meeting virtually, only two contributed. In contrast, everyone sitting in the meeting room said something.

4 Discussion and Conclusion

In this study, we analyzed office access card data for an agile company and investigated hybrid meetings by observing 23 meetings and conducting 9 interviews in two teams. Our analysis of the access card, interviews, and observations showed that many in the organization decided to work from home for several days, especially on Mondays and Fridays. A primary reason was not having to spend time commuting and that having a more flexible schedule contributed to a better work-life balance. These findings are similar to [4], and also other research that has found a better work-life balance to be one of the most common benefits of working from home [1, 18].

We identified significant discrepancies in the participation levels of co-located and virtual attendees in hybrid meetings. Our findings underscore that virtual participants are disadvantaged by both technological and social barriers, which diminish their ability to engage equally in the meeting dynamics. Our observations reveal that hybrid meetings often involve participation asymmetries, with virtual attendees consistently engaging less and contributing more sporadically than co-located participants. Furthermore, we found that being physically present in meetings was crucial for newly onboarded developers. Our findings align with those of [9], who studied the onboarding of globally distributed teams in a financial institution and found that physical co-location was important, while virtual participation in meetings proved troublesome.

Effective management of hybrid meetings is crucial for both team effectiveness and the emotional well-being of employees. Gerardi et al. [5] found that developers tend to feel more positive and satisfied when meetings are productive and constructive. On the other hand, as also reported in [20], lengthy and unconstructive meetings can evoke negative emotions and are considered a waste of time. Our findings are similar to [16], which found that the interaction in hybrid meetings was unequal and even unfair for virtual participants. Remote participants feel isolated from the meeting, while co-located participants dominate the interaction [16]. A recent study emphasizes that reducing barriers to participation is crucial for enhancing the design of hybrid meetings [7].

Saatçi et al. [16] argue that making meetings more inclusive for everyone is one of the primary challenges of hybrid meetings. Despite advanced technologies, practical issues still disrupt the inclusion of remote participants [15]. Virtual participants often find it confusing to remember who is in the meeting room if they are not visible to the camera [16]. Conversely, co-located participants face difficulties in including remote colleagues they cannot see, risking forgetting them entirely. The use of video during calls aids participants, particularly new team members, in understanding team dynamics and forming connections with peers [13]. To improve inclusivity in hybrid meetings, co-located participants might consider joining the call using their laptop cameras, which can make the meeting feel entirely virtual and treat everyone as equal participants. Additionally, having co-located participants manage turn-taking through meeting software features like "raise hand" can enhance inclusivity [15]. Sporsem et al. [19] also highlight that fully virtual meetings tend to achieve higher inclusion, as everyone has the opportunity to participate.

In light of these challenges, organizations must strive to create more inclusive hybrid environments. This can be achieved by investing in technological solutions that ensure seamless connectivity and clear audio-visual quality for all participants. Structuring meetings with clear agendas and predefined speaking orders can help ensure that all voices are heard equally, regardless of their physical location. The future of work is hybrid, and we must continue to evolve our understanding and methodologies to foster inclusivity and fairness in these settings. This study provides a foundation for further research and action toward optimizing hybrid meeting environments, ensuring that both virtual and co-located participants can collaborate equitably.

Acknowledgements. We would like to thank the studied company for their engagement in our research. The work was partially supported by the Research Council of Norway through the project 10xTeams (grant 309344).

References

1. Bao, L., Li, T., Xia, X., Zhu, K., Li, H., Yang, X.: How does working from home affect developer productivity? - A case study of Baidu during COVID-19 pandemic. Sci. China Inf. Sci. **65**(4), 142102 (2022)
2. Bennett, A.A., Campion, E.D., Keeler, K.R., Keener, S.K.: Videoconference fatigue? Exploring changes in fatigue after videoconference meetings during COVID-19. J. Appl. Psychol. **106**(3), 330–344 (2021)
3. Conboy, K., Moe, N.B., Stray, V., Gundelsby, J.H.: The future of hybrid software development: challenging current assumptions. IEEE Softw. **40**(02), 26–33 (2023). https://doi.org/10.1109/MS.2022.3230449
4. Ford, D., et al.: A tale of two cities: software developers working from home during the COVID-19 pandemic. ACM Trans. Softw. Eng. Methodol. **31**(2), 1–37 (2022)
5. Girardi, D., Lanubile, F., Novielli, N., Serebrenik, A.: Emotions and perceived productivity of software developers at the workplace. IEEE Trans. Softw. Eng. **48**(9), 3326–3341 (2022). https://doi.org/10.1109/TSE.2021.3087906
6. Gustavsson, T., Berntzen, M., Stray, V.: Changes to team autonomy in large-scale software development: a multiple case study of scaled agile framework (SAFe) implementations. Int. J. Inf. Syst. Proj. Manag. **10**(1), 29–46 (2022)
7. Hosseinkashi, Y., Tankelevitch, L., Pool, J., Cutler, R., Madan, C.: Meeting effectiveness and inclusiveness: large-scale measurement, identification of key features, and prediction in real-world remote meetings. Proc. ACM Hum.-Comput. Interact. **8**(CSCW1) (2024)

8. Khanna, D., Christensen, E.L., Gosu, S., Wang, X., Paasivaara, M.: Hybrid work meets agile software development: a systematic mapping study. In: IEEE/ACM 17th International Conference on Cooperative and Human Aspects of Software Engineering (CHASE 2024) (2024). https://doi.org/10.1145/3641822.3641863

9. Moe, N.B., Stray, V., Goplen, M.R.: Studying onboarding in distributed software teams: a case study and guidelines. In: Proceedings of the 24th International Conference on Evaluation and Assessment in Software Engineering, pp. 150–159 (2020)

10. Moe, N.B., Stray, V., Šmite, D., Mikalsen, M.: Attractive workplaces: what are engineers looking for? IEEE Softw. **40**(5), 85–93 (2023)

11. Moe, N.B., Ulsaker, S., Hildrum, J.M., Smite, D., Ay, F.C.: Understanding the difference between office presence and co-presence in team member interactions. In: Proceedings of the 57th HICSS. AIS Electronic Library (2024)

12. Redlbacher, F., Hattke, F.: How virtual meetings stimulate process innovations in organisations: mixed-methods evidence from emergency response providers. Innovation **26**(1), 1–22 (2024)

13. Rodeghero, P., Zimmermann, T., Houck, B., Ford, D.: Please turn your cameras on: remote onboarding of software developers during a pandemic. In: 2021 IEEE/ACM 43rd International Conference on Software Engineering: Software Engineering in Practice (ICSE-SEIP), pp. 41–50. IEEE, Madrid (2021)

14. Rogelberg, S.G., Shanock, L.R., Scott, C.W.: Wasted time and money in meetings: increasing return on investment. Small Group Res. **43**(2), 236–245 (2012)

15. Saatçi, B., Akyüz, K., Rintel, S., Klokmose, C.N.: (Re) configuring hybrid meetings: moving from user-centered design to meeting-centered design. Comput. Supported Coop. Work (CSCW) **29**(6), 769–794 (2020)

16. Saatçi, B., Rädle, R., Rintel, S., O'Hara, K., Nylandsted Klokmose, C.: Hybrid meetings in the modern workplace: stories of success and failure. In: Nakanishi, H., Egi, H., Chounta, I.-A., Takada, H., Ichimura, S., Hoppe, U. (eds.) CRIWG+CollabTech 2019. LNCS, vol. 11677, pp. 45–61. Springer, Cham (2019). https://doi.org/10.1007/978-3-030-28011-6_4

17. Smite, D., Moe, N.B., Hildrum, J., Gonzalez-Huerta, J., Mendez, D.: Work-from-home is here to stay: call for flexibility in post-pandemic work policies. J. Syst. Softw. **195**, 111552 (2023)

18. Smite, D., Tkalich, A., Moe, N.B., Papatheocharous, E., Klotins, E., Buvik, M.P.: Changes in perceived productivity of software engineers during COVID-19 pandemic. J. Syst. Softw. **186**, 111197 (2022)

19. Sporsem, T., Moe, N.B.: Coordination strategies when working from anywhere: a case study of two agile teams. In: International Conference on Agile Software Development, pp. 52–61. Springer (2022)

20. Stray, V., Gundelsby, J.H., Ulfsnes, R., Brede Moe, N.: How agile teams make objectives and key results (OKRs) work. In: Proceedings of the International Conference on Software and System Processes and International Conference on Global Software Engineering, pp. 104–109 (2022)

21. Stray, V., Moc, N.B., Bergersen, G., Kirkerud, J.: Behavioral aspects of agile software development: a case study on meeting practices in a fintech organization. In: Proceeding of the 57th HICSS. AIS Electronic Library (2024)

22. Tkalich, A., Šmite, D., Andersen, N.H., Moe, N.B.: What happens to psychological safety when going remote? IEEE Softw. (2022)

The 11th International Workshop on Large-Scale Agile Development Information on Submission

Agile Approaches in Critical Infrastructures

Geir Kjetil Hanssen$^{(\boxtimes)}$ and Martin Gilje Jaatun

SINTEF, Trondheim, Norway
ghanssen@sintef.no

Abstract. This paper explores the emergence of agile-inspired approaches in the critical infrastructure sector, with a focus on the current digital transformation of the Norwegian Oil & Gas industry. It addresses how traditional plan-driven development and strict architectural principles are challenged by the need to exploit the growing volume of operational data, in search for better, faster, and safer operations. We emphasize the increasing reliance on data for optimizing operations and the inherent risks and culture clashes between Information Technology (IT) and Operational Technology (OT). We furthermore discuss the role of cybersecurity in this transition, illustrating how increased connectivity and agile-like approaches can both mitigate and exacerbate security vulnerabilities.

Keywords: Agile Development · Critical infrastructures · Digital Transformation · Security · Safety

1 Introduction

All aspects of our society are being digitalized, where increasing amounts of data are gathered, shared, analyzed, and used to improve almost every conceivable aspect of our lives. Well-known examples are streaming services, where we consume media in totally different ways than before, where data about how we consume media is used to tailor content and increase consumption. Another example is banking services that only can be accessed via self-managed solutions. Following this development, we also see a very clear trend of digitalization also within critical infrastructures, such as energy production and distribution systems. This is however an industry that is "invisible" to the everyday consumer. It's based on traditional and trusted technologies and a conservative and change-resistant culture where the pace of change is moderated by strict regulations, where change must be restricted and controlled to minimize unintentional mistakes, which - in worst case scenarios - can lead to catastrophic events, and ultimately loss of lives [3].

In this paper, we look into the Norwegian Oil and Gas sector which is currently undergoing a massive digital transformation [3]. In short, operational technology (OT) systems, e.g., drilling systems on off-shore installations, are being

© The Author(s) 2025
L. Marchesi et al. (Eds.): XP 2024 Workshops, LNBIP 524, pp. 83–89, 2025.
https://doi.org/10.1007/978-3-031-72781-8_9

instrumented (e.g., via edge devices) and used as data sources to gather vast amounts of detailed data that are used to optimize drilling. Another example is data that are harvested from production equipment used to monitor wear and tear to enable predictive maintenance, where there are great cost savings in replacing expensive equipment only when needed, instead of at fixed service intervals. The main driver for such digitalization efforts is the search for faster and more efficient operations [9]. In the case of oil and gas production, it is about producing more energy resources, within shorter time, at lower cost, while also ensuring high operational availability and maintaining very strict safety requirements.

In Norway, oil and natural gas is produced at very large off-shore installations that rise hundreds of meters above the sea bed, and where resources are extracted through drilling holes reaching kilometres below the sea-bed. These are complex installations consisting of complex sub-systems, ranging from highly specialized operational technologies (OT) where the production happens (the so-called"sharp end"), to traditional IT-systems that are used by administrative personnel. In between, we find control systems, historians (time-series databases), functional safety systems (e.g. fire- and gas detection), etc. As a mean to enable overview and control, systems are logically arranged in layers, from layer 0 where we find the most critical operational technologies, to level 4 where we find traditional IT and office support systems. This layering of the system is often referred to as the Purdue model [13], illustrated in Fig. 1. Level 0 is the production level, where the consequences of failures are the highest and respectively, the need for protection is the highest. Level 1 is the control-level (controlling level 0), level 2 controls several sub-areas (e.g. drilling), level 3 controls the operation of a site (e.g. a well). Levels 0 to 3 is often known as the manufacturing zone. Over the past years, a level 3.5 has been introduced as a demilitarized zone, separating Level 4 and 5 which is called the enterprise zone (low-criticality) from Level 3-0 (high criticality). Level 4 and above are referred to as the IT-levels, while levels 0-3 are referred to as the OT-levels.

The rationale for organizing such complex systems in layered zones is that each layer can have varying levels of criticality, and that control and communication between layers are easier to manage, and that the flow between two layers have to pass through those in between.

This way of organising the system is however being challenged as a consequence of the digitalization of this industry. For example, we can now define a new (IT) level 6 - which is the cloud level that is connected via the Internet above the enterprise zone, and that even can be outside the organization itself in cases where one of the major cloud providers manage data at external infrastructures. Adding to this, new system providers enter the market to offer value-enhancing services (a.k.a. "AI magic") where large amounts of data (gathered from the operational level) are used to provide services that can increase efficiency. For example, data about production can be used to deliver operator support systems, where people, e.g., at the drilling deck, get better insight and decision support via handheld devices. This, however, means that the flow of data and control no longer always passes through the layers (and the protection that these offer) [3]. Furthermore, providers of such solutions may also want to gather data directly from lower levels to fully control the quality of data.

In sum, we see clear trends that the traditional control of *how* data flows between layers are challenged as a consequence of the digitalization of this industry with increasing amounts of data and - hence - increasing reliance on software-based systems.

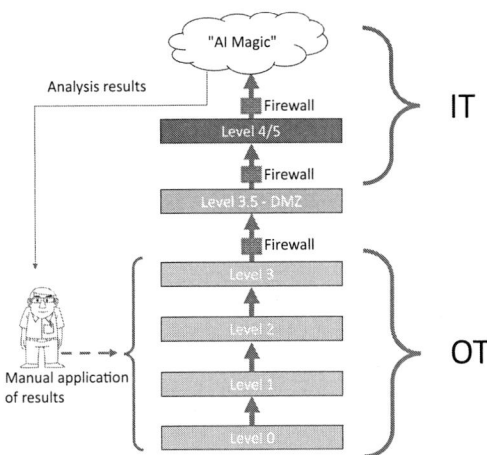

Fig. 1. To the cloud – and back again

2   The Challenge

2.1   Culture Shock

There are enduring culture differences between IT and OT. Traditionally, the speed of change can be perceived as lightning vs. glacial in IT and OT, respectively. Hence, we see that agile approaches are very relevant to the development of IT-systems, while development of OT systems are subject to plan-driven approaches. This is related to the need to enforce very strict control of change in OT-systems through certification procedures that ensure that changes are done according to very detailed international standards and regulations, which again requires high precision in traceability from requirements to implementation. The petroleum industry is a conservative domain, that now needs to deal with an increasing speed of change at the IT-levels and an expanding attack surface, exposing the OT levels.

Traditionally, there has been a hard separation of IT and OT, also because when bad things happen in the latter, really bad consequences tend to follow. This schism also manifests itself in the dichotomy between security and safety [8]

– IT usually only needs to worry about the former, whereas OT is predominately concerned with the latter. This is thus a very mature sector when it comes to safety; how can we capitalize on this in the area of security?

With new IT and software vendors are entering the critical infrastructure domain, culture is a major hurdle. Many of the players in the big data analytics space come from the IT side, and see no problems with siphoning sensor data from the lowest level, working their magic on the data in the cloud (Fig. 1), and using the results to optimize processes in the sharp end. Many of these new players are also relatively small, and do not have the rigid bureaucratic processes common in large enterprises, like suppliers of classical process control systems. It is therefore not surprising that a large number of these smaller, new IT vendors operate under agile principles that have become the norm for non-critical applications.

In a recent report by Vedere Labs [12] it is stated that OT vendors lack a fundamental understanding of security by design, and that existing security control designs are often broken.

Another consequence of this is that vendors often release low-quality patches. This situation is exacerbated by the fact that many industrial control systems still offer no appreciable security once the "hard crunchy shell" of perimeter security has been breached [1].

2.2   A Need for Agility?

In search of a way to respond to the described development and challenges we see that the mindset from agile software development practices may be relevant. Firstly, requirements tend to change more frequently from the dynamic thereat picture that follows the growing connectivity as well as the increasing amount of data-savvy services that are being offered from new actors. Such new actors may not have the safety-mindset that the established providers of traditional control systems have. Hence, frequent evaluation of the threat situation, and following, faster feedback-loops and reaction to threats (e.g. patches or other security measures) can be a good strategy for having a closer control with rapid change [5]. Secondly, an agile mindset may also offer better (and faster) innovation capabilities. Where access to richer data (and new technologies) can be used to create, test, and evaluate ideas faster. Thirdly, an agile approach can also offer a better strategy for following up new actors more closely to ensure that they adhere to the needed safety standards of this domain. Again, frequent evaluation and feedback (and corrections) is the key.

3   How to Tackle Challenges/Way Forward?

There is a lot of technology in OT, but unlike in IT, uptime and accessibility are extremely important and can only be sacrificed in situations where the safety of people or the environment is at risk. There is a need to handle the span between control and agility – where the conventional wisdom in OT goes beyond "if it's not broken, don't fix it" to the point where even in cases where there are known vulnerabilities in an OT system, the default stance is that change should be avoided, as it might break a safety certification, and thus lead to a halt in operation, which can be extremely costly. However, this stance is being challenged by the new players. The digitalization of OT, with more edge devices and sensors, and lots of data transferred to, and processed in the cloud, implies an agile transformation. The data is used for optimization of processes, but that means that the results need to be fed back into lower parts of the Purdue stack.

So, within this landscape of digitalization of previously isolated and strictly controlled - and thus, secure - systems, which principles could we turn to, in search of a more agile, but still secure (and safe) approach?

3.1   Safe&Secure Agile Development

With more data and more software in safety-critical systems, it becomes more attractive to work in an agile manner to increase responsiveness and efficiency when changes are needed. The challenge though is of course the need to maintain security and to not introduce new vulnerabilities. One viable approach could be to apply existing approaches for agile development of safety-critical systems, such as R-Scrum [2] or SafeScrum [4], but where cybersecurity considerations are managed in tandem with safety considerations. SafeScrum for example, is an agile development approach that is well aligned with the generic IEC 61508 [6] standard for functional safety. However, we believe that such approaches could be extended to consider safety and security, jointly. In fact, such an approach would be highly relevant in cases where cybersecurity directly relates to safety. Furthermore, it could also be relevant to extend such agile processes to adhere to both safety and security standards, like IEC 61508 and the IEC 62443 [7] standard series, which rapidly is becoming the go-to standard for cybersecurity for operational technology in automation and control systems (amongst others).

3.2   Zero Trust

Zero-trust [11] is currently a popular buzzword in OT, and for the particular case at hand it may be vital. Optimization decisions made in the cloud need to provide an audit trail and provenance, ensuring that no party have had the opportunity to tamper with the information on the way to or from the cloud. On the simplest level, it implies that any results need to be provided with a digital signature that can be verified before these results are being used to modify OT processes. Furthermore, if system engineering becomes more agile, security needs to follow, and security must be automated whenever possible.

3.3   Cybersecurity Barriers

The petroleum industry has a long tradition in implementing safety barriers, e.g. safety valves in connection with Emergency Shutdown Systems. Introduction of agile principles also highlights the need for additional *cybersecurity barriers*.

Preliminary studies and ongoing work indicate that cybersecurity barriers may integrate well with traditional safety barrier management, focusing on identifying and managing existing cybersecurity measures rather than solely deploying new ones. This integration is essential for maintaining the security and integrity of operations against new and evolving digital threats [10].

4   Conclusion

Critical infrastructures, exemplified here by the Oil & Gas-industry, are undergoing an inevitable digital transformation that leads to an increased flow of data and potential new cybersecurity vulnerabilities. Well-established principles for protection are being challenged and operational technologies are exposed to an increasingly more dynamic threat landscape. We argue that some of the key principles in agile development should be considered in search for better ways to ensure cybersecurity and system safety, and that there is a need for improved feedback loops to ensure better responsiveness to emerging threats.

We have identified three challenges: (1) The need for an integrated culture between IT and OT, (2) Newcyber-security challenges, and (3) The need for technological responsiveness. Further work will explore how these should be addressed.

Acknowledgements. This work has been funded by the Research Council of Norway as part of the Cybersecurity Barrier Management project, grant number 326717.

References

1. Dragos: PIPEDREAM: CHERNOVITE's emerging malware targeting industrial control systems. Whitepaper. https://hub.dragos.com/whitepaper/chernovite-pipedream
2. Fitzgerald, B., Stol, K.J., O'Sullivan, R., O'Brien, D.: Scaling agile methods to regulated environments: an industry case study. In: 2013 35th International Conference on Software Engineering (ICSE), pp. 863–872. IEEE (2013)
3. Hanssen, G.K., Onshus, T., Jaatun, M.G., Myklebust, T., Ottermo, M., Lundteigen, M.A.: Principles of digitalisation and IT-OT integration. Technical report, SINTEF Digital (2021). https://www.havtil.no/globalassets/fagstoff/prosjektrapporter/ikt-sikkerhet/sintef---report---principles-of-digitalisation-and-it-ot-integration.pdf
4. Hanssen, G.K., Myklebust, T., Stålhane, T.: SafeScrum®- Agile Development of Safety-Critical Software. Springer International Publishing, Cham (2018)
5. Hanssen, G.K., Thieme, C.A., Bjarkø, A.V., Lundteigen, M.A., Bernsmed, K.E., Jaatun, M.G.: A continuous OT cybersecurity risk analysis and mitigation process. In: Proceedings of the The 33rd European Safety and Reliability Conference (ESREL 2023). Research Publishing Services (2023). https://doi.org/10.3850/978-981-18-8071-1_P413-cd, https://ntnuopen.ntnu.no/ntnu-xmlui/handle/11250/3103209
6. IEC: IEC 61508-1:2010 functional safety of lectrical/electronic/programmable electronic safety-related systems

7. IEC: IEC/TS 62443-1-1:2009 Security for industrial automation and control systems - Part 1-1: Terminology, concepts and models (2009)
8. Line, M.B., Nordland, O., Røstad, L., Tøndel, I.A.: Safety vs security? In: PSAM Conference, New Orleans, USA (2006)
9. Lu, H., Guo, L., Azimi, M., Huang, K.: Oil and gas 4.0 era: a systematic review and outlook. Comput. Ind. **111**, 68–90 (2019)
10. Øien, K., Hauge, S., Jaatun, M.G., Flå, L., Bodsberg, L.: A survey on cybersecurity barrier management in process control environments. In: 2022 IEEE International Conference on Cloud Computing Technology and Science (CloudCom), pp. 113–120. IEEE (2022).https://doi.org/10.1109/CloudCom55334.2022.00026, https://ieeexplore.ieee.org/document/10005352/
11. Sanders, G., Morrow, T., Richmond, N., Woody, C.: Integrating zero trust and DevSecOps. Carnegie Mellon University Software Engineering Institute White Paper (2021). https://apps.dtic.mil/sti/trecms/pdf/AD1145432.pdf
12. Vedere Labs: OT:ICEFALL - the legacy of "insecure by design" and its implications for certifications and risk management. Technical report, Vedere Labs (2022). https://www.forescout.com/resources/ot-icefall-report/
13. Williams, T.J.: The Purdue enterprise reference architecture. Comput. Ind. **24**(2), 141–158 (1994). https://doi.org/10.1016/0166-3615(94)900175, https://www.sciencedirect.com/science/article/pii/0166361594900175

Social Capital in Software Product Management: A Case Study From a Large-Scale Agile Context

Astri Barbala[1]([envelope]) [ID], Nils Brede Moe[1] [ID], and Marthe Berntzen[2,3] [ID]

[1] SINTEF, 7034 Trondheim, Norway
astri.barbala@sintef.no
[2] University of Oslo, 0373 Oslo, Norway
[3] Knowit Solutions AS, Universitetsgata 1, 0164 Oslo, Norway

Abstract. Although large-scale agile software development increasingly is being organized in product areas, little research has to date looked into the skills needed for central roles to succeed with software product management (SPM) in a large-scale setting. Addressing this research gap, this paper provides insights into the skills and competencies deemed essential among Product Managers and Product Owners in ScanBank, a Scandinavian fintech organization counting over 10,000 employees. Our findings reveal that establishing and maintaining social networks are found to be paramount for successfully performing SPM-related tasks in a large-scale agile organizational context. We utilized a model for social capital consisting of three different dimensions to analyze our data material and highlight the value of social capabilities in enhancing collaboration and efficiency within large-scale agile SPM.

Keywords: Product Management · Large-Scale Agile · Social Capital · Coordination · SPM · Fintech

1 Introduction

In the rapidly evolving landscape of fintech, banks are increasingly adopting agile methodologies to enhance their responsiveness and competitive edge. This shift has not only transformed traditional banking practices but has also led to the organization of agile software development around distinct product areas. Such structuring is critical as it aligns development efforts with specific customer needs and strategic business goals, necessitating a reevaluation of the roles and competencies of product management within these organizations, first and foremost Product Owners (POs) and Product Managers (PMs) [9]. While current literature recognizes the structural and functional aspects of these roles [15], there is a significant research gap regarding what skills and competencies are deemed necessary for success in these positions, specially in agile companies with as many as 10,000 employees.

L. Marchesi et al. (Eds.): XP 2024 Workshops, LNBIP 524, pp. 90–99, 2025.
https://doi.org/10.1007/978-3-031-72781-8_10

This study delves into the importance of social networks in large-scale agile Software Product Management (SPM) by building on interviews from the Scandinavian fintech organization ScanBank (a pseudonym). We build on the concept of *social capital* [11,16] to discuss our findings, which is an established theory utilized within the strand of software engineering research focusing on human values and social networks. Our study was led by the following research question:

RQ: *What is the role of social capital in large-scale agile SPM?*

By aligning the principle of social capital with the dynamics of software product management in large-scale agile environments, we demonstrate how nurturing relational networks and social interactions can bolster collaborative efforts and efficiency in product management within large organizations engaged in agile practices.

2   Background

2.1   Software Product Management

The complexity and scale of large-scale organizations introduce three fundamental challenges when it comes to agile product management. First, the product development reaches the point where it is almost impossible to know everything about a system's development and evolution. Second, large-scale development efforts require the formation or scaling of new product teams [3]. Finally, in large product organizations there are many dependencies between products which requires constant planning, prioritization and stakeholder management. In a recent study, Berntzen et al. [2] found the use of seventeen coordination mechanisms in a product area with 8 teams. To manage the complexity, Bass [1] identified nine different functions that POs have in large-scale projects, which included architectural coordination, assessing risk, and ensuring project compliance with corporate guidelines and policies. As such, the PO role is a complex role with a broad set of responsibilities, which in large-scale settings may need to coordinate complex, interdependent tasks and team goals contributing to the overall goals of the product development. The key question is then; how can software PMs and POs in large-scale agile organizations efficiently cultivate the knowledge and skills needed in the product development?

Although studies conducted on SPM in large-scale agile settings still are scarce, previous research has attempted to map out activities typical of SPM roles. For instance, Maglyas et al. [8] outlined 12 activities commonly performed by Product Managers, with vision creation, product lifecycle management, roadmapping, release planning, and product requirements engineering highlighted as fundamental tasks. The many and complex tasks result in the PM role–at least the typical PM tasks–often being paramount for a product's success, and previous research found that there are many dangers connected to attempting to conduct SPM without a dedicated Project Manager [7]. These are connected to weakened leadership, decreased performance, greater rework, and delays, which highlights the essential role of dedicated product management in navigating the challenges of large-scale software development.

2.2   Social Capital

One concept that pinpoints the value-creating properties of social skills and communication competency is that of *social capital* [4, 11]. Social capital is the sum of the actual and potential resources derived from the network of relationships possessed by an individual or social unit. The term describes the social connections a person has, encompassing relationships with other individuals, organizations, and institutions. These social relations can in turn be capitalized on for achieving goals, as substantial social capital can result in benefits in the form of assistance and personal services from their relationships. The sociologist Pierre Bourdieu [4] is the theorist who many associate with the term, and central to his thinking is the idea that social capital constitutes an essential element in understanding the opportunities for cooperation and the dynamics between different actors.

Although Bourdieu primarily viewed social capital as a characteristic of the individual rather than the collective, organizational researchers have made use of the concept to discuss interaction processes within organizations. For instance, a widely cited study by Jane Dutton and Belle Ragins [6] examined how positive social capital is created and maintained in organizations. They uncovered that the underlying mechanisms for social capital that benefits both the organization and individuals are motivation and opportunity structures, such as favorable communication channels and sufficient resources. Furthermore, Dutton and Ragins highlight the importance of focusing both on the means with which social capital is created and the goals it is used for, in order for social capital to be linked to cross-organizational co-creation: "Social capital is positive if the means by which it is created expand the capacity of both individuals and groups. Social capital is positive if it helps people to develop, thrive and flourish in organizations, and thus achieve their goals in better ways".

In software development research, the social capital concept has also gained a foothold. Among others, Stol et al. [14] Wohlin et al. [16] and Moe et al. [10] are among those that have utilized the social capital concept to study the knowledge resources embedded in the networks of development teams, where "who you know" directly affects your knowledge.

Wohlin et al. [16] build on Nahapiet and Ghoshal [11], two other central social capital theorists, to formulate the following definition of social capital in a software development context: "The actual and potential resources that are embedded in, accessible through, and derivable from the relational network of an individual actor or a social group". We consider this definition advantageous also for our study of SPM in ScanBank. By applying the social capital theory in this article, we thus seek to create insight into how social networks are crucial for successfully performing the roles of PM and PO in a large-scale setting, which ScanBank is a prime example of.

3   Case, Method and Data Analysis

ScanBank, with its 10,000 employees primarily situated across three cities, boasts a substantial workforce. Over 130 individuals were actively involved in core SPM functions, predominantly as POs or PMs, during the time of the data collection. Their organizational landscape is marked by ongoing structural and technological transformations, notably accentuated by a significant technical transition following a recent merger. Over 70% of the POs and PMs possessed more than five years of experience within the company, hailing from diverse backgrounds encompassing technical domains, such as engineering, and business-related sectors. The introduction of the PO role in 2017 marked a pivotal shift in ScanBank's approach to product management. More details on SPM in the case can be found in Moe et al. [9].

We adopted a case study methodology [12] to investigate SPM skills and competencies within ScanBank. This approach offers a comprehensive and nuanced understanding, crucial for our study given the scarcity of research on SPM. To delve into these aspects, we conducted interviews with individuals engaged in SPM across five business areas (see Table 1). The aim was to grasp the complexities of product management in large-scale agile setups and gain insights into the skills and competencies PMs and POs felt were central in their roles.

Our data analysis utilized a thematic analytical approach [5]. We applied open coding techniques to gain a deep understanding of the content and to start identifying preliminary codes. This process led to the emergence of various themes, such as necessary skills for their role. Subsequently, we collectively examined these emerging themes by thoroughly discussing each interview, aiming to achieve consensus on the identified categories and themes. In the final stages, we refined these by sorting our results into overarching themes, and we used a model [11] for social capital in organizations as an analytical framework, described in the following section.

Table 1. Data sources

Data source	Details	#
Interviews	Product managers (5 female, 4 male)	19
	Product owners (5 male)	
	Other product development role (2 female, 3 male)	
Meetings	Managers and people responsible for improving product management	5
Documents	Strategic documents, product management survey, annual reports	3

4   Results

We identified 20 skills and competencies among PMs and 9 among the POs. The most common answers for PMs were (number of answers in parenthesis):

- Good communication skills (11)
- Understanding the costumer (7)

- Understanding product vision (7)
- Technical competence (7)
- People skills (6)
- Navigating ScanBank (6)

For the PO role, these were the most common answers:

- People skills (4)
- Technical abilities (3)
- Cross-functional cooperation (3)

Since the importance of the social aspects of product management roles were clearly the most dominating among our 19 informants, Nahapiet and Ghoshal's three-dimensional social capital model [11] was fitting for analyzing our results. The *structural dimension* of social capital has direct impact on the condition of accessibility to the network, the *cognitive dimension* influences accessibility through shared language, roles and narratives, while the *relational dimension* includes feelings of trust that are shared by the many actors. Although we separate these three dimensions analytically, they are highly interrelated [11].

4.1   Structural Dimension: Accessibility to the Network

The fact that that ScanBank is large and has various departments spread across both geographical and administrative levels seemed to often be the root of our informants' answers in regard to what was needed for product management to function smoothly in the organization. Several pointed to the importance of knowing the structure of the company (that is, who to reach and how to reach them) in order to get things done, with one interviewee saying: *"There are lots of experts and good people everywhere. You just have to know where to ask".*

One PM articulated the importance of managing the network of stakeholders: *"I have underestimated the importance of understanding how big our organization is. You can come from a smaller company[. . .] and know the [product management] theories very well. But that does not mean that it works in ScanBank".* He also commented on the importance of onboarding new people in the network: *"Especially during Covid, when we were working with recruitment, it was probably difficult to understand how big our organization was, and who to follow up. [...] In general, you should spend more time on it during onboarding processes".*

Although ScanBank's complexities meant it could not easily be compared to many other product management contexts elsewhere, we found that maneuvering the organizational structure and knowing who to connect with was a skill that experienced PMs and POs often would handle easier. One senior PM with only one year of experience in ScanBank quickly listed *"gathering information, sharing information, and talking to people"* when asked about the most valued skills for product management people, adding: *"I have worked so many years myself that I know who to talk to and what to do [despite being new in ScanBank]".*

4.2   Cognitive Dimension: Shared Understandings, Values and Goals

Although knowing the organizational structure and *where* to go to talk to the right people in ScanBank was central for achieving results in product management roles, knowing *how to* connect with people in a way that underpinned a sense of community was also underlined as essential by our interviewees. One PO who was praised by colleagues for his technical competence still highlighted 'soft skills' as crucial for his role, especially with regards to fostering shared values and understanding within the team. Questioned about key competences needed in his PO role, he said: *"Empathy towards our team members and give space for them to explain their stuff and understand their thought process is key. Because I always try to consider their inputs as the highest value, more than the requirements that comes directly from the business side".* This quote thus pinpoints that fostering a culture of understanding and common goals, where team members' knowledge was valued, was a central underpinning for product management success. Although we talked to more PMs and the answers were fairly similar for both roles, fostering team collaboration was especially mentioned for the PO role, with one person saying: *"[POs] need people skills because they need to get the developers to talk to each other, and the designers to talk to each other, on a daily basis. So that is, everyone actually needs people skills".*

Shared goals and values in the team was an important issue for the PMs we spoke to, yet more in regard to the wider success of the product. A PM underscored the importance of continuously backing each other and sharing both goals and attitudes, saying: *"It's about making sure that you have the right supporters on the team. That's important, and it's an important daily part of it".*

One central challenge we found amongst PMs and POs in ScanBank was connected to not having a shared language for product management as a discipline. This included using the same words for roles and contexts such as 'product area', but also a common understanding of the responsibilities of each role. Some pointed to how a lack of a common language could lead to conflicts, with one PM saying: *"One must [...]talk to the right people in the right way. So that you get them to help you, instead of it going into some sort of trench warfare. Get everyone to be friends and open up".*

4.3   Relational Dimension: Nature and Quality of Relationships

If one knows who in the organization to go to for which knowledge, per the structural dimension, as well as having established shared values and understandings, following the cognitive dimension in the social capital model, building relationships is often easier. In addressing some of the challenges she experienced as a PM in ScanBank, one person pointed to there being a lack of established relations between the different product areas in the organization. She said: *"We cannot work without talking a lot together. That is a very important point in relation to ScanBank".* This was echoed by a PO in a different area: *"The most important thing is the human relationships; that one has a good relationship in the team, that one is not afraid to speak up, that one can talk together and everyone can have opinions and that everyone can be heard. I find that extremely important."*

One PM also pointed to that although domain knowledge and technical competence were important for the success of the product, these skills were less important for the product management roles. He said: *"There are some who make it work (not having technical competence), because they manage to initiate very good conversations with others. [...] Not all decisions lie with the product, so to speak".* This outlook was common: Although other skills and competencies were frequently mentioned as also crucial for succeeding with product management in the organization, some pointed at how these were ideally spread around in the team, while PMs and POs were the ones maneuvering the relations for how these were best combined. One person said: *"You don't need to be a domain expert [...] if you can work well with people. That's the key to the 'product management' aspect [in ScanBank]: It's people who can work with people. You have so many other skilled, competent, technical people on the team. Often, mis-hirings in [ScanBank] has to do with the 'product management' aspect. We focus too little on the human aspect".*

5   Concluding Discussion

The adoption of Software Product Management (SPM) in large-scale agile companies is increasingly prevalent, with industry leaders such as Google, Facebook, Amazon, and Microsoft employing this practice. However, the implementation of SPM presents significant challenges. In this paper, we investigated the essential skills and competencies for product management, first and foremost PMs and POs, within a large-scale agile organization with 10,000 employees. We identified 29 skills, and we found social skills to be the most crucial, as they contributed significantly to the efficacy of PMs and POs. Accordingly, we adopted the concept of social capital [11,16] as an analytical framework.

5.1   The Role of Social Capital in Large-Scale Agile SPM

In large-scale organizations, where cross-functional and inter-departmental interactions are common, social capital can significantly enhance collaboration, information flow, and ultimately, product success [13,16]. In this article, we have pointed to how three different social dimensions need to be filled for agile SPM in the large-scale context. Firstly, the *structural dimension*, the accessibility to the network, needed to be in place in order for PMs and POs to be able to manoeuvre the large-scale organization. We found that this could be connected to the amount of experience people had in their SPM roles, which corresponds to the study of Wohlin et al. [16], who noted that "a combination of expertise and experience" was needed for people working in complex development contexts to succeed.

This is also in line with Smite et al. [13], who points to how social capital in large-scale settings is dependent on an adequate communication infrastructure.

In regards to the *cognitive dimension*, we found that shared understandings of goals, values and SPM as a discipline were paramount for fostering a thriving environment for product management in ScanBank. This emphasizes that SPM education and standardization of roles across the large-scale organization is key for people to understand each other [7]. However, standardization can also come at the expense of autonomy and adaptation, which points to a central dilemma for SPM in large-scale agile contexts.

Lastly, the *relational dimension* was in ScanBank crucial and regarded how a central task for PMs and POs was to link various roles and knowledge connected to the product without necessarily inhabiting this knowledge themselves. This adds to the findings of Bass [1] which focuses solely on the PO role in large-scale agile. Although separated analytically, the three social capital dimensions were intertwined, which can be illustrated by the hurdles experienced by our informants when organizing onboarding during Covid-19, when the network structures were harder to navigate for new hires due to a lack of communication and face-to-face meetings.

5.2   Limitations and Future Research

As we only studied the skills and competencies of POs and PMs, a limitation of this study is that we did not also look into the skills needed for other roles, such as Product Leads. Future studies would hence benefit from taking a broader approach in order to account for this. Furthermore, a longitudinal study could determine if the importance of social skills, as observed during the transitional period at ScanBank, remains consistent over time. Our upcoming research aims to investigate this further.

Future research should also delve into identifying and evaluating specific organizational strategies that can amplify social capital among SPM roles in a large-scale agile setting, assessing the consequent impact on organizational agility and product development success. Furthermore, cross-industrial and cross-cultural comparative studies would provide a broader understanding of the generalizability and specificities of these competencies and their influence on the success of product management. It would also be interesting to look into the skills needed for SPM roles in a small-scale agile setting.

Acknowledgments. The authors thank the informants for their willingness to share their experiences. This research was supported by the Research Council of Norway through the Transformit project (grant no. 321477).

References

1. Bass, J.M.: How product owner teams scale agile methods to large distributed enterprises. Empir. Softw. Eng. **20**, 1525–1557 (2015)
2. Berntzen, M., Engdal, S.A., Gellein, M., Moe, N.B.: Coordination in agile product areas: a case study from a large fintech organization. In: International Conference on Agile Software Development. pp. 36–52. Springer, Cham (2024)

3. Berntzen, M., Hoda, R., Moe, N.B., Stray, V.: A taxonomy of inter-team coordination mechanisms in large-scale agile. IEEE Trans. Softw. Eng. **49**(2), 699–718 (2022)
4. Bourdieu, P.: The forms of capital. In: The Sociology of Economic life, pp. 78–92. Routledge (1986)
5. Braun, V., Clarke, V.: Thematic Analysis. American Psychological Association (2012)
6. Dutton, J.E., Ragins, B.R.: Moving forward: positive relationships at work as a research frontier. In: Exploring Positive Relationships at Work, pp. 387–400. Psychology Press (2017)
7. Ebert, C., Brinkkemper, S.: Software product management-an industry evaluation. J. Syst. Softw. **95**, 10–18 (2014)
8. Maglyas, A., Nikula, U., Smolander, K.: What do we know about software product management?-a systematic mapping study. In: 2011 Fifth International Workshop on Software Product Management (IWSPM), pp. 26–35. IEEE (2011)
9. Moe, N.B., Berntzen, M., Barbala, A., Stray, V.: Software product management in large-scale agile. In: International Conference on Agile Software Development. Springer (2024)
10. Moe, N.B., Šmite, D., Šāblis, A., Börjesson, A.L., Andréasson, P.: Networking in a large-scale distributed agile project. In: Proceedings of the 8th ACM/IEEE International Symposium on Empirical Software Engineering And Measurement, pp. 1–8 (2014)
11. Nahapiet, J., Ghoshal, S.: Social capital, intellectual capital, and the organizational advantage. Acad. Manag. Rev. **23**(2), 242–266 (1998)
12. Runeson, P., Höst, M.: Guidelines for conducting and reporting case study research in software engineering. Empir. Softw. Eng. **14**(2), 131–164 (2009)
13. Šmite, D., Moe, N.B., Šāblis, A., Wohlin, C.: Software teams and their knowledge networks in large-scale software development. IST **86**, 71–86 (2017)
14. Stol, K.J., Schaarschmidt, M., Morgan, L.: Does adopting inner source increase job satisfaction? a social capital perspective using a mixed-methods approach. J. Strateg. Inf. Syst. **33**(1), 101819 (2024)
15. Tkalich, A., Ulfsnes, R., Moe, N.B.: Toward an agile product management: what do product managers do in agile companies? In: International Conference on Agile Software Development, pp. 168–184. Springer (2022)
16. Wohlin, C., Šmite, D., Moe, N.B.: A general theory of software engineering: balancing human, social and organizational capitals. J. Syst. Softw. **109**, 229–242 (2015)

The AI Scrum Master: Incorporating AI Into Your Agile Practices and Processes

ChatGPT for Tailoring Software Documentation for Managers and Developers

Saimir Bala[1]([⊠]) [iD], Kristina Sahling[1,2] [iD], Jennifer Haase[1,2] [iD], and Jan Mendling[1,2] [iD]

[1] Department of Computer Science, Humboldt Universität zu Berlin, Berlin, Germany
{saimir.bala,kristina.sahling,jennifer.haase,jan.mendling}@hu-berlin.de
[2] Group of Security and Transparency in Processes, Weizenbaum Institute, Berlin, Germany

Abstract. In many agile software development projects, documentation is often missing, outdated, or written with only a technical perspective. Existing literature recognizes the importance of documentation quality, especially when it comes to its readability for diverse audiences. While recent advances in Large Language Models (LLMs) offer the potential to tackle these issues, the use of LLMs for software documentation remains unexplored. This paper investigates the use of ChatGPT to improve and adapt documentation to specific audiences. We apply ChatGPT-4 for alternative documentation production and measure the resulting text characteristics and readability. Twenty-five experts from management and development rate these different versions. Results show the suitability of ChatGPT for generating high-quality text for both audiences, with managers benefiting more from an adapted version.

Keywords: LLM, ChatGPT · Software Development · Documentation

1 Introduction

Good documentation can make a difference in the overall progress of a software project because it can provide managers and developers with up-to-date information about the status of the software product [11]. However, the creation and maintenance of documentation is time-consuming and error-prone. That is why, in practice, many software projects tend to neglect or avoid this task, thus resulting in lower software quality [8]. When present, documentation is written by developers who have a technical rather than business view on the matter. This makes it hard for non-technical users to assess the status-quo of the project.

Existing literature [6] has studied various aspects of the quality of documentation and its relations to the overall software development process. In particular, there are many works [2] that point to ways to write documentation for better readability, taking into account the different target groups that consume it.

© The Author(s) 2025
L. Marchesi et al. (Eds.): XP 2024 Workshops, LNBIP 524, pp. 103–109, 2025.
https://doi.org/10.1007/978-3-031-72781-8_11

Recently, Large Language Models (LLMs) have been adopted in various areas of software engineering and have shown promising results [1,10], especially when it comes to text generation tasks [7]. However, we still lack detailed insights into the benefits of LLMs to support documentation. Therefore we ask the following research question: *how well do LLMs perform in tailoring documentation to the specific management or development audiences?*

This paper explores the use of an LLM, such as ChatGPT, to improve documentation quality. More specifically, it identifies two main issues in documentation: i) text quality and ii) text adjustment according to the audience. We applied ChatGPT-4 to different documentation and show its usefulness in addressing the above issues using metrics for text characteristics and readability. Furthermore, we asked managers and developers from practice to evaluate the different documentation versions. Our results show the suitability of ChatGPT when it comes to generating quality text for both development and business project management, with the latter gaining a better understanding from these adaptations. With this work, we pave the path to ChatGPT-supported and context-aware software documentation.

2   Method

To assess the capability of ChatGPT in producing audience-tailored software documentation, we adopt a two-step process: i) prompt ChatGPT to generate various versions and measure them via well-known readability metrics, and ii) perform evaluation by subject matter experts.

Prompt Formulation. For optimal adaptation of original software documentation using ChatGPT's zero-shot performance, we employ two distinct templates[1] predicated on the intended audience: management versus developers. Utilizing the templates in the colored boxes below when interfacing with ChatGPT ensures the generation of appropriately adapted texts, contingent on the incorporated documentation within the "Documentation Provided" segment.

Management Version

Documentation Provided: Insert the original code/documentation here
Audience: Non-technical managers
Purpose: To understand the high-level overview, the purpose of the code/tool, and its business or organizational benefits.
Details: Avoid deep technical jargon; focus on the "why" and "what" rather than the "how". Based on the above structure, please adapt the provided documentation for the specified audiences.

---

[1] For the generation of these templates, we followed the official guidelines provided by ChatGPT https://platform.openai.com/docs/guides/prompt-engineering/strategy-write-clear-instructions.

Developer Version

Documentation Provided: Insert the original code/documentation here
Audience: Developers/technical audience
Purpose: To understand the code/tool deeply, so they can implement and modify it.
Details: Highlight technical specification, intricacies, dependencies, and any other relevant information details. Based on the above structure, please adapt the provided documentation for the specified audience.

Metrics Used for Analysis. We measure i) text characteristics and ii) text readability. The characteristics refer to the structural properties of the documentation generated by ChatGPT, such as *number of paragraphs, number of headers*, etc. Next, we computed text readability metrics to assess the generated texts. More specifically we applied: i) Coleman-Liau Index [3]; ii) Flesch Reading Ease [5]; and iii) Difficult words [4]. We created Python scripts to compute the aforementioned metrics. We used standard Python libraries like `nltk` and `textstat` to compute the metrics. In particular, for each audience (Manager, Developer) our script takes as input 3 different documentation samples (Amazon, Facebook, Euronym) to which we apply the functions to compute the metrics. Each audience's documentation has 12 versions that were generated by the application of the same prompt. The source code and dataset are published on GitHub[2] and openly available under MIT License.

Expert Survey. We engaged subject matter experts in a structured survey methodology. The aim was to leverage their specialized knowledge and practical experience to critically assess the accuracy, coherence, relevance, and audience alignment of the AI-generated documents. Our sampling strategy intentionally follows the logic of purposeful sampling, targeting professionals with a demonstrated history of engaging with technical documentation in management or development roles [9]. The survey was conducted following ethical research standards, guaranteeing the anonymity and confidentiality of the participant's responses. The survey was methodically structured, starting with an introductory briefing, a consent form, and a self-identification step where respondents specified their role as either managers or developers. This was followed by a role-specific scenario to contextualize their evaluation of the technical documentation with a specific and typical task in mind. Participants were first randomly presented with one of the three original pieces of documentation, which they rated on clarity, detail adequacy, and suitability for either managerial or technical stakeholders on a Likert scale ranging from 1 (terrible) to 5 (excellent).

Subsequently, they were introduced to the ChatGPT-generated documentation, with the order of presentation for management and developer versions randomized to mitigate sequence bias. After reading, they rated these documents

---
[2] Source code and data: https://github.com/s41m1r/ChatGPT-Documentation.

on the same criteria used for the original, with additional queries concerning any factual errors, inconsistencies, or omissions relative to the source material.

The survey finished with demographic queries – age, gender, employment status, and years of professional experience – and an open-ended section for final remarks. This structured approach was designed to furnish a comprehensive evaluation of ChatGPT's performance in the realm of technical documentation, steering the investigation toward identifying potential disparities, gaps, and avenues for refinement in the AI-generated content.

3   Results

Document Analysis. The results for all the text characteristics metrics of the analyzed datasets can be found on our GitHub repository. Table 1 reports the characteristics with the most significant values. The columns in Table 1 list the average counts throughout the 12 versions of each type of audience. The audiences are indicated by the values of Dev (Developers), Man (Managers), and Ori (the original documentation text used as a baseline). From the data in Table 1, we can already notice the capacity of ChatGPT to lay out the text in a structured way. This is mostly evident by looking at the Amazon documentation text. We notice that the original text only had one paragraph, whereas the ChatGPT-generated texts had, on average, 22.67 paragraphs. Furthermore, we can observe that ChatGPT is also able to reduce the number of paragraphs based on the target audience. In the case of Euronym, the original text had 28 paragraphs. We can see here how the number of paragraphs reduced to 12.25 on average when it came to Managers. We assumed that ChatGPT expects managers to require more condensed information. This is also confirmed by the number of words (462.92 on average vs. 1066 words in the original text). Moreover, this behavior of ChatGPT to re-organize the text is consistently seen in the metrics Headers and Lists. Especially, comparing the original texts from Facebook and Amazon, which did not use or used at most one header or list, we can observe that the generated data contains several of such elements.

Table 1. Text characteristics for the different documentation versions

Project	Audience	Paragraphs	Headers	Lists	Sentences	Words
Amazon	Developers	22.67	3.33	14.25	29.67	571.33
	Managers	12.50	0.58	3.83	27.08	479.08
	Original	1.00	0.00	0.00	24.00	420.00
Euronym	Developers	27.75	7.67	12.75	33.58	730.00
	Managers	12.25	4.08	2.92	23.83	462.92
	Original	28.00	10.00	10.00	41.00	1066.00
Facebook	Developers	39.42	5.08	26.17	37.75	712.83
	Managers	16.75	1.33	4.17	32.42	562.42
	Original	12.00	0.00	1.00	61.00	1857.00

Table 2 shows the results of the readability metrics applied to the ChatGPT-generated documentation. We observe the differences between the metrics of the text for a management and development audience, compared to the original baseline. For all three documentation (Amazon, Euronym, Facebook), ChatGPT generated documentation shows different scores than the original. Developer-adapted ChatGPT documentation consistently scores lower readability compared to the baseline (i.e., higher Coleman-Liau, higher Difficult Words, and lower Reading Ease values). This is not necessarily a sign of worse readability; instead, it could potentially signal more technical-intense jargon usage. Manager-adapted ChatGPT documentation presents opposite scores compared to the baseline: lower Coleman-Liau, lower Difficult Words, and higher Reading Ease. In other words, these texts are easier to read and understand. We also looked into the texts qualitatively and noticed that most of the manager-adapted ChatGPT documentation has a summary or takeaway message at the end, different from the developer-adapted ChatGPT documentation.

Table 2. Readability metrics for three different technical documentations

Readability Metric	Documentation	Average			StdDev	
		Original	Developer	Manager	Developer	Manager
Coleman-Liau Index	Amazon	10.66	9.90	9.91	1.45	0.72
	Euronym	20.05	13.92	13.95	1.86	1.72
	Facebook	12.41	11.21	11.22	1.87	0.51
Difficult Words	Amazon	71.00	68.50	66.50	9.19	10.43
	Euronym	142.00	98.00	96.00	10.32	10.91
	Facebook	168.00	89.50	88.50	15.53	7.87
Flesch Reading Ease	Amazon	57.16	59.51	60.23	6.72	4.82
	Euronym	35.34	42.47	45.26	6.48	7.97
	Facebook	53.51	56.74	55.95	6.15	4.08

Expert Survey Results. The survey engaged a total of 25 professionals, consisting of 13 developers and 12 managers. Gender distribution included ten females, 14 males, and one participant preferring not to disclose their gender. Most respondents, 22 in number, were employed full-time, with two identifying as students and one categorized as 'other'. The age distribution predominantly fell within the 25–34 years range, encompassing 20 participants, while four were aged between 35 and 44, and one was between 45 and 54 years. Regarding professional experience, five participants had 1–2 years, 9 had 3–6 years, ten had 6–10 years, and one had less than a year of experience. This demographic composition provided a balanced perspective across different levels of professional experience and roles.

In terms of expert ratings, the evaluations were generally positive for all three versions of the documentation (cf. Table 3). All original documents aligned more closely with developer needs. However, both ChatGPT adaptations, intended for management and developer audiences, were rated as being better suited for the management audience, compared to the original documentation, likely due to an overall enhancement in readability by ChatGPT. This improvement was less pronounced for the technical audience and even reversed in the case of the Facebook documentation. The intended adaptation of documents was mostly successful for managers, less so for developers (compare grey areas in Table 3).

Table 3. Results of the expert survey. U=understandability of the text; D=provided level of detail; M=alignment with needs of a management audience; T=alignment with needs of a technical audience. A=Amazon; E=Euronym; F=Facebook

Eval	Doc	Average all experts (StdDev)			Average managers (StdDev)			Average developers (StdDev)		
		Ori	Dev	Man	Ori	Dev	Man	Ori	Dev	Man
U	A	4.50 (.93)	4.13 (1.13)	4.50 (.53)	4.00 (1.15)	3.75 (.50)	4.50 (.58)	5.00 (.00)	4.25 (1.50)	4.50 (.58)
D		2.89 (.78)	3.78 (.83)	3.78 (.83)	2.60 (.89)	3.80 (1.10)	4.00 (.00)	3.25 (.50)	3.75 (.50)	3.50 (1.29)
	F	4.13 (.83)	3.88 (.83)	3.88 (.99)	4.33 (1.15)	4.33 (.83)	4.33 (.58)	4.00 (.71)	3.60 (.89)	3.60 (.89)
D	A	4.00 (1.07)	3.88 (.83)	4.50 (.53)	3.50 (1.29)	3.75 (.50)	4.50 (.58)	4.50 (.58)	4.00 (1.15)	2.25 (1.26)
	E	3.11 (.93)	3.67 (.71)	3.67 (1.32)	3.20 (.84)	3.60 (.89)	4.40 (.55)	3.00 (1.15)	3.75 (.50)	2.75 (1.50)
	F	3.63 (1.06)	3.13 (1.25)	3.88 (.99)	2.67 (1.15)	3.33 (1.15)	3.00 (1.00)	4.20 (.45)	3.00 (1.41)	1.80 (.45)
M	A	2.75 (1.45)	3.63 (1.30)	4.75 (.46)	2.50 (1.29)	4.25 (.96)	5.00 (.00)	3.00 (1.83)	3.00 (1.41)	4.50 (.58)
	E	2.56 (1.13)	3.00 (.71)	4.56 (.73)	2.40 (1.14)	3.00 (1.00)	4.80 (.45)	2.75 (1.26)	3.00 (.00)	4.25 (.96)
	F	2.75 (1.16)	4.00 (.76)	3.00 (1.07)	2.33 (.58)	3.67 (.58)	3.33 (.58)	3.00 (1.41)	2.60 (1.14)	4.40 (.55)
T	A	3.88 (.83)	4.00 (.53)	2.50 (1.20)	3.75 (.50)	3.75 (.50)	2.75 (.96)	4.00 (1.15)	4.25 (.50)	2.25 (1.50)
	E	3.22 (.83)	3.56 (.73)	2.56 (1.24)	3.20 (.84)	3.40 (.89)	2.80 (1.10)	3.25 (.96)	3.75 (.50)	2.25 (1.50)
	F	4.00 (.76)	3.00 (1.51)	1.63 (1.06)	4.00 (1.00)	2.67 (1.53)	2.00 (1.73)	4.00 (.71)	3.20 (1.64)	1.41 (.55)

Often, the original documentation was better rated by developers than the developer version by ChatGPT. These differences in different measurements were partially supported by t-tests: the comparison between the original and management versions of Facebook documentation showed the management version as less aligned for the technical audience (two-tailed t-test, p = .00015); the original versus management versions of Euronym documentation indicated the management version as more aligned with manager needs (two-tailed t-test, p = .00039); and for Amazon, the management documentation was less aligned with developer needs (two-tailed t-test, p = .018) but more aligned for managers (two-tailed t-test, p = .0027).

4   Conclusion

In this paper, we addressed the problem of generating documentation that is targeted to specific audiences who work with different requirements and do not possess the same knowledge about software development details. Our approach uses ChatGPT version 4 to aid the restructuring and content according to management and development audiences. The results show clear distinction according to general document and readability metrics. An expert evaluation showed that managers reported improved readability and understandability of the catered versions from ChatGPT.

Acknowledgements. This research was supported by the Einstein Foundation Berlin under grant number EPP-2019-524 and the Weizenbaum Institute under grant number 16DII133.

References

1. Abrahamsson, P., et al.: Chatgpt as a fullstack web developer - early results. In: XP Workshops. Lecture Notes in Business Information Processing, vol. 489, pp. 201–209. Springer, Cham (2023)
2. Aghajani, E., et al.: Software documentation issues unveiled. In: Proceedings of the 41st International Conference on Software Engineering, ICSE 2019, pp. 1199–1210. IEEE Press, Montreal, Quebec, Canada (2019)
3. Coleman, M., Liau, T.L.: A computer readability formula designed for machine scoring. J. Appl. Psychol. **60**(2), 283 (1975)
4. Dale, E., Chall, J.S.: A formula for predicting readability: instructions. Educ. Res. Bull. 37–54 (1948)
5. Flesch, R.: A new readability yardstick. J. Appl. Psychol. **32**(3), 221 (1948)
6. Garousi, G., Garousi, V., Moussavi, M., Ruhe, G., Smith, B.: Evaluating usage and quality of technical software documentation: an empirical study. In: Proceedings of the 17th International Conference on Evaluation and Assessment in Software Engineering, EASE 2013, pp. 24–35. Association for Computing Machinery, New York (2013)
7. Pace AI: Chatgpt for technical documentation (2024). https://paceai.co/chatgpt-for-technical-documentation. Accessed 21 June 2024
8. Pan, W., Ming, H., Kim, D.K., Yang, Z.: Pride: prioritizing documentation effort based on a pagerank-like algorithm and simple filtering rules. IEEE Trans. Software Eng. **49**, 1118–1151 (2023)
9. Patton, M.Q.: Two decades of developments in qualitative inquiry: a personal, experiential perspective. Qual. Soc. Work. **1**(3), 261–283 (2002)
10. Ronanki, K., Daniel, B.C., Berger, C.: Chatgpt as a tool for user story quality evaluation: trustworthy out of the box? In: XP Workshops. Lecture Notes in Business Information Processing, vol. 489, pp. 173–181. Springer, Cham (2023)
11. Sommerville, I.: Sommerville Software Engineering, vol. 291. Pearson (2011)

The AI Scrum Master: Using Large Language Models (LLMs) to Automate Agile Project Management Tasks

Zorina Alliata[1], Tanvi Singhal[2(✉)], and Andreea-Madalina Bozagiu[3]

[1] Zorina Alliata, Munich, Germany
[2] Tanvi Singhal, Munich, Germany
Tanvi.singhal1990@gmail.com
[3] Andreea-Madalina Bozagiu, Bucharest, Romania

Abstract. There is a high demand across industries for intelligent devices to automate and optimize processes. Generative AI has soared in popularity and it is the first AI technology to be used by everyone. It is already automating junior-level office work, as well as highly complex creative tasks. This paper studies how Generative AI can automate some of the Agile project management tasks, such as reporting and creating requirements that correctly cover the scope.

Keywords: AI · Agile · Scrum Master · Project Management · LLM · Generative AI

1 Introduction

There has been a rise in the use of large language models (LLMs) as a method for creating synthetic data as a mean to automate some repetitive tasks, or to provide inputs for model training. Large language models (LLMs) such as ChatGPT and Claude can generate synthetic datasets through their remarkable in-context learning skills and enormous pre-trained linguistic information.

As examples, Josifoski et al. [6] artificially create a dataset consisting of 1.8 million data points in a reverse fashion and showcase the efficacy of this method in closed information extraction. Whitehouse et al. [7] employ multiple Language Models (LLMs) to enhance three datasets and evaluate the authenticity and logical consistency of the created examples.

The crucial factors are 1) ensuring that the use case aligns with the capabilities of this technology, and 2) ensuring that the data generated is suitable for this technology.

Use cases considered for this paper:

– Use Case 1: Generate status reports

o Interpret a burndown chart and create a narrative report

– Use Case 2: Expanding content from an outline or seed

o Create user stories from given Epics.

L. Marchesi et al. (Eds.): XP 2024 Workshops, LNBIP 524, pp. 110–122, 2025.
https://doi.org/10.1007/978-3-031-72781-8_12

2   Methodology

We use publicly available LLMs (Claude 3 Sonnet and Microsoft Copilot/ChatGPT 4.5) to generate synthetic data and measure accuracy of the new dataset. Prompting is needed for more meaningful data generation. We use ROUGE [1], METEOR [8] and BERTSCORE [2] evaluation methods to measure the generated data accuracy.

Use Case 1: Interpret a burndown chart and create a narrative report
Original data set:
1A. No context: Prompt: Please comment on this image (Fig. 1).

This is an image of a burndown chart for a team. The number of story points committed is 120, and they have 7 days to deliver. Looking at the graphic, it shows that first the team delivered slower than expected, and after day 4, they started delivering faster than expected. A possible explanation is that the team had a delay in testing the stories, and then released several at the same time. They finished the work on time and delivered all the committed story points.

1B. With context: Prompt: There are 3 days left in the sprint. Write a narrative status report of the burndown chart included (Fig. 2).

Looking at the burn down chart, it seems the team is behind the schedule in delivering user stories. With only three days left in the sprint, the team still has almost half the story points still not completed. It also looks like the actual hour spent by the time have been decreasing in the last two days. The cause is a team member who is out unexpectedly. Remediations include getting another developer to help out, descoping some of the stories, or moving some stories to the next sprint until the team is at the expected capacity again.

LLM Prompts:

– 1C. Only feed it the burndown chart image with no other context (Fig. 1)
– 1D. With context:

 o Prompt: The team sprint ends in 3 days. Please see attached burn-down chart and create a narrative report that explains the chart and the status of the delivery. (Fig. 2)

The result is a narrative that describes the burndown chart and reports on the work status for the team.

1C. This image appears to be a release burndown chart. A burndown chart is a graphical representation commonly used in agile software development to track the amount of work remaining over in a project or sprint. The chart plots the amount of work or story points remaining on the y-axis against the time periods (e.g., sprints or iterations) on the x-axis. In this particular burndown chart, the y-axis represents the "Story Points" or work items, while the x-axis represents the sprint or iteration numbers (1 to 7). The red line depicts the actual progress or "work done" over time, while the gray line represents the planned or "ideal" progress if work was completed at a constant rate. The chart shows that the team started behind schedule (the red line is above the gray line initially), but managed to catch up and even get ahead of the planned progress towards the end of the project or release cycle.

With context:

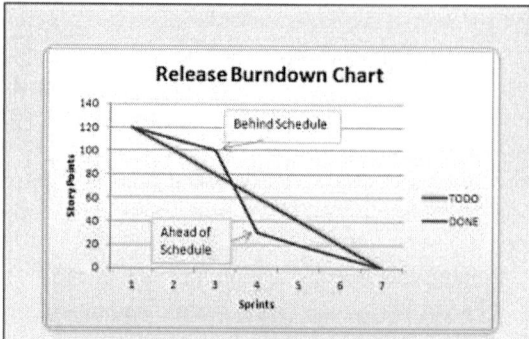

Fig. 1. No context prompting. (Color figure online)

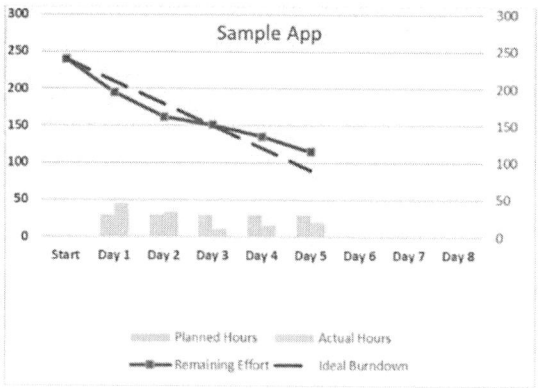

Fig. 2. Sample Burndown Chart (Color figure online)

Prompt: The team sprint ends in 3 days. Please see attached burndown chart and create a narrative report that explains the chart and the status of the delivery.

Claude 3 Sonnet:

1D. Based on the burndown chart for the Sample App, I can provide the following narrative report:

The chart displays the planned work hours, actual hours spent, remaining effort, and ideal burndown rate over an 8-day period for the project.

At the start of the project, the total planned effort was around 250 h. The ideal burndown line shows a steady, linear decrease in remaining work, representing the expected rate of progress if work proceeded perfectly as planned.

However, the actual remaining effort line (in blue) indicates that progress has been slower than the ideal rate. The team appears to have fallen behind the planned schedule, with more remaining work than expected at each day's point.

The green and yellow bars show the planned and actual hours spent each day, respectively. While the planned hours remain relatively consistent, the actual hours worked have fluctuated, sometimes exceeding the planned hours and other times falling short.

With 3 days remaining until the end of the sprint, there is still a substantial amount of remaining effort, approximately 100 h based on the latest data point. This suggests that the team may struggle to complete all the planned work within the allotted time unless they can significantly increase their productivity or reassess the scope.

Overall, the chart indicates that the project is behind schedule, and the team may need to take corrective actions, such as allocating additional resources, extending the timeline, or descoping certain features, to ensure a successful delivery.

Use Case 2: Create user stories from Epics

Starting data set: Backlog from auto insurance company (human generated). Data has been anonymized and any identifiable information removed. Goal: create a new mobile app for clients.

Original Epics:

Change of State; Copy Policy and Billing Account; Policy/Billing Notes; Renew Policy; Add/Update/Remove Specialty Vehicle; Multi-policy: group vehicle policy with home policy; Reissue/Reinstate/Resumption; Simple Add Driver; Simple Add Vehicle; Simple View Policy; Simple Remove Driver; Simple Remove Vehicle; Simple Update Driver; Simple Update Vehicle; Add Coverage; Integration with Other Systems; Remove Coverage; Update Coverage; Cancel Policy; Change In State; Complex Add Driver; Complex Add Vehicle; Complex Remove Driver; Complex Remove Vehicle; Complex Update Driver; Complex Update Vehicle; View Add/Remove Discounts; Cancel Rewrite Policy; Issue New Business; Recall Quote; View/Update Account Preferences.

2A. Original data set:

Epic	User Story
Add Coverage	Manage Coverages
Add Coverage	Renewal
Add/Update/Remove Specialty Vehicle	Assigned Risk Policies
Add/Update/Remove Specialty Vehicle	Specialty Vehicle Processing
Cancel Policy	Billing Auto/Cycle
Cancel Policy	Cancellation
Cancel Rewrite Policy	Cancel/Rewrite
Change In State	Change Mailing Address
Change In State	Change of Address In State
Change In State	Manage Coverages
Change In State	Process Out of Sequence Transaction
Change In State	Request Change of Address - Multi-Line
Change of State	Change of Address Out of State
Complex Add Driver	Activity Log
Complex Add Driver	Add Driver Endorsement
Complex Add Driver	Effective Date
Complex Add Driver	Manage Coverages

(continued)

(continued)

Epic	User Story
Complex Add Driver	Occurrences
Complex Add Driver	Usage/DVA
Complex Add Driver	View Policy
Complex Add Vehicle	Add Auto\Cycle Endorsement
Complex Add Vehicle	Effective Date
Complex Add Vehicle	Inspections
Complex Add Vehicle	Issue Endorse Policy Changes
Complex Add Vehicle	Manage Coverages
Complex Add Vehicle	Occurrences
Complex Add Vehicle	Usage/DVA
Complex Add Vehicle	Vehicle Customizations
Complex Remove Driver	Remove Driver Endorsement
Complex Remove Vehicle	Remove Auto\Cycle Endorsement
Complex Update Driver	Effective Date
Complex Update Driver	Issue New Business
Complex Update Driver	Remove Driver Endorsement
complex update driver	Renewal
Complex Update Driver	Update Driver Endorsement
Complex Update Vehicle	Add Auto\Cycle Endorsement
Complex Update Vehicle	Add Driver Endorsement
Complex Update Vehicle	Discounts
Complex Update Vehicle	Manage Coverages
Complex Update Vehicle	Update Auto\Cycle Endorsement
Complex Update Vehicle	Update Driver Endorsement
Copy Policy and Billing Account	Billing Auto/Cycle
Copy Policy and Billing Account	Billing Conversion
Copy Policy and Billing Account	Billing Download
Copy Policy and Billing Account	Copy Policy
Copy Policy and Billing Account	Policy Copy & Cloning
Integration with Privy	Security
Issue New Business	Documents/Forms
Issue New Business	Issue New Business
Issue New Business	Manage Changes to Policy
Issue New Business	Renewal

(continued)

(continued)

Epic	User Story
Multi-policy: group vehicle policy with home policy	Add Auto\Cycle Endorsement
Multi-policy: group vehicle policy with home policy	Add Driver Endorsement
Multi-policy: group vehicle policy with home policy	Automated Multiple Policy Processing (Multi-Line Orchestration)
Multi-policy: group vehicle policy with home policy	Cancel/Rewrite
Multi-policy: group vehicle policy with home policy	Cancellation
Multi-policy: group vehicle policy with home policy	Copy Policy
Multi-policy: group vehicle policy with home policy	Effective Date
Multi-policy: group vehicle policy with home policy	Issue New Business
Multi-policy: group vehicle policy with home policy	Manage Coverages
Multi-policy: group vehicle policy with home policy	Reinstate Policy
Multi-policy: group vehicle policy with home policy	Reissue Policy
Multi-policy: group vehicle policy with home policy	Remove Auto\Cycle Endorsement
Multi-policy: group vehicle policy with home policy	Remove Driver Endorsement
Multi-policy: group vehicle policy with home policy	Request Change of Address - Multi-Line
Multi-policy: group vehicle policy with home policy	Retrieve Quote
Multi-policy: group vehicle policy with home policy	Save Quote
Multi-policy: group vehicle policy with home policy	Update Auto\Cycle Endorsement
Multi-policy: group vehicle policy with home policy	Update Driver Endorsement
Multi-policy: group vehicle policy with home policy	Update Quote
Recall Quote	Policy Profile

(continued)

(*continued*)

Epic	User Story
Recall Quote	Retrieve Quote
Recall Quote	Save Quote
Recall Quote	Update Quote
Reissue/Reinstate/Resumption	Confirmation Page
Reissue/Reinstate/Resumption	Documents/Forms
Reissue/Reinstate/Resumption	Express
Reissue/Reinstate/Resumption	Reason Codes and Forms
Reissue/Reinstate/Resumption	Reinstate Policy
Reissue/Reinstate/Resumption	Reissue Policy
Reissue/Reinstate/Resumption	Resume Policy
Remove Coverage	Manage Coverages
Renew Policy	Renewal
Simple Add Driver	Add Auto\Cycle Endorsement
Simple Add Driver	Add Driver Endorsement
Simple Add Vehicle	Add Auto\Cycle Endorsement
Simple Remove Driver	Remove Driver Endorsement
Simple Remove Vehicle	Remove Auto\Cycle Endorsement
Simple Update Driver	Update Driver Endorsement
Simple Update Vehicle	Update Auto\Cycle Endorsement
Simple View Policy	View Policy
Update Coverage	Add Auto\Cycle Endorsement
Update Coverage	Manage Coverages
View Add/Remove Discounts	Discounts
View/Update Account Preferences	Account Preferences

LLM Prompt:

– Generate user stories for each Epic in the list, to accomplish the major goal of creating a mobile app for auto insurance customers, with the following functionality:

   o Policy Management

      Add/edit/delete policy
      Add/edit/delete vehicles, drivers, interested parties on a policy
      Add/edit coverage

   o Get Quote
   o Set up Account Preferences

– Context:

o The Auto insurance can have one or more drivers on each policy, and one or more Interested Parties (non-drivers)
o The Auto insurance can be combined with other policies such as home owner insurance or motorcycle insurance
o Each vehicle has a VIN that can be queried from public records and provides basic data about the vehicle
o There will be some integration work needed with the backend data lake where the company stores their data.

2C. No context:

Please generate user stories to accomplish the major goal of creating a mobile app for auto insurance customers, with the following functionality:

o Policy Management

  Add/edit/delete policy
  Add/edit/delete vehicles, drivers, interested parties on a policy
  Add/edit coverage

o Get Quote
o Set up Account Preferences

  Copilot:

  Certainly! Let's create some user stories for the auto insurance mobile app based on the provided functionality and context. User stories help us understand what users want to achieve and why. Here are some examples:

1. **Policy Management:**
   o **As an insurance agent**, I want to **add a new policy** for a customer, so they can have coverage for their vehicle.
   o **As a policyholder**, I want to **edit my existing policy**, so I can update my coverage details or add/remove vehicles and drivers.
   o **As an insurance administrator**, I want to **delete a policy**, so I can manage the policies effectively.
2. **Vehicle and Driver Management:**
   o **As a policyholder**, I want to **add a new vehicle** to my policy by providing its VIN, make, and model, so I can ensure it's covered.
   o **As a policyholder**, I want to **add a new driver** to my policy, including their license information, so they can drive the insured vehicle.
   o **As an insurance agent**, I want to **edit driver details**, such as updating their address or license number, so the policy remains accurate.
   o **As a policyholder**, I want to **remove a driver** from my policy, perhaps due to a change in household members.
3. **Interested Parties Management:**
   o **As a policyholder**, I want to **add an interested party** (such as a lienholder or leasing company) to my policy, so they receive notifications about the policy.
   o **As an insurance agent**, I want to **edit interested party details**, such as their contact information, to keep the records up to date.

o **As a policyholder**, I want to **remove an interested party** if they are no longer relevant to my policy.

4. **Coverage Management:**
   o **As a policyholder**, I want to **add or modify coverage options** (e.g., liability, collision, comprehensive) for my policy, so I can tailor it to my needs.
   o **As an insurance agent**, I want to **review and approve coverage changes**, ensuring they comply with company guidelines.

5. **Get Quote:**
   o **As a potential customer**, I want to **request a quote** for auto insurance by providing basic information (vehicle details, driving history), so I can compare prices.
   o **As an insurance agent**, I want to **generate a quote** based on the provided data and send it to the customer for review.

6. **Account Preferences:**
   o **As a policyholder**, I want to **set my communication preferences** (email, SMS, phone) for policy updates and reminders.
   o **As a policyholder**, I want to **manage my account settings**, including password changes and security options.
   o **As an insurance administrator**, I want to **integrate with the backend data lake**, ensuring seamless data synchronization between the app and our systems.

Remember, these user stories serve as a starting point. You can further refine them, prioritize, and break them down into smaller tasks during development.

2D. With context:

You

Epics: Change of State Copy Policy and Billing Account Policy/Billing Notes Renew Policy Add/Update/Remove Specialty Vehicle Multi-policy: group vehicle policy with home policy Reissue/Reinstate/Resumption Simple Add Driver Simple Add Vehicle Simple View Policy Simple Remove Driver Simple Remove Vehicle Simple Update Driver Simple Update Vehicle Add Coverage Integration with Other Systems Remove Coverage Update Coverage Cancel Policy Change In State Complex Add Driver Complex Add Vehicle Complex Remove Driver Complex Remove Vehicle Complex Update Driver Complex Update Vehicle View Add/Remove Discounts Cancel Rewrite Policy Issue New Business Recall Quote View/Update Account Preferences Please generate user stories for each Epic in the list, to accomplish the major goal of creating a mobile app for auto insurance customers, with the following functionality: o Policy Management ♣Add/edit/delete policy ♣Add/edit/delete vehicles, drivers, interested parties on a policy ♣Add/edit coverage o Get Quote o Set up Account Preferences Context: o The Auto insurance can have one or more drivers on each policy, and one or more Interested Parties (non-drivers) o The Auto insurance can be combined with other policies such as home owner insurance or motorcycle insurance o Each vehicle has a VIN that can be queried from public records and provides basic data about the vehicle o There will be some integration work needed with the backend data lake where the company stores their data. Please create multiple user stories per epic, and more granular in functionality.

Copilot.

Certainly! Let's dive deeper into each epic and create more granular user stories for the auto insurance mobile app:

1. **Change of State:**
   o As an auto insurance customer, I want to **suspend my policy temporarily** when I'm not using my vehicle (e.g., during a long vacation).
   o Benefit: This allows me to save on premiums while maintaining coverage.
   o As an auto insurance customer, I want to **reactivate my policy** after a suspension period.
   o Benefit: This ensures seamless coverage when I start using my vehicle again.
   o As an auto insurance customer, I want to **cancel my policy permanently** if I no longer need auto insurance.
   o Benefit: This simplifies the process and avoids unnecessary charges.
2. **Copy Policy:**
   o As an auto insurance customer, I want to **clone an existing policy** to create a new one with similar coverage.
   o Benefit: This streamlines policy setup for additional vehicles or drivers.
   o As an auto insurance customer, I want to **customize the cloned policy** by adjusting coverage limits or deductibles.
   o Benefit: This tailors the policy to my specific needs.
3. **Billing Account Policy/Billing Notes:**
   o As an auto insurance customer, I want to **view my billing history** within the app.
   o Benefit: This helps me track payments and understand my financial transactions.
   o As an auto insurance customer, I want to **add billing notes** (e.g., special payment arrangements) to my account.
   o Benefit: This ensures clear communication with the insurance company.
4. **Renew Policy:**
   o As an auto insurance customer, I want to receive a **renewal reminder** through the app before my policy expires.
   o Benefit: This prompts timely action to maintain continuous coverage.
   o As an auto insurance customer, I want to **renew my policy with a single click**.
   o Benefit: This simplifies the renewal process.
5. **Add/Update/Remove Specialty Vehicle:**
   o As an auto insurance customer, I want to **add a classic car** to my policy.
   o Benefit: This ensures proper coverage for my unique vehicle.
   o As an auto insurance customer, I want to **update the mileage** for my RV.
   o Benefit: This reflects accurate usage and affects premium calculations.
   o As an auto insurance customer, I want to **remove a specialty vehicle** (e.g., sold or no longer owned).
   o Benefit: This keeps my policy up-to-date.
6. **Multi-policy: Group Vehicle Policy with Home Policy:**
   o As an auto insurance customer, I want to **bundle my auto and home policies** for potential discounts.
   o Benefit: This simplifies management and may reduce costs.
   o As an auto insurance customer, I want to **view combined policy details** (auto and home) in one place.
   o Benefit: This provides a holistic view of my coverage.
7. **Reissue/Reinstate/Resumption:**

o As an auto insurance customer, I want to **reinstate my lapsed policy** after a missed payment.
o Benefit: This prevents gaps in coverage.
o As an auto insurance customer, I want to **resume my policy** after a temporary suspension.
o Benefit: This restores coverage quickly.

8. **Simple Add Driver:**
   o As an auto insurance customer, I want to **add a teenage driver** to my policy.
   o Benefit: This ensures proper coverage for new drivers.
   o As an auto insurance customer, I want to **specify the primary driver** for each vehicle.
   o Benefit: This affects premium calculations.

9. **Simple Add Vehicle:**
   o As an auto insurance customer, I want to **add a leased car** to my policy.
   o Benefit: This ensures coverage for the new vehicle.
   o As an auto insurance customer, I want to **upload vehicle documents** (e.g., registration, inspection) via the app.
   o Benefit: This simplifies paperwork.

10. **Simple View Policy:**
    o As an auto insurance customer, I want to **see my policy summary** (coverages, deductibles) at a glance.
    o Benefit: This provides quick access to essential information.
    o As an auto insurance customer, I want to **view my policy ID card** digitally.
    o Benefit: This helps during traffic stops or accidents.

11. **Simple Remove Driver:**
    o As an auto insurance customer, I want to **remove an ex-spouse** from my policy.
    o Benefit: This keeps my policy accurate after life changes.
    o As an auto insurance customer, I want to **specify excluded drivers** (e.g., high-risk individuals).
    o Benefit: This affects coverage and premium.

12. **Simple Remove Vehicle:**
    o As an auto insurance customer, I want to handle changes in policy status.

Results
While ROUGE and METEOR scores are low, we know that the data generated by the LLMs is quite accurate in accomplishing the tasks for both use cases. BERT Score is the metric that finds the similarity and correctly points out that the LLMs generated data that is close to the human-generated set.

For both use cases, the BERT Score is slightly higher when context is provided. Using better prompting or RAG in the future could lead to much more accurate results.

Generated versus actual	BERT Score	METEOR Score	ROUGE Score
1C versus 1A	tensor([0.8505])	0.28394412026 216626	{'rouge1': Score(precision=0.2484472049689441, recall=0.47058823529411764, fmeasure=0.3252032520325203), 'rougeL': Score(precision=0.14285714285714285, recall=0.27058823529411763, fmeasure=0.18699186991869918)}
1D versus 1B	tensor([0.8573])	0.28376450626 73121	{'rouge1': Score(precision=0.21397379912663755, recall=0.5051546391752577, fmeasure=0.3006134969325153), 'rougeL': Score(precision=0.13100436681222707, recall=0.30927835051546393, fmeasure=0.18404907975460125)}
2C versus 2A	tensor([0.7834])	0.08895303157 992328	{'rouge1': Score(precision=0.23040380047505937, recall=0.1471927162367223, fmeasure=0.17962962962962964), 'rougeL': Score(precision=0.1377672209026128, recall=0.08801213960546282, fmeasure=0.1074074074074074)}
2D versus 2A	tensor([0.7959])	0.16822527395 756623	{'rouge1': Score(precision=0.2911931818181818, recall=0.3110773899848255, fmeasure=0.3008070432868672), 'rougeL': Score(precision=0.16193181818181818, recall=0.17298937784522003, fmeasure=0.1672780630961115)}

3   Outcomes/Conclusion

Measuring how LLMs can help the Agile Scrum Master is their project management tasks can provide a basis for automating some of the repetitive tasks and enabling higher productivity. Providing business context is important, and can be done through prompting or a RAG approach for more complex situations. Using the right metric is also important, and in this case BERT Score was the measurement that correctly identified the accuracy of the generated data.

In practice, Scrum Masters and project managers can use publicly available LLMs to automate the reporting and requirements creation, with the understanding that the

Generative AI technology is creative by design, and it might contain hallucinations or other risks. The Scrum Masters and project managers need to review the outputs and keep testing that the answers are correct by employing the right measurements for LLM accuracy.

References

1. Lin, C.-Y.: ROUGE: a package for automatic evaluation of summaries. In: Text Summarization Branches Out, Barcelona, Spain, pp. 74–81. Association for Computational Linguistics (2004)
2. Zhang, T., Kishore, V., Wu, F., Weinberger, K.Q., Artzi, Y.: BERTScore: Evaluating Text Generation with BERT (2020). https://doi.org/10.48550/arXiv.1904.09675
3. Radford, A., Narasimhan, K., Salimans, T., Sutskever, I., et al.: Improving language understanding by generative pre-training (2018)
4. Radford, A., et al.: Language models are unsupervised multitask learners. OpenAI Blog 1(8), 9 (2019)
5. Brown, T., et al.: Language models are few-shot learners. In: Advances in Neural Information Processing Systems, vol. 33, pp. 1877–1901 (2020)
6. Josifoski, M., Sakota, M., Peyrard, M., West, R.: Exploiting asymmetry for synthetic training data generation: SynthIE and the case of information extraction. In: Bouamor, H., Pino, J., Bali, K. (eds.) Proceedings of the 2023 Conference on Empirical Methods in Natural Language Processing, (Singapore), pp. 1555–1574. Association for Computational Linguistics (2023)
7. Whitehouse, C., Choudhury, M., Aji, A.: LLM-powered data augmentation for enhanced cross lingual performance. In: Bouamor, H., Pino, J., Bali, K. (eds.) Proceedings of the 2023 Conference on Empirical Methods in Natural Language Processing, (Singapore), pp. 671–686. Association for Computational Linguistics (2023)
8. Banerjee, S., Lavie, A.: METEOR: an automatic metric for MT evaluation with improved correlation with human judgments. In: Proceedings of the ACL Workshop on Intrinsic and Extrinsic Evaluation Measures for Machine Translation and/or Summarization. Ann Arbor, Michigan, pp. 65–72 (2005)

Copilot's Island of Joy
Balancing Individual Satisfaction with Team Interaction in Agile Development

Viggo Tellefsen Wivestad[1]([✉]) [ID], Astri Barbala[1] [ID], and Viktoria Stray[1,2] [ID]

[1] SINTEF Digital, 7034 Trondheim, Norway
viggo.wivestad@sintef.no
[2] University of Oslo, 0373 Oslo, Norway

Abstract. This study assesses the integration of GitHub Copilot into agile software development practices in one of Norway's largest public sector organizations. Through a quasi-experimental survey of 115 participants, we differentiate the attitudes of users and non-users of GitHub Copilot regarding their development routines. Findings reveal that Copilot users experience significantly greater focus on engaging tasks and less dependence on colleagues compared to non-users, while non-users maintain a more cautious stance on AI use in the public sector. Further, while users generally showed more positive attitudes and fewer frustrations, these differences were not statistically significant. The study advocates for a mindful adoption of AI tools in agile settings, balancing individual benefits with interdependence and team unity.

Keywords: Agile Software Development · GitHub Copilot · AI Tool Adoption · Collaboration · Team dependence

1 Introduction and Background

AI Coding Assistants, a subset of Generative AI (GenAI), have recently emerged as popular tools, reshaping how coding tasks are approached and executed [15]. Developers, managers, and Scrum Masters are all trying to evaluate the impact of such tools on the agile software development process [15]. However, the adoption of these tools introduces significant uncertainty in agile software development, necessitating a fundamental shift in managerial planning and execution [4].

The role of the Scrum Master in agile projects has evolved significantly over the last decade [1,11], with recent studies offering new insights into this transformation. These studies explore various aspects of the Scrum Master role, such as servant leadership, facilitation, and mentorship, all crucial for enhancing team collaboration and overcoming organizational challenges [8]. Moreover, the emergence of GenAI technologies could further influence the Scrum Master's role and agile ways of working. Today, while some agile team members readily embrace these tools, others may exhibit hesitation, reflecting diverse attitudes toward technological adoption in agile environments.

© The Author(s) 2025
L. Marchesi et al. (Eds.): XP 2024 Workshops, LNBIP 524, pp. 123–129, 2025.
https://doi.org/10.1007/978-3-031-72781-8_13

While new research is continually appearing, the single largest study to our knowledge is still that of GitHub Research [6,17], which includes a survey with over 2000 respondents. The results from this study suggest several benefits of utilizing AI Coding Assistants, such as increased productivity, higher job satisfaction, and being able to spend time on more enjoyable tasks. Their study utilized the SPACE framework, which offers a comprehensive approach to understanding developer productivity beyond conventional metrics [5]. The framework encapsulates five critical dimensions: Satisfaction and well-being (S), Performance (P), Activity (A), Communication and Collaboration (C), and Efficiency and flow (E). In this study, we extend the original survey to answer the following research question: ***What benefits of using GitHub Copilot can be identified when comparing users to a control group?.***

To answer this RQ, we articulated a series of hypotheses based on an assumption that the adoption of AI Coding Assistants will yield predominantly favorable outcomes for its users, while simultaneously reducing challenges and friction in their daily routines.

To investigate whether the use or non-use of AI Coding Assistants made a difference in the everyday work of agile software developers, we conducted a quantitative study at the National Welfare Administration (NAV), a large public sector organization based in Norway. NAV has about 1000 employees in their IT department, and the teams follow agile principles of software development. The organization is known for being at the forefront in implementing new tools and practices for software development such as continuous software engineering [2], data-driven methods [3], and a widespread use of Slack as a coordination tool [14]. Recently, NAV has also looked into incorporating the use of GenAI tools in their software development work, and in September 2023 the organization gave 100 developers access to GitHub Copilot.

2   Method and Study Design

The research design can be described as an exploratory, cross-sectional, natural quasi-experiment involving two distinct groups: users and non-users of Copilot in NAV. While the non-users in the control group had not adopted Copilot, the experiment group consisted of 100 Copilot users who had volunteered and been pre-approved before our arrival, as well as external consultants who had obtained a license through other means. Our 114 respondents consisted of 67 users and 47 non-users. Among the respondents, 81% of respondents were in-house employees; 15% were women, 79% were men, 1% identified as "other" and 5% would not disclose gender.

The survey instrument was built upon GitHub Research's survey [16], which utilized the SPACE framework [5] to assess the perceived productivity of subjects participating in an unpaid technical preview of Copilot. Our study adapted a subset of relevant survey items and translated them. Given that the original survey was designed exclusively for users of Copilot, the survey items were transformed to fit a comparative analysis between users and non-users. Items that explicitly reference the Copilot were therefore rephrased and generalized, focusing on outcomes. Further, a few new items were added, based on ideas and concerns that were identified during a preceding interview process, and hypotheses we wanted to test. The hypotheses are listed in Table 1, and the complete survey instrument is available online at: https://doi.org/10.5281/zenodo.10987170.

The final questionnaire consisted of 57 questions (28 for both groups and an additional 29 for the users), most of them being 5-point Likert Agreement scale-type questions. The survey had a required, initial segmentation question that asked whether the respondent had used Copilot or not, which was used to label the participant as either a user or non-user.

The first part of the analysis consisted of a systematic comparison of the two groups, comparing the proportion of respondents who agreed with a statement (strongly agree + agree) against the total number of respondents. This approach, known as a Top 2-Box (T2B) analysis, is useful when focusing on an area of interest [12], but does not consider the entire distribution of replies (those who disagree or are neutral). The subsequent analysis entailed hypothesis testing. Considering the ordinal nature of Likert-scale responses, we employed the non-parametric Mann-Whitney U Test [9] to assess differences between the groups' distributions, complemented by the Rank-Biserial Correlation (RBC) [7] and the Common Language Effect Size (CLES) [10] for evaluating effect magnitude. We used Bonferroni corrected $p < 0.0056$ $(0.05/9)$ as the threshold of statistical significance, to account for the multiple hypothesis testing problem. The analysis was predominantly done using Python.

3   Results

The final survey collected a total of 115 responses, comprising 67 users and 48 non-users of GitHub Copilot. The results from the Top 2-Box (T2B) analysis are depicted as a barplot in Fig. 1, and the results from the hypothesis testing are detailed in Table 1.

A key finding related to user benefits was the enhanced ability to focus on satisfying work; over 70% of users reported this benefit compared to only half of the non-users. Our related hypothesis, that users would experience a higher ability to focus on satisfying work, was statistically validated using the Mann-Whitney U test, and confirmed to be significant, with a meaningful effect size evidenced by both the Rank-Biserial Correlation (RBC) and the Common Language Effect Size (CLES). Note that had we not corrected for multiple hypothesis testing, our hypothesis that users experience higher job satisfaction would also have been confirmed ($p = 0.031$). This finding indicates that using AI Coding Assistants enables users to move faster past frustrating and demotivating tasks, spending more time on things they enjoy.

As shown in Fig. 1, users generally had higher agreement rates regarding job satisfaction, flow, and productivity, and disagreed more that they felt frustrated while coding. However, none of these were found to be significant, as shown in Table 1.

Table 1. Results from the Mann-Whitney U test, comparing attitudes differences between users and non-users. For each item, information is provided related to the one-sided test ($\mathbf{H_a}$), sample size of the user/non-user ($\mathbf{N_U}$, $\mathbf{N_{NU}}$), Mann-Whitney U value ($\mathbf{U}$), P-value ($\mathbf{P}$), Rank-Biserial Correlation ($\mathbf{RBC}$), Common Language Effect Size ($\mathbf{CLES}$), and whether or not to reject the null hypothesis given the Bonferroni corrected threshold.

Item	H_a	(N_U, N_{NU})	U	P	RBC	CLES	Reject H_0
Copilot is valuable	$\mu_U > \mu_{NU}$	(61, 35)	592	0.000	0.446	0.723	✓
Can focus on satisfying work	$\mu_U > \mu_{NU}$	(60, 36)	740	0.002	0.315	0.657	✓
Satisfied with job	$\mu_U > \mu_{NU}$	(61, 37)	894	0.031	0.207	0.604	
Is in flow when coding	$\mu_U > \mu_{NU}$	(63, 40)	1175	0.273	0.067	0.534	
Productive when coding	$\mu_U > \mu_{NU}$	(63, 40)	1256	0.490	0.003	0.502	
Critical of AI in public sector	$\mu_U < \mu_{NU}$	(59, 38)	660	0.000	-0.411	0.705	✓
Dependent on colleagues	$\mu_U < \mu_{NU}$	(60, 39)	800	0.003	-0.317	0.658	✓
Frustrated when coding	$\mu_U < \mu_{NU}$	(63, 40)	1054	0.075	-0.163	0.582	
Searches for information online	$\mu_U < \mu_{NU}$	(61, 39)	1142	0.360	-0.040	0.520	

Another finding was a significantly lower dependency on colleagues among the users of Copilot. This confirmed our hypothesis, with nearly half of the users disagreeing with the notion that they rely on assistance or guidance from colleagues, compared to just a fifth of the non-users.

We also confirmed our hypothesis that users are noticeably less concerned about using AI in the public sector, with "strongly disagree" being the most frequent answer (41%), with 64% disagreeing. For non-users, the answers were spread out on both sides, indicating a more nuanced and skeptical view. One non-user stated in the open-text field in the survey: *"I am uncomfortable with the idea that data collected by AI is used for purposes that I am unaware of, especially from a privacy perspective."*

The most prominent finding, aligning with our hypothesis and expectations, indicated that users perceived Copilot as significantly more valuable than non-users. Determining the cause is however difficult, as the groups were not randomly selected. Positive responses might reflect genuine benefits derived from using the tool, or simply capture the user's initial motivation. It is also worth noting that half of the non-users also agreed with the statement, suggesting a generally positive attitude towards the tool across both groups.

4   Discussion and Implications for Practice

In this paper, we outline the findings from a survey conducted among users and non-users of Github Copilot in a large, public-sector organization. When comparing the attitudes between the two groups, we identified only one significant user benefit: the enhanced ability to focus on satisfying work. Regarding other

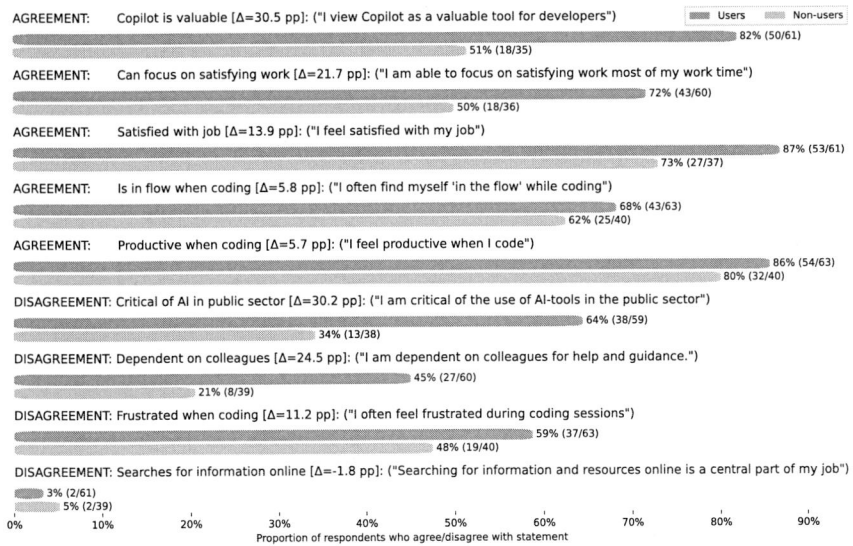

Fig. 1. Top 2-Box plot comparing the proportion of users and non-users who agreed/disagreed with statements related to attitudes and experiences among software developers.

proclaimed benefits, our study found no significant differences. This is surprising, given the proclaimed benefits by users in GitHub Research's study [6,17], such as productivity and flow. This divergence could be a user expectancy effect or an artifact of our general, and slightly vaguer, survey statement formulations.

Users also reported a notably higher job satisfaction than the non-users, with 87% of the users agreeing that they felt satisfied in their job, as compared to 73% of the non-users. While this could be a result of self-selection bias, it echoes the study of Ulfsnes et al. [15] who found that usage of GenAI tools empowered software developers by reducing tedious and repetitive tasks and freeing up time for more satisfying work. The same study also pointed out some negative consequences, with developers preferring to get help from their AI Coding Assistant rather than their colleagues. This finding resonates with our findings, with evident signs of decreased dependence, with 45% of the users outright disagreeing that they are dependent on colleagues for help and guidance.

Given these findings, we speculate that while AI Coding Assistants might enhance individual satisfaction and independence, they could pose long-term threats to teamwork, knowledge sharing, unity, and overall team interactions. Remote workers might be especially vulnerable, as the threshold to approach, and potentially disturb, a colleague is higher [13]. Such challenges would pose extraordinary disruption for agile teams and Scrum Masters, whose main tasks are to facilitate collaboration and remove team obstacles [11].

Scrum Masters can leverage these insights to balance the use of AI Coding Assistants within agile frameworks, thereby upholding the core agile value of prioritizing individuals and interactions over processes and tools. Although AI Coding Assistants seem to enhance focus and satisfaction among developers, it is imperative to ensure that these benefits do not lead to isolation, where each team member finds themselves on a solitary 'island of joy.'

References

1. Alliata, Z., Alliata, D., Berzin, L.: Get IT! How to Start a Career in the New Information Technology: How to Start as an Agile Scrum Master. Better Karma LLC (2016)
2. Barbala, A., Sporsem, T., Stol, K.J.: A case study of continuous adoption in the norwegian public sector (2024)
3. Barbala, A., Sporsem, T., Stray, V.: Data-driven development in public sector: how agile product teams maneuver data privacy regulations. In: International Conference on Agile Software Development, pp. 165–180. Springer, Cham (2023)
4. Cleveland, S., Moschoglou, G., Millisor, E.J., Hansen, D.D.: Exploring project uncertainty and leadership strategies: domains, factors, categories, and competencies. Int. J. Smart Educ. Urban Soc. (IJSEUS) **13**(1), 1–13 (2022)
5. Forsgren, N., Storey, M.A., Maddila, C., Zimmermann, T., Houck, B., Butler, J.: The SPACE of developer productivity. Queue **19**(1), 20–48 (2021). https://doi.org/10.1145/3454122.3454124
6. Kalliamvakou, E.: Research: quantifying GitHub Copilot's impact on developer productivity and happiness (2022). https://github.blog/2022-09-07-research-quantifying-github-copilots-impact-on-developer-productivity-and-happiness/
7. Kerby, D.S.: The simple difference formula: an approach to teaching nonparametric correlation. Compr. Psychol. **3**, 11.IT.3.1 (2014)
8. Kristensen, S.H., Paasivaara, M.: What added value does a scrum master bring to the organisation? - a case study at nordea. In: 2021 47th Euromicro Conference on Software Engineering and Advanced Applications (SEAA), pp. 270–278 (2021). https://doi.org/10.1109/SEAA53835.2021.00041
9. Mann, H.B., Whitney, D.R.: On a test of whether one of two random variables is stochastically larger than the other. Ann. Math. Stat. **18**(1), 50–60 (1947). https://doi.org/10.1214/aoms/1177730491. http://projecteuclid.org/euclid.aoms/1177730491
10. McGraw, K.O., Wong, S.P.: A common language effect size statistic. Psychol. Bull. **111**(2), 361–365 (1992). https://doi.org/10.1037/0033-2909.111.2.361. https://doi.apa.org/doi/10.1037/0033-2909.111.2.361
11. Shastri, Y., Hoda, R., Amor, R.: Spearheading agile: the role of the scrum master in agile projects. Empir. Softw. Eng. **26**, 1–31 (2021)
12. Shull, F., Singer, J., Sjøberg, D.I.K. (eds.): Guide to Advanced Empirical Software Engineering. Springer, London (2008). https://doi.org/10.1007/978-1-84800-044-5
13. Smite, D., Mikalsen, M., Moe, N.B., Stray, V., Klotins, E.: From collaboration to solitude and back: remote pair programming during COVID-19. In: Gregory, P., Lassenius, C., Wang, X., Kruchten, P. (eds.) XP 2021. LNBIP, vol. 419, pp. 3–18. Springer, Cham (2021). https://doi.org/10.1007/978-3-030-78098-2_1
14. Stray, V., Barbala, A.: Slack use in large-scale agile organizations: ESN tools as catalysts for alignment? In: International Conference on Agile Software Development, pp. 20–35. Springer, Cham (2024)

15. Ulfsnes, R., Moe, N.B., Stray, V., Skarpen, M.: Transforming software development with generative AI: empirical insights on collaboration and workflow. In: Nguyen-Duc, A., Abrahamsson, P., Khomh, F. (eds.) Generative AI for Effective Software Development, pp. 219–234. Springer, Cham (2024). https://doi.org/10.1007/978-3-031-55642-5_10

16. Ziegler, A., et al.: Productivity assessment of neural code completion. In: Proceedings of the 6th ACM SIGPLAN International Symposium on Machine Programming, MAPS 2022, pp. 21–29. Association for Computing Machinery, New York (2022)

17. Ziegler, A., et al.: Measuring GitHub copilot's impact on productivity. Commun. ACM **67**(3), 54–63 (2024). https://doi.org/10.1145/3633453. https://dl.acm.org/doi/10.1145/3633453

Can ChatGPT Suggest Patterns? An Exploratory Study About Answers Given by AI-Assisted Tools to Design Problems

João José Maranhão Junior[1]([✉]) [iD], Filipe F. Correia[2] [iD],
and Eduardo Martins Guerra[3] [iD]

[1] Institute for Technological Research, São Paulo, Brazil
`joao.junior@ensino.ipt.br`
[2] Faculty of Engineering, University of Porto, Porto, Portugal
`filipe.correia@fe.up.pt`
[3] Free University of Bozen-Bolzano, Bolzano, Italy
`eduardo.guerra@unibz.it`

Abstract. General-purpose AI-assisted tools, such as ChatGPT, have recently gained much attention from the media and the general public. That raised questions about in which tasks we can apply such a tool. A good code design is essential for agile software development to keep it ready for change. In this context, identifying which design pattern can be appropriate for a given scenario can be considered an advanced skill that requires a high degree of abstraction and a good knowledge of object orientation. This paper aims to perform an exploratory study investigating the effectiveness of an AI-assisted tool in assisting developers in choosing a design pattern to solve design scenarios. To reach this goal, we gathered 56 existing questions used by teachers and public tenders that provide a concrete context and ask which design pattern would be suitable. We submitted these questions to ChatGPT and analyzed the answers. We found that 93% of the questions were answered correctly with a good level of detail, demonstrating the potential of such a tool as a valuable resource to help developers to apply design patterns and make design decisions.

Keywords: ChatGPT · Design Patterns · Artificial Intelligence · AI-assisted tools

1 Introduction

The use of design patterns [1–3] in software development is a practice that brings several advantages, including code reuse, better code organization, ease of maintenance, better scalability, and software quality [4,5]. In the context of agile methods, these characteristics are essential to keep the code ready to change, enabling adjustments in requirements in small iterations. However, becoming proficient in understanding and applying these patterns can take time and

© The Author(s) 2025
L. Marchesi et al. (Eds.): XP 2024 Workshops, LNBIP 524, pp. 130–138, 2025.
https://doi.org/10.1007/978-3-031-72781-8_14

effort [6], requiring a high degree of abstraction and practice in object-oriented programming. Educational institutions use various learning techniques [7,8] to engage students with real-world problems in recognizing and interpreting these patterns.

ChatGPT is an AI-assisted tool capable of answering questions in a conversational way. Recently, this kind of tool has received a lot of attention from the media and the general public, raising questions about the potential of its application in several fields, such as public health [9] and academia [10]. Some recent works suggest its use for software engineering applications, such as solving programming bugs [11] and improving other kinds of activities, like requirements engineering and code quality [12]. GitHub Co-Pilot[1] is an example of another tool in this direction.

The goal of this paper is to investigate if an AI-assisted tool can help developers to make design decisions, like suggesting appropriate design patterns to apply in a given scenario. To reach that goal, we performed an exploratory study considering 56 exercises and exam questions obtained from educational institutions and public tenders, which present a concrete context and ask which pattern should be applied. We used ChatGPT for this study, and we evaluated how many answers it answered correctly based on the question's official answer and what elements that can help in the pattern implementation is present in the answers. For wrong answers, we also assessed if they could mislead the developer to the wrong path.

We found that the AI-assisted tool answered 93% of the questions correctly, always referring to specific details of the scenario and, in several cases providing guidance to the pattern implementation, including the classes and interfaces that should be created. In the few cases where the tool provided wrong answers, we found that they could be misleading and guide the developers in the wrong direction. Based on that, we consider the results of this initial assessment promising, pointing to the potential of such tools to assist in software design decisions. However, we also believe an experienced professional is still needed to evaluate the suitability of the suggested solution.

2 Research Design

Based on the goal of investigating if an AI-assisted tool can help developers in choosing the appropriate design pattern to apply in a given scenario, we formulated three more specific research questions:

1. RQ_1 - How is the success rate of the AI-assisted tool in suggesting design patterns?
2. RQ_2 - Do elements provided in the answer of the AI-assisted tool help in the pattern implementation?
3. RQ_3 - In questions where the wrong pattern is pointed, does the AI-assisted tool answer mislead the developers?

---

[1] https://github.com/features/copilot.

To answer these research questions, we collected preexisting questions prepared by higher education professors or public tenders in which a scenario is described, and it asks which design pattern should be applied. Since these questions are used to evaluate the student's knowledge of patterns, we believe they can also be used to evaluate the tool's performance. We chose ChatGPT as the AI-assisted tool for the study and submitted the selected questions to it, registering the answers. The content of the answers was analyzed, not only comparing to the exercise correct answer (RQ_1) but also analyzing what elements that can help the developers in the pattern implementation were present (RQ_2). A qualitative analysis was done on the wrong answers to evaluate if they could mislead the developers (RQ_3).

To select the answers, we contacted professors that teach design patterns in universities asking for exam questions and exercises they give students. We've received the material from three professors from different countries: Italy, the United States, and Portugal. We also analyzed available exams of public tenders for 26 Brazilian institutions. As a question inclusion criteria for this study, we considered the following criteria: (a) the solution should be one of the "Gang of Four" (GoF) patterns; (b) the question should describe a scenario and ask which pattern should be applied; and (c) the question should describe a concrete scenario and not just give general requirements.

The first criterion was included to restrict the scope of the study to these patterns, which are well known by the software development community and taught in university courses, which enabled finding a good number of questions. The two other criteria were considered to choose questions that better simulate the decision of applying a pattern in a real scenario.

The qualitative analysis inspected each correct answer and evaluated the following criteria: (C1) If the answer mentions the described context (instead of just giving a generic answer); (C2) If the answer explains the pattern;(C3) If the answer describes the classes and interfaces that need to be created to implement the pattern; (C4) If the answer describes the methods that should be created to implement the pattern; (C5) If the answers included a UML diagram to represent the solution; (C6) If the answer described any trade-off or negative consequence in using of the proposed pattern.

3   Questions Database

In selecting questions, we obtained a total of 56 Design Pattern questions. There are 19 questions from university courses: 9 questions from the United States, 6 from Portugal, and 4 from Italy. All of these questions were formulated in English. We also found 37 questions in Portuguese from public tenders in Brazil, inspecting selection exams of twenty-nine different institutions. Since the questions obtained from teachers are used in exams and some asked to keep them private, we did not make the questions dataset open.

From the selected questions, all patterns in the study scope were covered with at least one question. Figure 1 presents how many questions have each pattern as a correct answer. Considering the pattern categories, there are 25 questions about *behavioral* pattern, 22 about *structural* patterns, and 17 about *creational* patterns. We consider that the question database is reasonably balanced among the pattern categories, having a good amount of questions that cover each one. Two questions accepted more than one pattern as a correct answer; in such cases, we consider any one of them as right. Four questions asked for a combination of patterns as an answer; in this case, we considered that the right answer should include all of them.

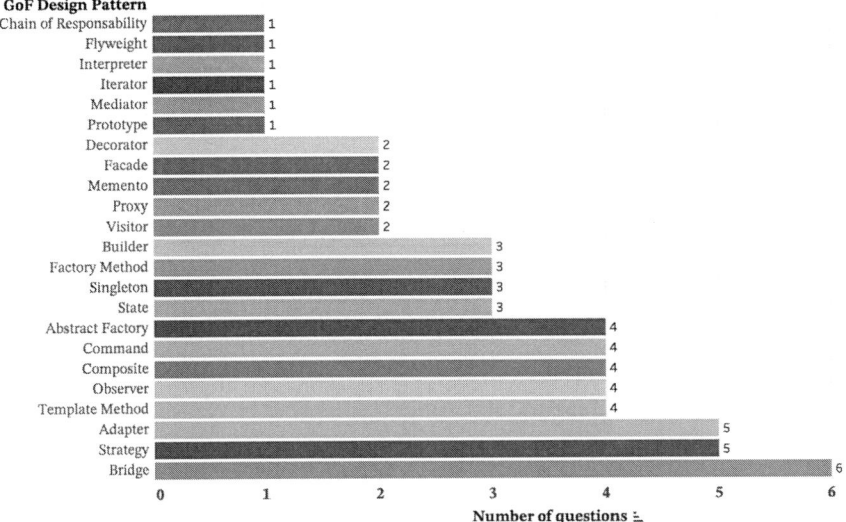

Fig. 1. Number of questions collected by design patterns.

4 Results

The questions were sent to ChatGPT (version 3.5) in the period comprised between 2023-03-03 and 2023-04-16. Based on the results, ChatGPT was generally effective in answering our questions, with an overall accuracy rate of 93%. Most of the questions were in Portuguese, with 31 of the 34 questions answered correctly, while 21 of the 22 in English were answered correctly.

The answers have an average number of 1033 chars with a standard deviation of 657, varying from a minimum of 247 to a maximum of 3127. Considering the number of words, the average is 155, with a standard deviation of 89, varying from a minimum of 37 to a maximum of 390 words. We used the Pearson correlation coefficient to evaluate if the number of words on the question would be related to the number of words in the answer. The value of 0,09 obtained showed that there was no significant relation.

Information Present in the Answers. A qualitative analysis evaluated the six criteria proposed in Sect. 2. The following are the results:

- (C1) 100% of the correct answers (52/52) mention the described context (instead of just giving a generic answer)
- (C2) 57.69% of the correct answers (30/52) explain the pattern;
- (C3) 32.69% of the correct answers (17/52) describe the classes and interfaces that need to be created to implement the pattern;
- (C4) 26.92% of the correct answers (14/52) describe the methods that should be created to implement the pattern;
- (C5) 3.85% of the correct answers (2/52) include a UML diagram to represent the solution;
- (C6) None of the correct answers (0/52) describe any trade-off or negative consequence in using the proposed pattern.

Assessment of Wrong Answers. This section presents an analysis of the questions that received a wrong answer (the ID will be used to refer to that question later):

- (WA1) The question presented a problem in creating a solution for reports needing two dimensions: the report type and the report format. While the correct answer was using the Visitor pattern, the tool suggested Strategy. In the answer, one of the dimensions of the question was ignored, and the proposed solution focused only on the report format.
- (WA2) The question asked how the representation of more complex devices could be dynamically created by reusing the behavior of more simple devices that are part of it. While the correct answer was Composite, the given answer was Factory Method. In this case, the solution described does not help in solving the design problem presented.
- (WA3) The question presented the context of exchanging messages between different cell phone operating systems platforms, handling distinct message formats transparently. While the correct answer was Adapter, the answer given was Bridge. In this case, even if the patterns share some structural similarities, the described solution does not help solve the problem.
- (WA4) The question presented an abstract class that is responsible for transparently creating objects corresponding to different types of databases. Concrete subclasses are responsible for instantiating specific connections and queries for each type of database. The correct answer was Abstract Factory, and the given answer was Factory Method. Even if both are creational patterns, the given answer does not help to solve the problem because it was necessary to create a family of objects for each type of database.

5   Discussion

This section performs a discussion based on the obtained results, answering each research question. We also point out some limitations of the present study.

5.1 RQ_1 - How is the Success Rate of the AI-Assisted Tool in Suggesting Design Patterns?

The study showed an efficient result with 93% correct answers in 56 questions. We highlight that the questions selected do not just ask for information about the patterns but present a specific and concrete scenario. To correctly answer the question by choosing the right pattern, the relevant factors that point to the usage of that specific pattern need to be identified in the context description. We also highlight that in the four questions that required a combination of patterns as an answer, the correct answer was provided by the AI-assisted tool.

ChatGPT performance can be considered good compared to other works that proposed more specific techniques for pattern suggestion [13, 14]. Consequently, it can be considered a suitable assisting tool for developers, which can describe the design scenario in their application and receive suggestions from the tool.

5.2 RQ_2 - Do Elements Provided in the Answer of the AI-Assisted Tool Help in the Pattern Implementation?

One positive point is that all responses mentioned the problem's context instead of just pointing to the pattern and providing a generic explanation. Around one-third of the answers also provided the name of the classes and interfaces that should be created in that case. Additionally, around one-quarter described the methods that should be created. Few answers, only 2, also provided UML diagrams with the structure that should be used.

Most of the answers, but not all, brought a more theoretical explanation of the pattern, which can be useful in case the developer is unfamiliar with the pattern. A piece of important information that was not present in any of the answers is the trade-off in the usage of the suggested pattern since knowing possible bad consequences is important to make design decisions.

To avoid any kind of bias, the questions used in this study were not modified; however, we acknowledge that if we explicitly included in the question what information we wanted in the answer, the tool would include it. We did some exploratory experiments on some of the questions, rephrasing them to ask explicitly for some missing information. As a result, the missing information was included correctly in the new answers. That fact highlights the importance of how the questions are formulated, a new disciple called prompt engineering [12].

5.3 RQ_3 in Questions Where the Wrong Pattern is Pointed, Does the AI-Assisted Tool Answer Mislead the Developers?

We analyzed the four questions that received wrong answers to see if there was any inconsistency or ambiguity in the way they were formulated, and all authors agreed that they were clearly described and there was no doubt about the correct answer. For all the patterns that were the correct answer for these questions, there is at least another question with the same pattern answered correctly.

In the case of WA1, the answer given by ChatGPT considered the described context partially, and the Strategy implementation that it described could be evolved to a Visitor. However, in WA2, WA3, and WA4, the answer leads to a way that does not solve the problem. The answers are assertive and well-described, and we believe can easily be accepted by a less experienced developer. Because of that, we advise that the answers given by an AI-assisted tool should be reviewed and understood instead of being blinded implemented. In other words, there should be a professional that should be responsible for its analysis and adoption.

We also noticed that some of these questions used terms and expressions closely connected to other patterns. So, we suggest avoiding expressions like "family of algorithms" or "composite objects" that can drive the tool to a specific pattern.

5.4   Study Limitations

Our study focused only on "Gang of Four" (GoF) design patterns, which are well-known and widely used in the software development community. The performance of ChatGPT may differ for other design patterns that are newer and have less material available.

Our study was conducted in a controlled setting using preexisting questions. These questions were formulated by teachers with software design knowledge, focused on scenarios suitable for applying one of the patterns, and included all the necessary information relevant to direct the answer to one of the patterns. Using such a tool in a real project would require skills to identify the relevant forces in the scenario and formulate them properly [12]. Asking which pattern should be used might force the choice of one pattern in cases where none of them is suitable.

6   Conclusion

This paper described an exploratory study that investigated using an AI-assisted tool, in our case ChatGPT, to suggest design patterns using scenarios from existing exam questions. The tool answers have good accuracy, being correct in 93% of the cases, and always mention specific details of the scenarios, which provide guidance for the pattern implementation. In some cases, the answers also included information on classes, interfaces, and methods to be created, which we believe could be improved even more using prompt engineering techniques [12]. Another finding is that wrong answers, even if given in only a few cases, could be misleading and lead the developers in a direction that does not help the design problem described. In conclusion, our study suggests that AI-assisted tools can be a valuable resource for developers in understanding and applying design patterns; however, they should not replace human expertise, and the solutions should be reviewed before their adoption.

Future studies in this direction can focus on a different set of patterns that have less documentation and material available on the Internet. The result of this new study can be compared with the one made with the GoF patterns to assess if the AI-assisted tool can have a similar performance. Other studies can be conducted in more realistic scenarios using the description of design challenges faced by development teams and comparing the solutions suggested by an AI-assisted tool with the ones adopted in the projects.

References

1. Gamma, E., Helm, R., Johnson, R., Vlissides, J.: Design Patterns: Elements of Reusable Object-Oriented Software. Addison-Wesley Professional, Boston (1994)
2. Joshua, K.: Refactoring to Patterns. Addison-Wesley Professional, Boston (2004)
3. Martin, R.C.: Agile Software Development, Principles, Patterns, and Practices. Prentice Hall, Upper Saddle River (2002)
4. Holub, A.: Holub on Patterns: Learning Design Patterns by Looking at Code. Apress, New York (2004)
5. Barros-Justo, J.L., Benitti, F.B.V., Cravero-Leal, A.L.: Software patterns and requirements engineering activities in real-world settings: a systematic mapping study. Comput. Standards Interfaces **58**, 23–42 (2018)
6. Shalloway, A., Trott, J.: Design patterns explained: a new perspective on object-oriented design. Addison-Wesley Professional, Boston (2004)
7. Warren, I.: Teaching patterns and software design. Conferences in Research and Practice in Information Technology Series, vol. 42 (2005)
8. Chatzigeorgiou, A., Tsantalis, N., Deligiannis, I.: An empirical study on students ability to comprehend design patterns. Comput. Educ. **51**(3), 1007–1016 (2008)
9. Biswas, S.S.: Role of chat GPT in public health. Ann. Biomed. Eng. 1–2 (2023)
10. Lund, B.D., Wang, T.: Chatting about chatgpt: how may AI and GPT impact academia and libraries? Library Hi Tech News (2023)
11. Surameery, N.M.S., Shakor, M.Y.: Use chat GPT to solve programming bugs. Int. J. Inf. Technol. Comput. Eng. (IJITC) **3**(01), 17–22 (2023). ISSN: 2455-5290
12. White, J., Hays, S., Fu, Q., Spencer-Smith, J., Schmidt, D.C.: Chatgpt prompt patterns for improving code quality, refactoring, requirements elicitation, and software design. arXiv preprint arXiv:2303.07839 (2023)
13. Hussain, S., Keung, J., Sohail, M.K., Khan, A.A., Ilahi, M.: Automated framework for classification and selection of software design patterns. Appl. Soft Comput. **75**, 1–20 (2019)
14. Hasheminejad, S.M.H., Jalili, S.: Design patterns selection: an automatic two-phase method. J. Syst. Softw. **85**(2), 408–424 (2012). Special issue with selected papers from the 23rd Brazilian Symposium on Software Engineering

Education Track

Towards Improving Behavior-Driven Development and Acceptance Testing-Driven Development Teaching in a University Project Course

Marina Filipovic$^{(\boxtimes)}$ ⓘ and Fabian Gilson ⓘ

University of Canterbury, Christchurch, New Zealand
{marina.filipovic,fabian.gilson}@canterbury.ac.nz

Abstract. Behavior-Driven Development (BDD) improves the collaboration between developers and stakeholders following agile software development practices. Acceptance Test-Driven Development (ATDD) is an extension of BDD where requirements are accompanied by automated acceptance tests, translating functional acceptance criteria linked to requirements. While BDD and ATDD have been successfully applied in industry, few universities report on teaching BDD and ATDD principles as part of their curriculum. However, there is a need for education providers to teach industry-relevant practices so that junior developers' skills are better aligned to industry's expectations. Therefore, we report on how BDD and ATDD techniques have been taught in a two-semester software engineering project, including (i) the lack of observed evidence on the implications of applying BDD and ATDD on the functional suitability of software products, (ii) the lack of engagement with BDD and ATDD from students, and (ii) recommendations to educators to improve students' engagement with these practices.

Keywords: agile software development · behavior-driven development · acceptance test-driven development · Scrum · tertiary education

1 Introduction

Behavior-Driven Development (BDD) aims at helping software development teams to build reliable products that are closely aligned with the needs of customers [1]. BDD focuses on specifying the system's behavior in natural language so that it can be easily automated [2]. Specifically, user interactions are described with specific keywords for preconditions, actions, and post-conditions (or effects), i.e. *Given <precondition>, When <action>, Then <post-condition>* (GWT). In Acceptance Test-Driven Development (ATDD), test code is derived from GWT criteria to drive the design of a feature.

When successfully implemented, BDD and ATDD exhibit many benefits [3], such as improved communications between customers and developers, improved

© The Author(s) 2025
L. Marchesi et al. (Eds.): XP 2024 Workshops, LNBIP 524, pp. 141–149, 2025.
https://doi.org/10.1007/978-3-031-72781-8_15

productivity and decreased code defects, and automated testing of software at the "business" level. However Farooq et al. report on challenges in using BDD in industry, suggesting it is difficult for inexperienced developers [4]. Therefore, particular attention needs to be put into teaching BDD and ATDD so junior developers can be better prepared for the industry.

In this report we investigate the effects on students' learning outcomes of a *learning-by-doing* with *just-in-time learning* [5]. We observed 8 teams of 3rd year undergraduate students over 5 Scrum sprints, where they applied Scrum, BDD, ATDD, and DevOps principles, within a continuous integration pipeline. Specifically, we investigate the following questions: **RQ1:** Can we observe a correlation between BDD and ATDD engagement levels and functional suitability [6] of a product developed in a project course? **RQ2:** To what extend learning-by-doing is a suitable approach for 3rd year students to adopt BDD and ATDD practices? **RQ3:** What challenges and success factors do 3rd year undergraduate students face when implementing BDD and ATDD practices for the first time?

Our main findings are: (i) BDD and ATDD practices were not used to their full potential, with teams partially disengaging around mid-project; (ii) students needed more timely guidance to overcome technical challenges with the implementation of complex acceptance test scenarios; and (iii) despite students indicating they found the workshops useful (e.g., git, ATDD, DevOps), they were not sufficient for students to engage with BDD/ATDD in the long term.

2   Related Work

While reports on BDD implementations in industry settings are well documented, there is limited research focused on teaching BDD [4].

Goulart reports on a successful application of BDD into a capstone project conducted by a team of 3 students [7]. Amongst the lessons learned, the author reported that students needed close mentoring, regular revision of acceptance tests, and frequent deliveries to ensure the full benefits of applying BDD. Our project course also implements close mentoring of teams, as well as frequent deliveries (Scrum sprints).

Rocha et al. report on their experience with students applying TDD and BDD in a software project course where they observed better grades and faster delivery [8]. Where limited details are given on how the authors calculated the grades, we focus on successful product deliveries instead of grades, which matches more closely the expected outcome in industry.

Sarinho applies an "unplugged" and "gamified" paper-based teaching method for students to get familiar with BDD principles [9]. However, they do not evaluate the effectiveness of their method beyond anecdotal observations.

Nascimento et al. suggest that an active learning methodology such as *"Challenge-Based Learning"* improves students' learning and engagement [10]. Our project-based course, applying both problem-based learning and learning-by-doing principles, closely matches these recommendations.

Compared to existing works, we observe the effects on product deliveries of teaching and applying BDD in an active-learning environment over five Scrum sprints. We also investigate students' engagement with BDD practices over a rather long period of time (multiple months) on a sizeable software product (approx. 20KLOC).

3   Study Design

3.1   Context

This study was carried on a whole-year project course in the 3rd year of the Software Engineering degree at the University of Canterbury. Before taking the course, all students have experience in imperative (python) and object-oriented (Java) programming, design principles, and relational databases. As a co-requisite, students take a software engineering course that covers Scrum, BDD, ATDD, and continuous integration. This research was conducted from February to September 2021 (21 study weeks). 80 students were enrolled at the start of the course, with 70 completing it. Out of these, 7 identified as women, and 63 as men. We obtained appropriate approval from the University Ethics Committee and students to use their anonymised data for research purposes.

3.2   Project Organisation

The project follows the Scrum framework [11] and is divided in 6 sprints lasting 3 to 4 weeks each. Because students start in sub-teams for the first sprint (for on-boarding purposes), we gathered data from the second sprint onwards. All teams start with the same project template containing the initial technology stack, i.e. SpringBoot with Gradle, and Vue.js, configured to interact with a Gitlab pipeline and virtual machines hosted by the University.

Each team of 7–8 students is mentored by a scrum master being a 4th year student who successfully passed the course previously. A more experienced teaching team is composed of lecturers and senior tutors playing the roles of product owner (PO), technical leads, or training consultants. The PO, a lecturer, overlooks the product backlog with acceptance criteria where technical leads and training consultants approve additional technologies and give students a technical and methodological guidance (i.e. predefined workshops, ad-hoc support, marking of deliverables).

Each sprint implements all Scrum events (i.e. planning, daily scrums, review, retrospective), with each team negotiating their sprint commitment separately with the PO during sprint planning. Each product is marked at the end of each sprint in terms of delivered stories in regards to each team's sprint backlog.

3.3   Workshops

During the course, specific workshops were offered (e.g. Git, Testing including BDD and ATDD, code review). These workshops were mandatory. The dedicated Testing workshop was delivered at the beginning of the project, in sprint

2. During this workshop students learned how to write automated acceptance tests using Cucumber[1]. To emphasise BDD principles, the product backlog was made out of user stories with detailed acceptance criteria. Stories and acceptance criteria were written by the PO while students had to translate them into (automated) acceptance tests.

Students worked in pairs during most workshops, as working in small groups leads to improved learning outcomes [12]. We paired students on their engagement and abilities demonstrated during the first sprint to encourage knowledge sharing. From that workshop on, students were required to follow BDD practices, including automated acceptance testing, into their project.

3.4 Data Sources and Metrics

To answer our RQs, we collected metrics via four sources: SonarQube with JaCoCo[2], Cucumber feature files, manual test scripts in spreadsheets, and a survey students filled in at the end of the year where they reflected on their own learning, including how they evaluated the content of the workshops.

Unit test code coverage: These were obtained from JaCoCo reports uploaded to SonarQube (triggered by the Gitlab pipeline) after each sprint. Because of the technology stack, back-end JUnit (Java) unit tests are referred to as BEUT, while front-end Jest (Javascript) unit tests are denoted FEUT.

Automated acceptance test coverage: Students wrote automated acceptance tests in *Gherkin* syntax, i.e. *Given-When-Then*, using Cucumber scenarios. We manually mapped scenarios to acceptance criteria attached to user stories after each sprint, denoted as AAT. The acceptance criteria were considered fully covered if there was at least one Cucumber scenario per criterion.

Manual acceptance test coverage: The coverage of acceptance criteria with manual tests is denoted MAT. The data was aggregated from manual inspection of manual test scripts in spreadsheets mapped to acceptance criteria for all stories, on a sprint basis.

Assessment of functional suitability: Each sprint delivery was assessed by a teaching team member in terms of passed story points, denoted PSP, compared to the team's own sprint commitment (i.e. team sprint backlog).

End-of-year survey: As part of their end-of-year survey, students were given optional questions to comment on their learning experience in the course and on the material covered during the testing workshop.

4 Results

We report on the main findings from observations and analysis of 8 out of 10 initial teams in the project over 5 sprints[3]. Raw data are available on Zenodo[4].

---

[1] See https://cucumber.io/.

[2] See https://www.sonarqube.org/ and https://www.jacoco.org/jacoco/.

[3] Two teams were discarded as only partial manual testing data could be retrieved.

[4] R sources and data: https://zenodo.org/doi/10.5281/zenodo.10064914.

RQ1 - BDD and Functional Suitability. We have undertaken statistical modelling in R to analyse potential relationships between different levels of testing and product deliveries. We have chosen to fit a Linear Mixed-Effect model (LMER) as we have repeated observations of clusters of data, i.e. testing metrics per team, where teams can be considered as the random effect. Following industry results [4], we postulate that any increase in ATDD-related test coverage (i.e. AAT metric) would predict an increase in passed stories (i.e. PSP metric). We reproduce the results of the LMER model calculation in Table 1 where we also added the other testing coverage metrics for comparison purposes. Teams' PSP averages (over all sprints) ranged from 43.59% (Team A) to 77.61% (Team H).

Table 1. Results from LMER model calculation (in R).

	Estimate	St.Error	t value	Pr(>|t|)
(Intercept)	0.3159	0.1723	1.834	0.07522
FEUT	0.6323	0.2188	2.890	0.00657 **
BEUT	−0.3307	0.2950	−1.121	0.26984
AAT	0.1731	0.2179	0.794	0.43230
MAT	0.3895	0.1401	2.779	0.00871 **

Asterisks next to probability values indicate significance levels (R `summary` function).

From Table 1, front-end unit testing (FEUT) and manual acceptance testing (MAT) have statistically significant effects on passed story points (PSP). However we couldn't find any strong correlation between AAT (automated acceptance testing) and passed stories, i.e. functional suitability of delivered products.

RQ2 - Engagement with BDD and ATDD. In Fig. 1 we plot the AAT metrics for all teams over all relevant sprints, as proxy for their engagement with BDD and ATDD practices.

Two teams engaged straight after the ATDD workshop, Team F slowly disengaging sprints after sprints, and Team G showing a spike in sprint 5. Teams C, D and H engaged with automated acceptance testing from sprint 3 onwards, Team A picking up from sprint 4. However Team D disengaged from mid-year. The remaining two teams, B and F, never really engaged throughout the year. All but Team C put less effort in AAT coverage during the last sprint, which is often considered as a wrap-up sprint by students wanting to "polish" their products. Overall, only 3 out of 8 teams did put a regular effort into their automated acceptance scenarios, still with rather low coverage around 50%.

RQ3 - Challenges and Success Factors: The survey ran for two weeks after the end of the course, was anonymous, optional, and accessible online using Qualtrics. It was composed of 17 distinct questions, with 9 directly related to

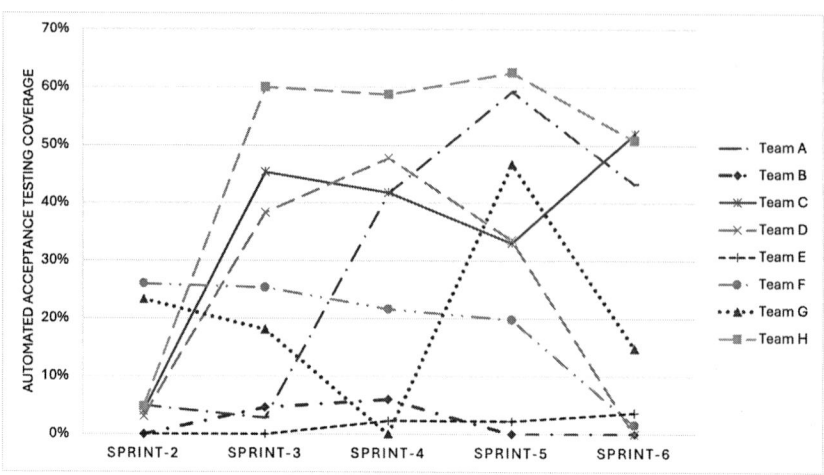

Fig. 1. Acceptance testing coverage per team per sprint.

the Testing workshop. Seven questions were using a 5-point Likert scale, accompanied by a free-text box for students' comments (lower values indicate a dissatisfaction), and two were open-ended. Out of 70 students enrolled in the course, 35 responded to the survey, out of which 23 were complete answers. Table 2 reproduces an excerpt of the survey questions, with students' ratings and number of respondents.

Table 2. Questions of the survey and mean of answers, with number of respondents.

ID	Question	Mean	Resp.
1.	How satisfied were you with testing workshops in SENG302?	3.63	35
2.	What do you think about timing of testing workshop?	2.89	35
3.	Testing workshop has covered Unit testing, Mocking and Acceptance testing. Did you find it beneficial to cover them all in one workshop?	3.46	28
4.	For the ATDD part of the Testing workshop we have covered best practices to write scenarios. How useful have you found this material?	3.91	23
5.	Have you been using material related to best practices of scenario writing while working on the project?	2.86	23
6.	One of the tasks during Acceptance testing part of the testing workshop was to write all possible scenarios for one of the stories from your backlog. Was this exercise helpful? Consider your confidence in implementing these techniques after the workshop.	3.95	23
7.	During ATDD part of the testing workshop was to implement the test steps for one or more scenarios for a story from your project backlog. How helpful have you found this exercise?	3.69	23
8.	Overall, what other improvements can we make in the future to make testing workshops more useful?	n/a	17
9.	Reflect on the year as a whole. What has helped you the most in improving your testing skills?	n/a	17

Most students found the content of the workshop valuable (Q1, Q3, and Q4), but many would have preferred to have it scheduled earlier (Q2 and Q8) as they felt they were already too far away in the project. Students mentioned that they typically did not refer to the material later on, in line with the disengagement with ATDD discussed in RQ2 (Q5). The hands-on approach taken in the workshop was well appreciated, but some students mentioned that the growing complexity of the backlog caused challenges regarding test modularity, or mocking (Q6 and Q7). Students mostly mentioned that they needed more time and support to learn how to mock properly (Q8). Many also suggested to decompose each subject (i.e. best practices, BDD principles, and mocking) in separate workshops, so all aspects are covered in more details (Q8, Q9).

5 Discussion

Summary of Results: Unlike some results in the industry (e.g., [2,13]), we observed that implementing BDD practices cannot predict a high functional suitability when applied by 3rd year undergraduate students in a two-semester long project. As visible in Table 1, front-end and manual tests were better predictors of a high passing rate of stories (RQ1).

Furthermore, despite hands-on workshops coupled to academic expectations to engage with an ATDD framework (i.e. Cucumber), the level of engagement varied across teams, as well as with time. Students mentioned that a growing complexity in the product backlog and resulting software hindered their ability to write automated acceptance tests on the long run. Still, students appreciated the learning-by-doing approach, including the ability to work on their project during the workshop (RQ2).

Combining our statistical analysis and survey results, we identified that the schedule of the workshop is primordial, and must come as early as possible when students start working on their code base. We also identified that academic requirements are not enough for students to fully engage with BDD and ATDD practices, but more pro-active and continuous support is needed to get them started and keep writing automated acceptance tests, or they may fall back to manual testing (RQ3).

Recommendation 1: Offer early and continuous hands-on guidance on testing, BDD, ATDD and DevOps practices to students, and do not rely on theoretical course content to increase practical engagement with the content.

Recommendation 2: Apply pair programming in hands-on workshops, using the project code base itself, in the early stages of the project, and decompose the content in focused sessions.

Threats to Validity: The calculation of automated acceptance and manual coverage metrics have been performed manually by one author, with random crosscheck by the other author. A potential error rate can be compensated by the amount of data, the number of measures, and the usage of statistical analysis, openly accessible for review (internal validity). All teams had access to the same content, same support, working on the same product backlog (construct validity). Our recommendations follow clear trends observed, or feedback given by students, however a different project course with a different method than Scrum may lead to different conclusions, especially since not all students provided feedback in the survey (external validity).

6   Conclusion

We have discussed our lessons learned from teaching BDD in a two-semester project course. We combined code coverage metrics and survey results to understand the adoption level of BDD and ATDD practices by teams of 3rd year undergraduate students while developing a software following the Scrum framework. We also analysed whether the application of ATDD would predict higher degrees of functional suitability. We observed that the engagement vary across teams and with time, despite academic expectations to do so. Students reported that the timing of practical training is important, as well as creating focused sessions for each aspects of testing, e.g., best practices, BDD, ATDD, mocking, DevOps. Students also appreciated the hands-on approach where they could learn these techniques in workshops on the actual product that they were developing in the project.

References

1. North, D., et al.: Introducing bdd (2006). Accessed 28 Mar 2024
2. Dookhun, A.S., Nagowah, L.: Assessing the effectiveness of test-driven development and behavior-driven development in an industry setting. In: International Conference on Computational Intelligence and Knowledge Economy (2019)
3. Latorre, R.: A successful application of a test-driven development strategy in the industrial environment. Empir. Softw. Eng. (2014)
4. Farooq, M.S., Omer, U., Ramzan, A.: Behavior driven development: a systematic literature review. IEEE Access (2023)
5. Brandenburg, D.C., Ellinger, A.D.: The future: just-in-time learning expectations and potential implications for human resource development. Adv. Dev. Hum. Resour. 5(3), 308–320 (2003)
6. ISO/IEC: ISO/IEC 25010 system and software quality models (2010)
7. Goulart, A.E.E.: Using behavioral driven development (bdd) in capstone design projects. In: ASEE Annual Conference and Exposition (2014)
8. Rocha, F.G., Souza, L.S., Silva, T.S., Rodríguez, G.: Enhancing the student learning experience by adopting tdd and bdd in course projects. In: IEEE Global Engineering Education Conference, pp. 1116–1125 (2021)
9. Sarinho, V.T.: "BDD Assemble!": a paper-based game proposal for behavior driven development design learning. In: Entmt Computing & Serious Games. (2019)
10. Nascimento, N., Santos, A., Sales, A., Chanin, R.: Teaching bdd in active learning environments: a multi-study analysis. In: International Conference on Computer Supporting Education (2022)

11. Schwaber, K., Sutherland, J.: The definitive guide to scrum (2020)
12. Hanks, B., Fitzgerald, S., McCauley, R., Murphy, L., Zander, C.: Pair programming in education: a literature review. Comput. Sci. Educ. **21**(2), 135–173 (2011)
13. Nascimento, N., Santos, A.R., Sales, A., Chanin, R.: Behavior-driven development: an expert panel to evaluate benefits and challenges. In: Brazilian Symposium on Software Engineering. (2020)

Agile Software Engineering Capstone Courses: Exploring the Impact of Gender

Gyda Elisa Sæter[ID], Camilla Kielland Lund[ID], and Viktoria Stray[✉][ID]

University of Oslo, 0373 Oslo, Norway
{gydaes,camilltk,stray}@ifi.uio.no

Abstract. The wide adoption of agile methodologies in software development necessitates an educational approach that prepares students for industry practices. This study aims to explore an agile capstone course, focusing on student learning experiences in teamwork while examining the gender dynamics affecting team roles and engagement. We conducted a comprehensive study of the capstone course "Software Engineering with Project Work" at the University of Oslo, analyzing 27 presentations and interviewing 10 students and two teaching assistants. The course is designed to immerse informatics students of different specializations in agile methodologies and collaborative project work. Our findings suggest that the students learn essential collaboration and technical skills. However, during their final presentations, significant gender differences emerged in the topics discussed: women predominantly spoke about design and process, whereas men focused more on technical aspects such as architecture, technical solutions, and algorithms. Our results underscore the need for educational strategies that promote inclusivity and equal participation in agile software development courses.

Keywords: Collaboration · Knowledge sharing · Human and social aspects of agile software development · Gender diversity · Teaching experiences · Empirical studies with students

1 Introduction

With the rise of agile methodologies in the software development industry, there has been a corresponding need to adapt educational practices to better prepare students for these environments. Research indicates that teamwork is critical in agile settings, as it significantly affects the development outcomes of software projects [18].

Meier et al. [10] underscore the importance of having students work in self-organized, agile teams, where agile values are not only taught but also experienced through practical projects. Team autonomy is a crucial aspect of agile work [6]. Similarly, Sahin et al. [14] highlight a deficiency in non-technical skills among students, advocating for an integration of soft skills training through collaborations with social sciences and industry. Such soft skills are crucial for thriving in agile software development [15].

© The Author(s) 2025
L. Marchesi et al. (Eds.): XP 2024 Workshops, LNBIP 524, pp. 150–158, 2025.
https://doi.org/10.1007/978-3-031-72781-8_16

Multiple studies show that the formation of agile teams is crucial [20]. This naturally follows from the importance of teamwork in software development [3]. Team formation is especially important in agile education, impacting both learning outcomes and project success [8]. In line with previous studies, it is essential to form teams that have a diverse mix of skills and gender representation to ensure well-rounded team composition. [16]. There are strategies for forming effective teams that include both instructor-formed and self-formed teams. Instructor-formed teams, in particular, can serve as a powerful enabler for learning by ensuring a diverse and balanced group that might not naturally form in a student-driven setting.

The "IN2000 Software Engineering with Project Work" is a course at the University of Oslo, and is a typical Softwar Engineering capstone course [17]. It is conducted over a semester and is structured as a team-based project course with teams of six students (slightly larger than the most common size found in [17]). Unlike many courses that lack an external client, our projects involve a real-world client, providing students with practical, hands-on experience. We adhere closely to agile development methodologies, emphasizing the production of key deliverables such as artifacts, project reports, and presentations.

The course had 240 informatics students in 2023, placed in teams with different gender and expertise compositions. We aimed to explore how gender affects their agile teamwork and learning experience by investigating the following research question:

RQ1: *"How does gender affect role allocation and team dynamics in an agile software engineering capstone course?"*

To investigate this research question, we conducted interviews and observations within IN2000. This approach provided a comprehensive view of the agile methodologies taught, the complexities of teamwork faced, and how these elements interact with gender dynamics to influence the students' learning experiences.

2 Methodology

2.1 About IN2000

In the software engineering capstone course examined in this study, students work on a project for 12 weeks to build a software application that meets certain given requirements. They conclude this period by delivering a report that outlines the software they developed and their approach to the project, they also give a presentation and have an exam. In 2023, the course enrolled around 240 students who were organized into 40 teams, each composing six students. Teams are formed by the instructors, but students can pre-assemble a team consisting of 2–3 members. Each team receives guidance and mentorship from designated teaching assistants. For many students, this project often represents the initial exposure to applying agile techniques within a collaborative environment.

The course is offered in the fourth semester and is mandatory for bachelor's degree students in three distinct programs: 1) Programming and Systems Architecture, 2) Digital Economics and Management, and 3) Design, Use, and Interactions. The course aims to deepen students' understanding of the foundational aspects of software engineering beyond just coding. This includes learning about Agile methodologies, how to manage a project, and the importance of working well in a team.

2.2   Data Collection and Analysis

As part of the course's evaluation, all teams presented their collaboration process and demonstrated their Kotlin-developed app to the instructors at the end of the course in May/June 2023. During these presentations, each member's gender and speaking topic during the presentations were noted down, categorized, and analyzed for patterns. Only teams with at least one woman were included in the analysis, yielding observations from 27 teams' project presentations; see Appendix A for an overview.

In March 2024, we conducted 12 semi-structured interviews, including 10 students and 2 teaching assistants, as part of an ongoing research effort to understand teamwork dynamics. These interviews were recorded and transcribed with participants' consent, and the transcripts were analyzed using Nvivo. This analysis was guided by the principles of thematic analysis as defined by Braun and Clarke [1]. The interviewees were involved in the course in 2023. Six women and six men were interviewed. Three teams had two interviewees representing different viewpoints from the same team. For a detailed overview of the interviewees, see Appendix B. This study builds on our earlier analysis of two surveys conducted within the same course, reported in [13].

3   Results

A total of 40 teams presented their projects and teamwork. The majority, approximately 84% of the teams, reported having used ScrumBan in their project work, 7.5% chose to implement Scrum as their agile methodology, 7.5% Kanban, while 1% reported others.

Our findings indicate that students acknowledged the importance of learning to collaborate in teams. They viewed teamwork as essential for effectively mastering agile software development techniques. One student explained:

> *"It was a very positive experience working in a team. It was also very beneficial to finally try programming in groups. Until then, I had mostly worked alone due to the coronavirus, thinking programming was something you had to do alone at home, requiring brilliance to understand. But what was great about the group work in IN2000 was that I gradually realized it's actually about programming together and discussing code, which is how you truly improve."*

Students reported that the opportunity to select up to two peer students in their teams made it easier and safer to give feedback and build on a somewhat existing dynamic. They also stated that being placed in teams with strangers made the teamwork more challenging but also more of a learning experience, compared to being in a team only with friends:

> *"It was definitely educational, while at the same time, one should not sweep under the rug that there were challenges in our teamwork at times."*

Students emphasized the significance of leadership being a significant factor in successful teamwork. Teams with an abundance of dominant personalities experienced power struggles over decision control. When more submissive students worked in teams with assertive students, the submissive students reported not feeling like there was room for their opinions and preferences. This results in most decisions being in the dominating person's favor. This was prominent in teams with few women, as men tend to be more assertive, and women more agreeable [4].

3.1 Gender Distribution in Speaking Topics

A crucial part of the course is to present the work at the end of the teamwork period. As described in the method section, we observed these presentations and analyzed the speaking topic with regard to gender. After analyzing these notes, eight categories of interest were identified, namely *Introduction, Development Process, App Demo, App Architecture, Design, Technical solution, Algorithm, Requirements and Modelling.* Findings revealed a significant gender difference between five of the topics as illustrated in Fig. 1. A total of 34 women and 51 men presented within these five topics. Topics within designs include user testing, user interface, and user experience. Architecture encloses apps' technical implementation of MVVM architecture, folder structure, third-party libraries supporting architecture implementation, and object-oriented principles. Technical Solutions include speaking about programming language-related details, git and version control, chosen APIs, and third-party libraries supporting front-end or back-end code. The topic includes agile methodology, project timeline, teamwork experiences, and chosen cooperation tools. Design processes are excluded from this topic and considered within the broader design topic. Algorithm topics describe the technical and mathematical details of the app's main algorithm. Typically going into the details of code makes the algorithm of apps. The topic is only relevant to a few teams, as few app cases demand advanced computing or non-API-related back-end code.

Importantly, students were free to choose their presentation topics and compositions, theoretically allowing any member to present any topic. This suggests that the observed gender patterns in topic selection are not strictly a function of the male-majority enrollment.

Furthermore, all men who spoke about design were in the men-dominated teams with only one or two women. Moreover, the women who spoke about

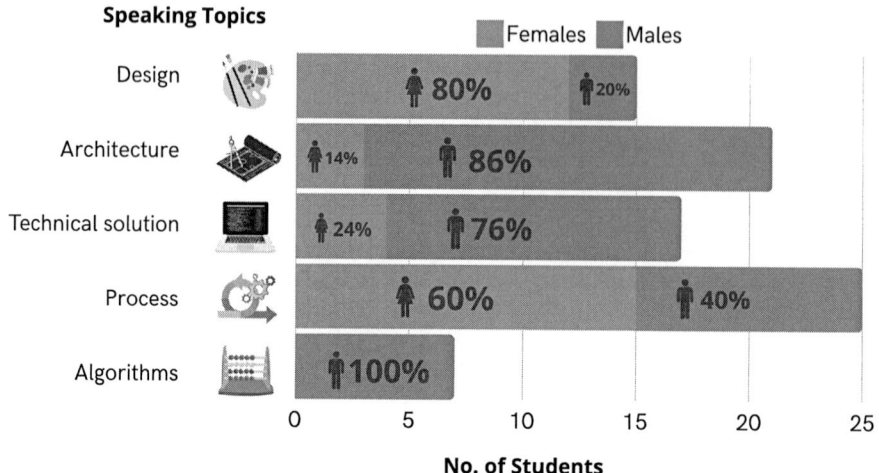

Fig. 1. Gender distribution of students' speaking topics in the project presentations. Percentages are calculated from all speakers on that topic.

architecture were in balanced or women-dominated teams with three or four women.

Reflects the Work Roles Throughout the Project. When asked to elaborate on how their team decided which members were to speak about what topics, most students said that it naturally followed the pattern of the team's role distribution. Those who had designed throughout the project talked about design, while those who programmed presented the technical aspects of the app. Students also found it natural to delegate the task of speaking about design, to the students who belonged to the design informatics study program. About their speaking topic delegation, a male student stated:

> "Partly because that's what we had been working on. I'm now seeing that it's not optimal, though." [M4]

Through this, a gender role pattern emerged. As the gender distribution of students in this course enrolled in the design study program is balanced, the role delegation could not only reflect the student's study program. Students identified an unconscious gender bias in the project's role delegation, where many of the students acknowledged how the role and speaking topic delegation would have changed with a different gender team composition. A woman stated:

> "I find it irritating. I want the girls to talk just as much about algorithms and programming as the guys." [W3]

Women Have Overview, Men Are Specialized. Another explanation for the gender division in the presentations is gender stereotypes about qualities and strengths traditionally associated with each gender. Women were described as having a broader project overview, encompassing team processes, design choices, and selected technology. Conversely, male students tended to specialize in specific technological facets. As one male student explained:

"The one girl on our team was more thoughtful about the process than all five of us boys combined ... I believe she had a better overview of the entire project, while us boys were very focused on detailed issues, especially on the technical side." [M4]

Furthermore, due to the historic gender division in aesthetic and design domains, a gender bias follows:

"It may have something to do with norms, that everyone thinks it's natural for girls to talk about design. Because, yes, design is associated with, like, people, aesthetics, and usability. And it's something the at has been female-dominated in all other areas of society, in a way." [W1]

The High Stakes of Speaking About Tech. Several female students expressed apprehension about presenting the technical aspects of the app, fearing they were not competent enough to present it. This imposter syndrome was suggested to be due to men's greater confidence in technical aspects and their tendency to dominate these areas. A woman who did not engage in programming throughout the project, despite studying programming and wanting to, explained:

"I feel like that might be the reason why boys take on more of the technical aspects; you need a bit firmer control. In contrast, when discussing design, you can speak more freely. Even though I feel confident in my abilities, I still tend to hold back because I'm afraid of saying something wrong."

Men on the other hand usually reported that they found it natural to speak about the technical aspects, as they felt they excelled in it individually or among the team members: *"The API part that I worked on, I felt like I knew a lot about... I worked more on it than anyone else." [M3]*

This aligns with a confidence difference between boys and women. One teaching assistant's observation supported this:

"So there was this girl who had done the entire architecture by herself, and I was like, 'why aren't you talking about this? You're the one who knows this better than anyone here.' [TAM2]"

4   Discussion and Conclusion

This study presents our experiences running a software engineering capstone course [17] and teaching students agile methodology and teamwork. We have examined how gender affects agile student teamwork through observing student presentations and conducting in-depth interviews with 12 participants,

Aligning with former research [5,10], we found the Scrum Master role and good leadership to be a crucial variable to the student's teamwork experience. This relates to gender as research has found women to naturally fit the Scrum Master role [12].

Moreover, we found the personalities of the team members to affect the teamwork. A study from 2020 examining agile teams found members' ability to get along with the team members to have a significant positive influence on the teamwork [19]. Conversely, we found members with non-agreeable personalities to have a destructive effect on collaboration, resulting in imbalanced decision-making and workloads, and inefficient meetings. We suggest that dominant personalities threaten shared leadership in student teams that opt to rotate the role, as they are inclined to dominate meetings. Women are more exposed to this challenge, as men are perceived as more assertive and dominating within the context of technical domains in this course.

Furthermore, we found that gender differences in speaking topics, when presenting their teamwork, revealed barriers keeping women from presenting technical aspects and men from presenting the design and process. Furthermore, students' choices in speaking topics indicate a gender difference in role distribution. Results highlight the importance of building confidence and providing support for women in agile student teams, as well as addressing gender stereotypes that may hinder learning in teamwork courses. This aligns with research identifying lack of confidence as a significant barrier keeping women from participating in software engineering education, recognizing the necessity of providing women with greater exposure to programming [2,7]. Some research found that girls show increased enthusiasm for programming when they can learn in settings exclusive to their gender, providing a more comfortable environment for exploration [9].

A structured onboarding process and regular feedback mechanisms significantly enhance the self-efficacy and social integration of team members [11]. These findings support our emphasis on carefully designed team compositions to ensure that all members, regardless of gender or background, can effectively contribute to and benefit from the collaborative learning experience.

Future work should explore measures empowering students to step outside the gender stereotypes and roles. Specifically, one could investigate the impact of gender-inclusive leadership training to enhance the confidence and engagement of female students in technical discussions. Additionally, examining the effectiveness of mixed-gender team configurations and their influence on equitable participation across different project roles could provide deeper insights into fostering a balanced educational environment in software engineering capstone courses.

Appendix A: Team presentation observations

An overview over the observed team presentations is available online:

https://doi.org/10.5281/zenodo.10996589.

Appendix B: Overview of the interviews

An overview over the interviews is available online:
https://doi.org/10.5281/zenodo.10996595.

References

1. Braun, V., Clarke, V.: Using thematic analysis in psychology. Qual. Res. Psychol. **3**(2), 77–101 (2006)
2. Chachra, D., Kilgore, D.: Exploring gender and self confidence in engineering students: a multi method approach. In: 2009 Annual Conference & Exposition, pp. 14–614 (2009)
3. Chow, T., Cao, D.B.: A survey study of critical success factors in agile software projects. J. Syst. Softw. **81**(6), 961–971 (2008)
4. Costa, P.T., Jr., Terracciano, A., McCrae, R.R.: Gender differences in personality traits across cultures: robust and surprising findings. J. Pers. Soc. Psychol. **81**(2), 322 (2001)
5. Fernandes, S., Dinis-Carvalho, J., Ferreira-Oliveira, A.T.: Improving the performance of student teams in project-based learning with scrum. Educ. Sci. **11**(8), 444 (2021)
6. Gustavsson, T., Berntzen, M., Stray, V.: Changes to team autonomy in large-scale software development: a multiple case study of scaled agile framework (SAFe) implementations. Int. J. Inf. Syst. Proj. Manag. **10**(1), 29–46 (2022)
7. Happe, L., Buhnova, B.: Frustrations steering women away from software engineering. IEEE Softw. **39**(4), 63–69 (2021)
8. Løvold, H.H., Lindsjørn, Y., Stray, V.: Forming and assessing student teams in software engineering courses. In: Proceedings of the 21st International Conference on Agile Software Development: Agile Processes in Software Engineering and Extreme Programming–Workshops: XP 2020 Workshops, Copenhagen, Denmark, 8–12 June 2020, Revised Selected Papers, pp. 298–306. Springer International Publishing (2020)
9. Marquardt, K., Wagner, I., Happe, L.: Engaging girls in computer science: do single-gender interdisciplinary classes help? In: 2023 IEEE/ACM 45th International Conference on Software Engineering: Software Engineering Education and Training (ICSE-SEET), pp. 128–140. IEEE (2023)
10. Meier, A., Kropp, M., Perellano, G.: Experience report of teaching agile collaboration and values: agile software development in large student teams. In: 2016 IEEE 29th International Conference on Software Engineering Education and Training (CSEET), pp. 76–80. IEEE (2016)
11. Moe, N.B., Stray, V., Goplen, M.R.: Studying onboarding in distributed software teams: a case study and guidelines. In: Proceedings of the 24th International Conference on Evaluation and Assessment in Software Engineering, pp. 150–159 (2020)
12. Petrescu, M.A., Motogna, S., Berciu, L.: Women in scrum master role: Challenges and opportunities. In: 2023 IEEE/ACM 4th Workshop on Gender Equity, Diversity, and Inclusion in Software Engineering (GEICSE), pp. 49–55. IEEE (2023)

13. Sæter, G., Stray, V., Almås, S., Lindsjørn, Y.: The role of team composition in agile software development education: A gendered perspective. In: šmite, D., Guerra, E., Wang, X., Marchesi, M., Gregory, P. (eds.) Agile Processes in Software Engineering and Extreme Programming, LNBIP, vol. 512, pp. 1–16. Springer, Cham (2024)

14. Sahin, Y.G., Celikkan, U.: Information technology asymmetry and gaps between higher education institutions and industry. J. Inf. Technol. Educ. Res. **19**, 339 (2020)

15. Stray, V., Florea, R., Paruch, L.: Exploring human factors of the agile software tester. Softw. Qual. J. **30**(2), 455–481 (2022)

16. Tafliovich, A., Petersen, A., Campbell, J.: Evaluating student teams: do educators know what students think? In: Proceedings of the 47th ACM Technical Symposium on Computing Science Education, pp. 181–186 (2016)

17. Tenhunen, S., Männistö, T., Luukkainen, M., Ihantola, P.: A systematic literature review of capstone courses in software engineering. Inf. Softw. Technol. **159**, 107191 (2023)

18. Villavicencio, M., Narvaez, E., Izquierdo, E., Pincay, J.: Learning scrum by doing real-life projects. In: 2017 IEEE Global Engineering Education Conference (EDUCON), pp. 1450–1456. IEEE (2017)

19. Vishnubhotla, S.D., Mendes, E., Lundberg, L.: Investigating the relationship between personalities and agile team climate of software professionals in a telecom company. Inf. Softw. Technol. **126**, 106335 (2020)

20. Zainal, P., Razali, D., Mansor, Z.: Team formation for agile software development: a review. Int. J. Adv. Sci. Eng. Inf. Technol **10**(2), 555–561 (2020)

PhD Symposium Track

Towards Continuous Certification of Software Systems for Aerospace

J. Eduardo Ferreira Ribeiro$^{(\boxtimes)}$ (ID)

Department of Informatics Engineering, Faculty of Engineering, University of Porto,
4200-465 Porto, Portugal
`jose.eduardo.ribeiro@fe.up.pt`
`https://pt.linkedin.com/in/joseeduardoribeiro`

Abstract. Safety-critical systems are subject to strict regulation by domain-specific standards and documents. One such example is the *DO-178C* standard for aerospace, which provides guidance to organizations to ensure system safety and produce the necessary evidence for certification. In these regulated environments, most organizations rely on traditional development processes, unlike the widespread adoption of Agile in the broader software industry. This PhD research is a collaboration between academia and industry, involving the Faculty of Engineering at the University of Porto (FEUP), the University of Coimbra (UC), and Critical Software SA (CSW), as part of the Doctoral Program in Informatics Engineering at FEUP. The study focuses on integrating Agile methods and practices into safety-critical software development for aerospace applications, specifically adhering to the *DO-178C* standard. The goal is to define a new process that enhances safety-critical software development, moving towards continuous certification of software systems for aerospace. The research aims to establish a quasi-continuous certification process by evaluating new guidelines, practices, and tools, thereby ensuring high-quality and traceable software releases. Preliminary results are promising, as the initial case study involving a real industry project demonstrated positive outcomes using our innovative process. The findings are anticipated to advance the adoption of Agile methods and practices in safety-critical domains.

Keywords: Agile, Aerospace · DO-178C · FAA · Safety-critical · Software development

1 Introduction

This PhD research originates from an ongoing collaboration between academia and industry, specifically involving the Faculty of Engineering at the University of Porto (FEUP)[1], the University of Coimbra (UC)[2], and Critical Software SA (CSW)[3], under the Doctoral Program in Informatics Engineering at

---

[1] https://sigarra.up.pt/feup/en/web_page.inicial.
[2] https://www.uc.pt/en/.
[3] https://criticalsoftware.com/en.

© The Author(s) 2025
L. Marchesi et al. (Eds.): XP 2024 Workshops, LNBIP 524, pp. 161–168, 2025.
https://doi.org/10.1007/978-3-031-72781-8_17

FEUP. Section 1 presents an overview of the research context, theme, and motivation, outlining the research problem, objectives, hypotheses, and expected outcomes.

In Sect. 2, we discuss the challenges faced in our research and seek feedback and guidance to enhance and refine our research and validation efforts. Section 3 summarizes previous studies on the application of Agile methods and practices to safety-critical software development, aiming to improve existing software development lifecycle processes. We also assess their applicability to aerospace software development, particularly in compliance with the *DO-178C* [1] standard.

The study focuses on integrating Agile methods and practices into safety-critical software development for aerospace applications while adhering to the *DO-178C* standard. The objective is to define a novel process that enhances safety-critical software development, moving towards continuous certification of software systems for aerospace. This research aims to create a quasi-continuous certification process by evaluating new guidelines, practices, and tools, thus ensuring high-quality and traceable software releases. This approach seeks to streamline the certification process by implementing shorter, more frequent certifiable delivery cycles.

Section 4 addresses the limitations and threats to validity identified so far and the measures being taken to mitigate them. Finally, Sect. 5 provides an overview of the research progress, preliminary results, and future plans.

1.1 Research Theme and Motivation

CSW specializes in developing and validating safety-critical software systems for major organizations such as NASA, ESA, and AIRBUS, among others. Additionally, CSW has been at the forefront of using Agile software development methods for their projects, influencing their clients' adoption of such methods.

In our review of previous work related to Agile methods and practices in safety-critical systems, more precisely for aerospace, we observed that most studies focus on Agile principles and values, with only a limited exploration of specific Agile practices. This indicates a need for further research in this area. Our aim is to investigate the feasibility of enhancing agility in the development of aerospace software systems while adhering to the *DO-178C* standard [2,3].

A core value of the Agile manifesto is "responding to change over following a plan" [4]. We believe this value underscores a significant challenge in current processes: the difficulty in accommodating shorter feedback loops and increasing the maturity of requirements. Our research seeks to integrate Agile methods and practices into safety-critical software development for aerospace applications in compliance with the *DO-178C* standard. The objective is to develop a new process that improves safety-critical software development. Ultimately, our goal is to transition towards a quasi-continuous and iterative certification process.

1.2   Research Problem and Goals

Our research focuses on exploring innovative approaches to enhance the development of safety-critical software systems for aerospace. Specifically, we aim to investigate how Agile methods and practices can be employed to improve the development of these systems while moving towards continuous certification in line with relevant guidelines and standards, such as *DO-178C*.

In light of these considerations, this work aims to propose and evaluate guidelines, activities, practices, and tools in an industrial context to ensure the certifiability of smaller, independent software releases. Essentially, this involves evolving towards more frequent and incremental certifications.

1.3   Hypothesis and Expected Results

We hypothesize that it is possible to enhance aerospace software development towards a quasi-continuous certification process that incorporates Agile practices while maintaining the quality and traceability required by existing standards such as the *DO-178C*. Our goal is to refine the current software development lifecycle processes to achieve a quasi-continuous certification model for aerospace software.

2   Seeking Guidance

As an author, I encounter several challenges in my research journey that require valuable advice and insights. First, industry confidentiality presents a significant obstacle, limiting the availability of scientific publications and hindering my exploration of specific topics in depth. This scarcity of accessible literature poses a considerable challenge.

Second, I face cultural resistance to publishing findings related to integrating Agile methods with safety-critical development practices. This resistance is driven by stringent compliance standards within the safety-critical domain, making introducing novel approaches deviating from traditional practices difficult.

Furthermore, I seek advice on various methods to validate my proposed innovative processes. The limited availability of industry projects for study and industries' reluctance to participate in case studies present significant hurdles. Thus, exploring alternative validation methods is crucial in this context.

In summary, I am eager to receive guidance on navigating these challenges and finding effective strategies.

3   Building on the Past

Firstly, building on our initial study [2], Fig. 1 illustrates the progression from the planning phase, where software requirements are defined, to the use of system lifecycle process outputs in developing High-Level Requirements (HLR). The software design process then utilizes the HLR to refine and create the software architecture and Low-Level Requirements (LLR), which serve as a basis for implementing the source code. The figure also maps the relationships between integration, V&V, HLR, design, LLR, and source code. Additionally, Fig. 1 shows when each State of Involvement (SOI) event should achieve successful V&V and certification-ready status.

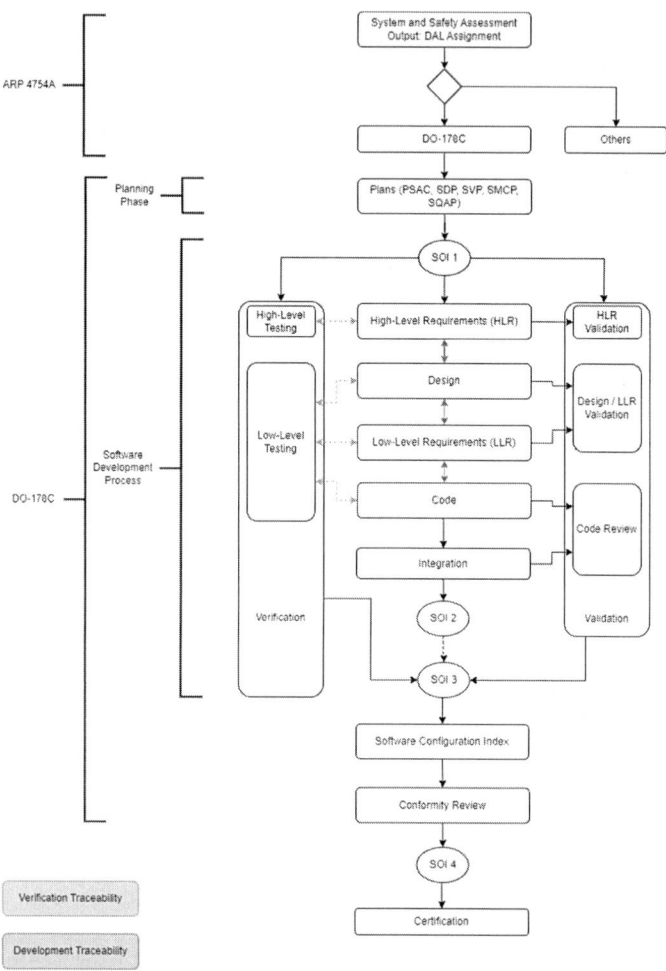

Fig. 1. *DO-178C* Software Development Process, adapted from [1].

Our analysis in [2] reveals that the *DO-178C* standard does not prescribe any specific software development method. Instead, it delineates the software-level activities and outputs necessary for successful certification, thus aligning with Agile methods. This conclusion solidifies that the *DO-178C* standard is conducive to adopting Agile methods and practices.

Secondly, we conducted a Systematic Literature Mapping (SLM) to gain a comprehensive overview of relevant literature. Following the guidelines of [5], an SLM results in an inventory of publications mapped to a classification, facilitating the identification of research gaps and trends. To ensure the transparency and reproducibility of our SLM, we developed a replication package using a Replication Package Builder (RPB) [6]. This package includes the resulting datasets and provides detailed information about our search strategy, including inclusion and exclusion criteria, data extraction forms, and outcomes. These resources empower other researchers to replicate our study and leverage its findings. Additionally, we explored data from post-mortem analyses of concrete aerospace industry projects provided by CSW. While these industry projects offer valuable information for research, access to their data is often restricted due to confidentiality concerns.

Our work in [3] was guided by two main objectives: to investigate the major concerns and challenges associated with adopting Agile methods and practices in safety-critical software development, particularly within the aerospace industry, and to identify key opportunities for enhancing such development using Agile approaches in the same context.

The study aimed to assess the adoption of Agile methods and practices in the aerospace domain, pinpoint existing concerns and challenges, and uncover potential opportunities for further research and development. The insights and conclusions from these efforts are presented in our causal loop diagram (Fig. 2) and detailed in our publication [3].

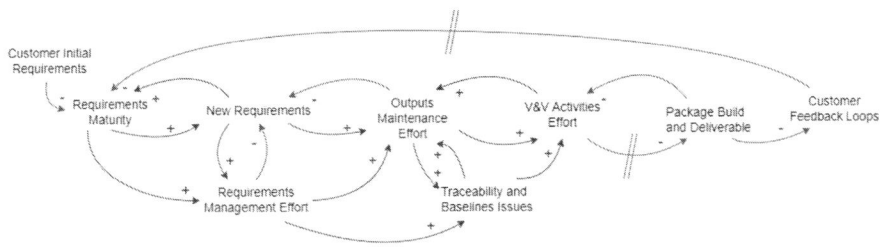

Fig. 2. Current System Causal Loop Diagram, adapted from [3].

Figure 2 illustrates our understanding of the causes and effects associated with the interactions among key system variables, highlighting the major concerns and challenges. This demonstrates that even with a complete initial requirements specification, there is a risk of immaturity due to limited system knowledge. These issues heighten the effort for requirements and output management and V&V, leading engineering teams to have fewer but larger and less frequent deliveries [3].

4   Validity Threats

During the research, we identified several limitations and threats to validity and are actively working to mitigate them. Since the review of publications was conducted by a single author, there was a potential bias in the selection process that could have influenced the outcome of the mapping study. We developed and utilized a replication package builder (RPB) incorporating defined inclusion and exclusion criteria to address this internal threat to achieve reliable results. We have also made the replication package of our Systematic Literature Mapping (SLM) available here [6] to ensure reproducibility and transparency.

Another aspect affecting validity was the limited access to detailed information during the post-mortem analysis. To overcome this, we obtained additional data on three aerospace industry projects provided by CSW, including interviews with some of the project participants. These projects served as valuable complements to the analysis, enabling a deeper understanding of past mistakes and identifying opportunities for improvement. Strict adherence to confidentiality constraints was crucial for maintaining privacy and protecting data. We primarily relied on project documentation to investigate the activities, outputs, and documents required for *DO-178C* certification. The project names were anonymized to safeguard privacy, and the data and conclusions were presented abstractly.

Regarding the previous external threats to validity-limited access to detailed information during post-mortem analysis and the necessity of strict adherence to confidentiality constraints-both the first and third authors followed a well-defined process of reporting and publication. They conducted a comprehensive analysis using appropriate methods and techniques suitable for the available data. A detailed report meticulously documented this study's findings, lessons learned, and recommendations. When presenting the results, utmost care was taken to preserve project confidentiality.

To address the potential threat of non-representative results due to project similarities, we defined an approach to normalize project data per HLR contracted when comparing results between projects for the case studies. Second, we established and followed a detailed implementation of the novel process during the study execution in a controlled manner to reduce internal threats to validity, particularly related to the team adapting to a new process during the case study. Third, we identified ways to address the limitations of our novel process in accommodating safety-critical requirements by incorporating additional V&V steps and quality gates. We validated the process using an actual aerospace project, selecting the *DO-178C* software level A requirements, the most demanding requirement level, to ensure the research's applicability to similar safety-critical software development projects.

In summary, we employed several strategies to enhance the robustness and generalizability of the research findings. However, further research is required to confirm these findings in additional contexts.

5   Research Progress Overview and Future Plans

Upon completing the analysis of the *DO-178C* standard and confirming that it does not prescribe any specific software development methodology [2], we achieved the first critical milestone in our research. Building on this analysis, we reviewed existing scientific literature and gathered data from real industry projects to understand the challenges and opportunities of adopting Agile methods and practices in safety-critical software development for aerospace, particularly in compliance with the *DO-178C* standard. This foundation enabled us to identify key challenges and opportunities for improvement, leading to the initial iteration of our novel process definition [3].

Our research is ongoing. We have completed our first case study with a real industry project using our novel process for validation, which yielded positive outcomes. We are currently finalizing a publication to share our findings with the broader research community. At the same time, we are actively refining our process by incorporating improvements identified during the case study. Additionally, we are increasing automation in our process steps to reduce the risk of manual errors.

In summary, while we have made significant progress in our research, important steps remain as we continue to refine our findings and contribute to advancements in Agile methods for safety-critical software development.

Acknowledgments. The author would like to thank Critical Software SA for supporting the access to data on concrete aerospace projects and the analysis of the outputs.

Disclosure of Interests. The authors have no competing interests to declare that are relevant to the content of this article.

References

1. DO-178C, Software Considerations in Airborne Systems and Equipment Certification. *RTCA*. (2011)
2. Ribeiro, J., Silva, J., Aguiar, A.: Beyond tradition: evaluating agile feasibility in DO-178C for aerospace software development. ArXiv Preprint ArXiv:2311.04344 (2023)
3. Ribeiro, J.E.F., Silva, J.G., Aguiar, A.: Weaving agility in safety-critical software development for aerospace. IEEE Access **12**, 52778–52802 (2024)
4. Beck, K., et al.: Manifesto for agile software development http://agilemanifesto.org/ (2001)
5. Petersen, K., Vakkalanka, S., Kuzniarz, L. Guidelines for conducting systematic mapping studies in software engineering: an update. Inf. Softw. Technol. **64**, 1–18 (2015)
6. Ferreira Ribeiro, J., Gabriel Silva, J., Aguiar, A.: Replication package for a systematic literature mapping of agility in safety-critical software development within the aerospace industry. Zenodo, December 2023. https://doi.org/10.5281/zenodo.10354398

Shared Leadership for Better Understanding Agile Teams

Jakub Perlak[✉]

AGH University, Krakow, Poland
j.perlak@gmail.com

Abstract. Leadership has been considered from every angle (almost) and the efforts are going strong. New ideas, books and trends, fads are popping out frequently. It's not a secret that leadership in Agile is a fundament, started looking from attitude and roles up to practice at every level of the organization. Leadership in Agile Teams is still under dispute. It is time to embrace shared leadership, a very helpful concept in describing an emergent team phenomenon whereby leadership roles and influence are distributed among team members. This approach has surprising support in studies about team performance, well-established history, and even anecdotal evidence from practitioners. This very short paper presents results from the initial research of the author using SNA method.

Keywords: Agile Teams · Self-Organized Team · Shared Leadership

1 Introduction

The software development environment has been evolving over the years as long as the different forms of teams have been adopted. Agile methods and the manifesto proposed over the last two decades [1] have become a widespread phenomenon since then. One of the most common forms of teams is self-organizing teams. Inherently, the question of the leadership nature of such teams has been raised [2]. In this very short summary, the author presents initial results from PhD research on shared leadership in Agile Teams. Beginning with an overview of shared leadership and studies based on social network analysis (SNA) then the paper is finished with early results.

2 Shared Leadership Within Research

Leadership can be examined from many angles. Looking at the top-down reporting line in an organization can tell a lot about the formal leaders. Examining the horizontal influences among team members can bring more understanding of leadership in a team [4]. Especially this second approach brings the concept of shared leadership, which can be described as a team-level emergent phenomenon where one or more team members take responsibility for leaders [3]. The body of empirical research on shared leadership mentions multiple benefits like team performance, team confidence, cohesion, and creativity

© The Author(s) 2025
L. Marchesi et al. (Eds.): XP 2024 Workshops, LNBIP 524, pp. 169–174, 2025.
https://doi.org/10.1007/978-3-031-72781-8_18

[4]. Shared leadership among many possible leadership concepts that can help better understand the teams working with Agile methods, shared leadership brings promising light [2]. Shared leadership is a vivid concept and is under profound research by many scholars [4]. One of the interesting research streams in Shared Leadership is the usage of social network analysis [4]. In contrast to the aggregation method, which is based on examining the formal leader using a typical questionnaire [4].

The author takes inspiration from the classification of shared leadership [5] divided into four categories (Fig. 1). The categories are created on a level of parameters, from low to high levels of density and decentralization. The first category concerns the lowest level of shared leadership, which is potentially hierarchical, where a low level of decentralization (or, conversely, a high level of centralization) indicates leadership still based on a certain hierarchy of the dominant person in the middle of the network, with the density of connections is high, which indicates that the connections are strong with people at the center of the network. The second category, defined as a low level of shared leadership, is characterized by a low level of both decentralization and the level of density of connections and corresponds to low shared leadership in the proposal of Carson and colleagues [3]. The third category, originally called moderate level, concerns an egalitarian distribution of leadership but with a low level of interaction, defined by low density [4]. Here, the more the level of density increases, but still only to the medium level, we have the equivalent of the medium level of shared leadership [3]. The last category is the category with a high level of shared leadership, where the network of connections is highly decentralized (or in other words the level of centralization is low) and the level of network density is high.

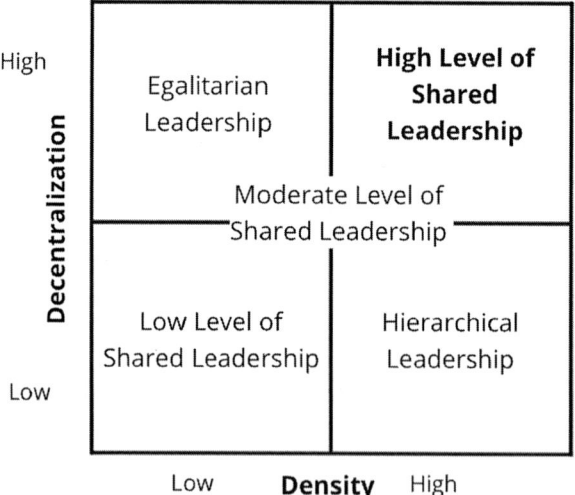

Fig. 1. Shared leadership classification

3 Method

The data collected as part of the survey was used for network analysis. Social network analysis, abbreviated SNA (Social Network Analysis), is widely used in social sciences including its rising popularity in management sciences [6]. Examples of research focus on social capital, interrelations between organization up to influence among people [6]. Studying the systems of social relations between various actors and their connections is a research challenge. Network analysis tools allow for a comprehensive capture of such dependencies [5]. It is no coincidence that SNA is commonly used in studying constructs such as shared leadership in a team [4].

The typical method of using SNA is creating an adjacency matrix (Fig. 2) representing relations among every actor in the network. The author used the method proposed by Carson and others [3] using a question to every team member on how to rely on a person in terms of leadership on a scale of 1 – never to 5 always then the data was dichotomized from 0 to 1 if the answer was at least 3 on scale 1–5.

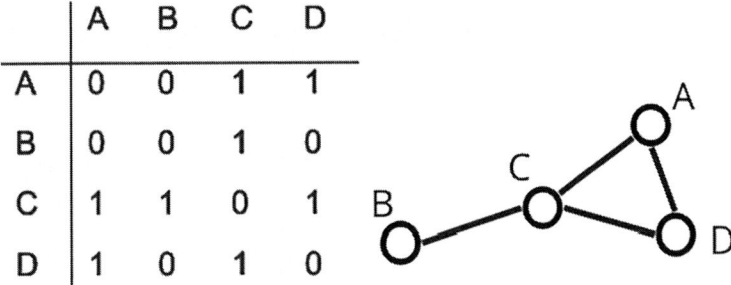

	A	B	C	D
A	0	0	1	1
B	0	0	1	0
C	1	1	0	1
D	1	0	1	0

Fig. 2. Adjacency matrix and network graph

The advantage of the graphical presentation of the network, as it can be seen on Fig. 2, is visual evaluation [5]. We can draw a first intuition on the potential dynamics in the network.

Data analysis in the case of social networks offers many possibilities and has a very rich number of measures [6]. The study in this paper focuses on two measures of network density and decentralization. Density (G) in a directed network is the number of nodes (m) divided by the number of all possible nodes (n), which can be represented by the formula:

$$G = \frac{m}{n(n-1)}$$

The common measure in SNA is the centrality measure [5]. The group degree centrality (GDC) is the sum of the difference of the maximum degree centrality of a vertex (maxDC) to the specific degree centrality of a given vertex (DC) by the number of vertices in the network, which can be expressed by the formula:

$$GDC = \frac{\sum(\text{maxDC}' - \text{DC}')}{(N-1)(N-2)/(2N-1)}$$

The group degree centrality measure takes values from 0 to 1. Where 0 means that all vertices in the network are equal, and when the value is 1, we have a case where one node completely dominates other nodes. Those two measures allow sufficient examination of the data and usage of the Shared leadership categorization.

4   Results

As part of PhD research, the author surveyed Agile practitioners from March to October 2023. The collected data was sufficient for examining the 9 teams. Most of the researched teams were working in the IT industry, then some teams pointed the banking and finance sector or telecommunication sector. Regarding the software development method used by the teams, Scrum was the most popular one, second Kanban and the rest was a mixture of multiple methods, including an in-house approach. The team members were on average at least 3 years experienced. Responders of the survey work mostly in large multinational organizations.

The teams network representations were plotted on the graph (Fig. 3). Looking the results most of teams were around the average level of shared leadership. Missing responses from most team members, as in the case of teams 4 and 1, placed the shared leadership score in the "egalitarian leadership" quadrant, or in the low level of shared leadership, as in the case of teams 8 and 7. Only team number 5 presents high level of shared leadership.

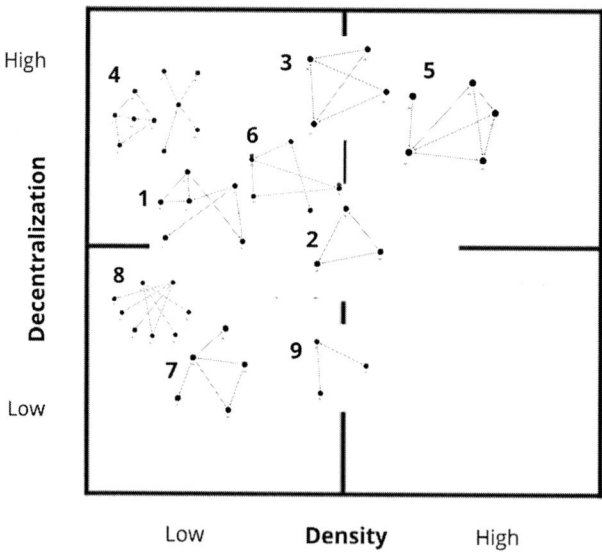

Fig. 3. Results of SNA analysis

Network visualization along with the definition of shared leadership allows for a deeper look at the situation in each team and provides for recommending improvements. Details of obtained data with sociograms and shared leadership categorization are presented in Table 1.

Table 1. Shared leadership vs distributed leadership

Id.	Density and GDC	Team size	Sociogram	Shared leadership
1	0.23 and 0.44	6		Egalitarian leadership
2	0.66 and 0.5	3		Moderate level shared leadership
3	0.5 and 0.22	4		High level of shared leadership
4	0.11 and 0.24	10		Egalitarian leadership
5	0.55 and 0.24	5		High level of shared leadership
6	0.45 and 0.38	5		Moderate level shared leadership
7	0.25 and 0.63	5		Low level shared leadership
8	0.13 and 0.51	8		Low level shared leadership
9	0.5 and 0.75	3		Low level shared leadership / Hierarchical leadership

As part of the SNA analysis conducted, data such as a measure of network density and centralization, calculated according to the group degree of centralization (GDC), and visualization of connections in the form of a sociogram of the network were obtained. The results collected in this way were placed collectively in a table along with determining the level of shared leadership.

5 Discussion

Shared leadership studied using Social Network Analysis can be a useful lens for examining leadership in teams, including Agile Teams. The amount of data collected from individual teams did not allow for a full SNA analysis. However, the collected sample showed the possibility of the method in the study of shared leadership. Self-organizing teams on average have a moderate level of shared leadership. It can be an implication for collaboration that is important in Agile methods [1].

Presenting the above analysis to assembled teams demonstrates the potential of social network analysis in exploring the issue of shared leadership. The undoubted advantage of the graphical illustration of the network in the form of a sociogram allows conclusions about its potential characteristics. Of course, this is a fragment of a rich method of social network analysis [6] and is only a foretaste of the possibilities offered by SNA, with a larger number of responses from teams.

Further research on leadership in self-organizing teams is recommended.

Disclosure of Interests. The author has no competing interests to declare that are relevant to the content of this article.

References

1. Highsmith, J., Fowler, M.: The agile manifesto. Softw. Develop. Mag. **9**(8), 29–30 (2001)
2. Srivastava, P., Jain, S.: A leadership framework for distributed self-organized scrum teams. Team Perform. Manag. **23**(5–6), 293–314 (2017)
3. Carson, J.B., Tesluk, P.E., Marrone, J.A.: Shared leadership in teams: an investigation of antecedent conditions and performance. Acad. Manag. J. **50**(5), 1217–1234 (2007)
4. Zhu, J., Liao, Z., Yam, K.C., Johnson, R.E.: Shared Leadership: a state-of-the-art review and future research Agenda. J. Organ. Behav. **39**, 834–852 (2018). https://doi.org/10.1002/job.2296
5. Pastor, J.C., Mayo, M.: Shared Leadership In Work Teams: A Social Network Approach. Working Papers Economia wp02–10, Instituto de Empresa, Area of Economic Environment (2002)
6. Borgatti, S.P., Mehra, A., Brass, D.J., Labianca, G.: Network analysis in the social sciences. Science **323**, 892–895 (2009)

Design Framework for Software Startups Applying Remote Work

Triando(⊠) 🆔

Free University of Bozen-Bolzano, Bolzano, Italy
Dtriando@unibz.it

Abstract. Remote work is commonplace nowadays, with software startups actively embracing it. However, remote work poses various challenges, among which team challenges are prominent and highly relevant to early-stage software startups, since effective team collaboration is one key factor for them to operate and succeed in uncertain environments. Challenges faced by early-stage software startup teams are less explored, especially in remote work settings. This research will propose a design framework to address the challenges faced by early-stage software startup teams in remote work settings. This research uses multi-case study to facilitate a deeper understanding of the phenomenon. Expected significance of findings lies in the identification of unique challenges and key practices to tackle those challenges, offering actionable insights and innovative solutions.

Keywords: software startups · team challenges · remote work · design framework

1 Introduction

Remote work is on the rise in recent years. The advancement of technology enables an increasing number of people to fulfil their tasks not only from their workplaces but from wherever they want. Already in 2013, Fried and Hansson [5] stated that "the future (referring to remote work) is already here - it's just not evenly distributed". With the outbreak of the COVID-19 pandemic, remote work has become an evenly distributed reality. Many software startups were among the early adopters of remote work and have fully embraced it ahead of the mass adoption wave triggered by the pandemic. GitLab[1] and Basecamp[2] are the well-known examples. The global pandemic extended remote work to numerous other startups.

Remote work brings many benefits to companies, such as more engaged and productive employees, reduced real estate costs, "talent on the cloud", reduced attrition, and better employee retention [2,12]. However, it also poses various

---

[1] www.gitlab.com.
[2] www.basecamp.com.

© The Author(s) 2025
L. Marchesi et al. (Eds.): XP 2024 Workshops, LNBIP 524, pp. 175–180, 2025.
https://doi.org/10.1007/978-3-031-72781-8_19

challenges, among which are those associated with teamwork. Brainstorming and problem-solving can be less effective when workers are distributed across different time zones and rely more on asynchronous communication because of reduced business-hour overlap [1]. Knowledge sharing may happen less frequently. Distributed colleagues cannot just tap one another on the shoulder to ask questions or get help. Another major worry for remote workers is the potential to feel isolated socially and professionally, missing the camaraderie feeling [10].

These team challenges in remote work can be exacerbated in the context of early-stage startups because of the pivotal role the team plays and the nature of the work in the early phases. The team behind a startup is often as important as the idea itself, if not more so. The right team can navigate the challenges of starting a business, drive innovation, and significantly increase the chances of success.

Building a startup team is one of the key challenges faced by early-stage software startups, together with other team challenges including managing multiple tasks and, staying focused and disciplined [6]. What remain unclear are how these challenges are manifested when the startup teams work remotely and how the challenges can be tackled effectively.

2   Research Questions

In this research, the research questions are as follow:

1. What are the team challenges faced by early-stage remote software startups?
2. How to tackle those unique challenges within remote software startups?
3. What are the keys practices in the design of framework for remote software startups?

3   Related Work

3.1   Software Startups Team Challenges

There was a survey study of ten key challenges in early-stage software startups, among which three challenges are pertinent to startup teams [6]:

- **Building entrepreneurial teams**
  Create and inspire a team that embodies entrepreneurial qualities, including the capacity to assess and respond to unexpected circumstances.
- **Managing multiple tasks**
  Handle multiple tasks within a limited time frame, such as managing responsibilities ranging from business to technical matters.
- **Staying focused and disciplined**
  Maintain a level of insensitivity to external influences from various stakeholders, including customers, partners, investors, and both current and potential competitors.

In the same study, the authors substantiated these challenges with two cases of early-stage software startups. For the two startups studied, building an entrepreneurial team implies several specific challenges related to teamwork, team motivation, as well as appropriate composition of the team. In both cases, the two teams are overburdened with lots of activities in a short time. Staying focused and disciplined is particularly challenging for a startup that has distributed team members.

3.2 Remote Work Challenges

The transition to remote work has been facilitated by technological advancements, yet it also poses several challenges. The first challenge is in effectively utilizing technology to support remote work [3,4,8]. While tools like video conferencing and project management software are readily available, there can be a learning curve associated with their implementation and integration into daily workflows.

Inefficient collaboration is another significant challenge in remote work environments [3,4,8]. Without the physical presence of coworkers, spontaneous interactions and idea exchanges are limited. Moreover, poor communication is also a challenge that sometimes lead to misinterpretation or incomplete information sharing [3,4,11]. Lack of clarity in instructions or expectations can affect progress on tasks and projects.

Striking a balance between work and personal life becomes increasingly difficult in a remote setup [4,9,11]. The boundaries between work hours and personal time blur, making it challenging for employees to make a physical separation of office and home. Remote work also introduces a gap in personal connections among team members [7,11]. Casual interactions that build team cohesion are less frequent in virtual environments.

Decreased engagement among team members is a common consequence of remote work, without the social dynamics and accountability present in traditional office settings, employees may feel isolated from their colleagues [8,9]. Furthermore, remote work can lead to reduced visibility into team members' tasks and progress [3,7,8,11]. Without physical proximity, managers may struggle to monitor workload distribution and identify potential bottlenecks or inefficiencies.

3.3 Remote Work Challenges as Contributing Factors in Software Startups Team Challenges

Building entrepreneurial teams is influenced by several factors, including inefficient collaboration, characterized by a lack of synchronized efforts among members; poor communication, leading to misunderstandings and affecting work progress; gaps in personal connections, which can affect trust and cooperation; decreased engagement among team members, resulting in lowered morale and productivity; and reduced task visibility, making it challenging to track progress and allocate resources effectively.

Managing multiple tasks is affected by several key elements: the challenge of leveraging technology to facilitate remote work, affecting seamless coordination and communication among team members; inefficient collaboration, where efforts are not harmonized, leading to redundancy and delays; poor communication, resulting in misunderstandings and inefficiencies; struggles with maintaining work-life balance, potentially causing burnout and reduced productivity; decreased engagement among team members, decreasing motivation and synergy; and reduced task visibility, making it difficult to prioritize and allocate resources efficiently.

Staying focused and disciplined is influenced by several factors: inefficient collaboration, where the lack of streamlined teamwork leads to distractions and wasted efforts; poor communication, which can result in confusion and disrupt workflow; and struggles with managing work-life balance, impacting one's ability to allocate time effectively and maintain a consistent level of concentration. Overcoming these challenges requires strategies to enhance collaboration, improve communication channels, and establish boundaries to achieve a harmonious balance between professional and personal commitments, promoting sustained focus and discipline.

4   Timeline

The research is planned to be run on three years as follow:

1. Literature review and identify team challenges
2. Collect data and design framework
3. Validate design framework in startups

5   Study Plan

Topics that require a deepening of expertise and the suitable means of study:

1. Remote team dynamics and challenges
2. Designing effective framework

6   Summary of the Current Status of the Research Project

Currently, a literature review is conducted, which serves as the foundation for subsequent phases and undertaking empirical research to analyze the unique challenges faced by software startup teams operating within remote environments.

7   Plans for Publications

1. XP2024 (PhD symposium and workshop paper)
2. ICSOB2024 (PhD symposium and workshop paper)
3. XP2025 (PhD symposium and full paper)
4. ICSOB2025 (PhD symposium and full paper)
5. XP2026 (PhD symposium and full paper)
6. ICSOB2026 (PhD symposium and full paper)

8   Future Work

I intend to refine it through a comprehensive review of software startups literature, followed by empirical studies. In the empirical investigation, I particularly
plan to conduct interviews and case studies. Therefore, good practices for effective remote work will be identified, focusing on successful startups and online
communities (e.g. open-source software development community, online gaming
community). Finally, I aim to evaluate design framework in startups, to support the identified successful practices and mitigate remote work challenges in
software startups.

References

1. Choudhury, P.: Our work-from-anywhere future. Harvard Business Review **98**(6)
   (2020)
2. Coffey, R., Wolf, L.: The challenge and promise of remote work: a brief study of
   remote work and best practices. Technical Report, Argonne National Lab.(ANL),
   Argonne, IL (United States) (2018)
3. Ferreira, R., Pereira, R., Bianchi, I.S., da Silva, M.M.: Decision factors for remote
   work adoption: advantages, disadvantages, driving forces and challenges. J. Open
   Innov. Technol. Market Complexity **7**(1), 70 (2021)
4. Flores, M.F.: Understanding the challenges of remote working and it's impact to
   workers. Int. J. Bus. Market. Manage. (IJBMM) **4**(11), 40–44 (2019)
5. Fried, J., Hansson, D.H.: Remote: office not required. Currency (2013)
6. Giardino, C., Bajwa, S.S., Wang, X., Abrahamsson, P.: Key challenges in early-
   stage software startups. In: Agile Processes in Software Engineering and Extreme
   Programming: 16th International Conference, XP 2015, Helsinki, Finland, 25–29
   May 2015, Proceedings 16, pp. 52–63. Springer (2015)
7. Koehne, B., Shih, P.C., Olson, J.S.: Remote and alone: coping with being the
   remote member on the team. In: Proceedings of the ACM 2012 conference on
   Computer Supported Cooperative Work, pp. 1257–1266 (2012)
8. Lenka, R.M.: Unique hybrid work model-the future of remote work. PalArch's J.
   Archaeol. Egypt/Egyptol. **18**(7), 2687–2697 (2021)
9. Popovici, V., Popovici, A.L.: Remote work revolution: current opportunities and
   challenges for organizations. Ovidius Univ. Ann. Econ. Sci. Ser **20**(1), 468–472
   (2020)
10. Schieffer, L.: The benefits and barriers of virtual collaboration among online
    adjuncts. J. Instruct. Res. **5**, 109–125 (2016)

11. Wang, B., Liu, Y., Qian, J., Parker, S.K.: Achieving effective remote working during the covid-19 pandemic: a work design perspective. Appl. Psychol. **70**(1), 16–59 (2021)
12. Wiik, N.: The remote revolution: preparing for the boom in distributed work with data-based insights. AV Technol. **13**(3), 42 (2020)

Bridging Silos: Amplifying InnerSource Adoption Using an Activity Theory Perspective

Clare Dillon(✉) 🆔

University of Galway, Lero, Ireland
clare.dillon@live.ie

Abstract. My research explores the adoption of InnerSource, a practice that integrates open source methodologies within organizations to foster collaboration and overcome the traditional silo mentality. InnerSource and Agile implementations share many values such as transparency, employee empowerment, and a flexible response to change. InnerSource adoption can come before, after, or in parallel with Agile transformations. Despite the increasing recognition of InnerSource as a pivotal driver for developer productivity and its growing presence in industry discussions, academic research on the subject remains in its infancy. Leveraging my involvement with the InnerSource Commons community and drawing from Activity Theory, my research aims to fill critical gaps in our understanding of InnerSource adoption. Specifically, it investigates the activities organizations engage in to enable InnerSource, identifies blockers hindering its implementation, and proposes effective strategies to counteract these challenges. At the XP 2024 PhD Symposium, I intend to share some preliminary findings of my research, derived from a Systematic Literature Review and a pilot study with an InnerSource practitioner working group. My research not only seeks to advance theoretical knowledge in the field but also offers practical insights for organizations striving to change software development practices, contributing to a more collaborative and efficient software development environment.

Keywords: innersource · inner source · collaborative software development

1 Introduction

The adoption of open source practices and tools within an organization, referred to as InnerSource, is now part of a larger management strategy to change the typical enterprise silo-based mentality and enable collaboration across an organization [1]. InnerSource adoption has grown in the past number of years. In 2023 InnerSource appeared in the Gartner Hype Cycle for Software Development [2] and was listed as one of Gartner's top 6 strategic technology trends for Software Engineering[3]. Industry surveys have reported that InnerSource is perceived as a top driver of developer productivity [4]. Furthermore, the InnerSource Commons [5], a community of over 3000 InnerSource practitioners, has tracked over 100 public mentions and case studies of InnerSource adoption across a wide variety of industries and geographies.

L. Marchesi et al. (Eds.): XP 2024 Workshops, LNBIP 524, pp. 181–186, 2025.
https://doi.org/10.1007/978-3-031-72781-8_20

I have been involved in the InnerSource Commons (ISC) community since 2018, and served as the inaugural Executive Director of the ISC Foundation from 2021–2023. The motivation for my research originated through my involvement with the ISC community, and the wish to advance knowledge in the area.

While some InnerSource case studies and experience reports have been referenced in software development literature ([6–9]), research in the area has remained in a nascent state. A survey in 2020 identified only 25 empirical studies and concluded that "theorising the inner source approach is important since there is lack of cohesion, cumulative tradition and clarity" [10]. In fact, it has been noted that there is still less research literature on InnerSource than there are practitioner reports [11]. A more recent review of the literature reveals a gap in terms of examining the contradictions or barriers that inhibit InnerSource activities, and that may demotivate practitioners and limit InnerSource roll-outs.

In 2022, Morgan et al. explored how InnerSource has been adopted with Agile practices over time [12]. They conclude that "inner source is a complimentary value add to agile, providing companies with the capability to build on existing solutions whilst not conflicting with their ability to work fast and adapt to change." InnerSource practitioners are also interested in the topic of how InnerSource can be adopted with other methodologies such as Agile.

I have identified Activity Theory as a theoretical lens to examine efforts to accelerate InnerSource adoption within organizations. Activity Theory has been used to examine Agile implementations and maturity ([13, 14]). However, no research has been conducted so far on InnerSource transformations using an Activity Theory lens, and research on InnerSource in the Information Systems domain as a whole is relatively sparse.

2   Research Questions

I propose to address the following research questions on the activity systems relating to InnerSource, which have not been studied in academic research to date. These include:

1. What activities are organizations engaging in to enable or amplify InnerSource adoption within their organizations?
2. What are the blockers (contradictions or tensions within related activity systems) to InnerSource implementations within organizations?
3. What activities are effective in counteracting InnerSource blockers?

3   Areas for Advice

Research Theme: Feedback from InnerSource practitioners indicates that InnerSource is often practiced alongside Agile. I would welcome insights into activities that can enable or accelerate both InnerSource and Agile implementations.

Theoretical Framework: Activity Theory has been used to examine obstacles in agile implementations ([13, 14]). I would value feedback on my choice of Activity Theory as a theoretical lens for development methodologies.

Research Methodology: What are the most effective strategies for conducting qualitative and longitudinal studies on software development teams?

Emerging Trends: I seek insights into emerging trends in Agile software development, in particular how AI bots and agents are being incorporated into Agile practices.

Publication and Dissemination: Advice on targeting the right venues for publishing interdisciplinary research that spans software engineering and another field.

4   Current Research Progress

4.1   Systematic Literature Review

My research is an article-based PhD. In order to more accurately identify research problems and identify gaps, I began a Systematic Literature Review (SLR) within the InnerSource and open source fields of literature. That review has revealed a gap in terms of examining the contradictions or barriers that inhibit InnerSource activities, and in particular how this may demotivate practitioners and limit InnerSource roll-outs.

4.2   Theoretical Lens

An initial review of literature on Information Systems theories has identified Cultural Historical Activity Theory (Activity Theory) as an excellent lens through which I could explore the activities organizations engage in while implementing InnerSource. CHAT, originated by Lev Vygotsky and further developed by scholars such as Engeström, focuses on the study of how human activities are socially situated and mediated by tools, signs, and systems of activity [15]. Activity Theory allows for the analysis of blockers or barriers to change and examines the broader impact of InnerSource activities, where human interaction, cultural norms, and collaborative practices play a central role alongside the adoption of tools and processes. The theory aligns with many aspects of InnerSource:

- **Emphasis on social and cultural context:** InnerSource initiatives are deeply influenced by the social and cultural context of an organization. Activity Theory's emphasis on these aspects helps to analyze how organizational culture, norms, and values affect the adoption and effectiveness of InnerSource practices.
- **Focus on the whole work system:** Activity Theory looks at the entire work system, including the tools, tasks, rules, community, and the division of labor. 4GAT includes the concept of interacting activity systems. This holistic view is essential for understanding InnerSource, which impacts not just the technical aspects of software development but also organizational structures, collaboration patterns, and cultural elements.
- **Interactions between tools and people**: InnerSource relies heavily on tools (e.g., source code repositories, communication platforms). Activity Theory's focus on the interaction between tools and people can help unpack how these tools enable or hinder collaboration, knowledge sharing, and community building.
- **Role of communities**: Activity Theory acknowledges the importance of communities and networks of practice within activity systems. InnerSource initiatives thrive on the formation of communities of practice, and Activity Theory can provide insights into how these communities form, function, and contribute to InnerSource adoption.

- **Understanding of contradictions:** Activity Theory includes the idea that there may be contradictions and tensions within and between different components of an activity system. In the context of InnerSource, these contradictions could be between traditional siloed development practices and the collaborative approach of InnerSource. Identifying and exploring these contradictions can provide insights into what may be blocking InnerSource implementations and how to address those constraints.
- **Dynamic perspective**: Activity Theory recognizes that activity systems are constantly evolving. This perspective aligns well with InnerSource, which is recognized as an evolving practice.

The fourth generation of Activity Theory (4GAT) extends these ideas into a more interconnected and networked analysis of activities, emphasizing systemic contradictions and their resolution as the primary drivers of change and development within activity systems ([16, 17]). The latest generations of Activity Theory focus more on networked activity systems, and the complexity and contradictions that may arise when actors have different motivations. As Activity Theory has been used to examine Agile implementations and maturity ([13, 14]), I anticipate that it will also be a useful framework with which to explore InnerSource.

4.3   Pilot Study

In 2023, I embarked upon a pilot study with members of the new InnerSource Program Office Working Group (ISPO WG) at InnerSource Commons using Activity Theory as a theoretical lens. InnerSource Program Offices (ISPOs) are a relatively new concept that has not as yet been explored in academic literature. In their nascent efforts to define what is an ISPO, the ISPO WG references the concept of Open Source Program Offices (OSPOs). OSPOs have been defined as an "the center of gravity for an organization's open source operations and structure. This can include training developers, ensuring legal compliance, engaging with and building communities, and defining policies that govern code usage, distribution, selection, auditing and more." [18]. The WG members have defined an ISPO in similar terms. One definition lists an ISPO as acting as a "central governing body responsible for overseeing and facilitating the adoption of InnerSource practices across different departments and teams."

The ISPO WG is a group of individuals who are explicitly employed to enable or accelerate InnerSource adoption within their organizations. I have conducted hour-long semi-structured interviews with 10 individuals from 10 organizations and am in the process of analyzing the results. An examination of the activities ISPO WG community members engage in, and the barriers they face will allow me to generate insights to help further address my research questions. The aim of my research is not only to comprehend the foundational aspects of ISPOs but also to distil and share the insights gained from pioneers in this domain. By doing so, I intend to provide valuable guidance for organizations that are considering the adoption of InnerSource practices through the establishment of an ISPO.

Through my pilot study and my engagements with InnerSource practitioners, I continue to identify priorities and emerging themes that may warrant further research. Some of the emerging themes in the last year include automated tooling to support InnerSource implementations within enterprises (e.g. to create Software Bills of Materials or SBOMs); how bots and GenAI code generation will impact InnerSource implementations; how global culture impacts InnerSource implementations (e.g. with feedback from emerging Asian communities); and how InnerSource implementations impact other software development methodologies, specifically Agile practices.

As this research progresses, my objective is to shed light on the complex dynamics of InnerSource adoption through a rigorous academic lens. I also aim to offer actionable strategies and insights that organizations can use to address any blockers that might occur as they implement InnerSource.

References

1. Morgan, L., Gleasure, R., Baiyere, A., Dang, H.P.: Share and share alike: how inner source can help create new digital platforms. California Manag. Rev. **64**(1), 90–112. bth. (2021)
2. Hype Cycle for Software Engineering, 2023. (n.d.). Gartner, https://www.gartner.com/en/documents/4590099. Accessed on 02 Apr 2024
3. Gartner Identifies the Top Strategic Technology Trends in Software Engineering for 2023. (n.d.). Gartner. https://www.gartner.com/en/newsroom/press-releases/gartner-identifies-the-top-strategic-technology-trends-in-software-engineering-trends-for-2023. Accessed on 02 Apr 2024
4. Linux Foundation FINOS Annual Report 2022. https://project.linuxfoundation.org/hubfs/LF%20Research/FINOS%20Annual%20Report%202022%20-%20Report.pdf?hsLang=en. Accessed on 02 Apr 2024
5. InnerSource Commons, I. (n.d.-b). InnerSource Stories. https://innersourcecommons.org/stories/. Accessed on 02 Apr 2024
6. Dinkelacker, J., Garg, P. K., Miller, R., & Nelson, D. Progressive open source. Proceedings of 24th International Conference on Software Engineering, 177–184. (2002)
7. Gurbani, V.K., Garvert, A., Herbsleb, J.D.: A case study of a corporate open source development model. In: Proceedings of 28th International Conference on Software Engineering, pp. 472–481 (2006)
8. Riehle, D., et al.: Open collaboration within corporations using software forges. IEEE Softw. **26**(2), 52–58 (2009)
9. Wesselius, J.: The bazaar inside the cathedral: business model for internal markets. IEEE Softw. **25**(3), 60–66 (2008)
10. Edison, H., Carroll, N., Morgan, L., Conboy, K.: Inner source software development: current thinking and an agenda for future research. J. Syst. Softw. **163**, 110520 (2020)
11. Riehle, D., Capraro, M., Kips, D., Horn, L.: Inner source in platform-based product engineering. IEEE Trans. Softw. Eng. **42**(12), 1162–1177 (2016)
12. Morgan, L., Gleasure, R., Baiyere, A.: Is inner source the next stage in the agile revolution? In: Co-creating for Context in the Transfer and Diffusion of IT, pp. 130–136. Springer International Publishing (2022)
13. Chita, P.: Agile Software Development – Adoption and Maturity: An Activity Theory Perspective. In: Garbajosa, J., Wang, X., Aguiar, A. (eds.) Agile Processes in Software Engineering and Extreme Programming, pp. 160–176. Springer International Publishing (2018)
14. Stray, V., Hoda, R., Paasivaara, M., Kruchten, P.: Agile implementation and expansive learning: identifying contradictions and their resolution using an activity theory perspective. In: Agile Processes in Software Engineering and Extreme Programming, vol. 383. Springer (2020)
15. Engeström, Y.: Learning by expanding: An activity-theoretical approach to developmental research. OrientaKonsultit (1987)

16. Karanasios, S., Allen, D.K., Finnegan, P.: Activity theory in information systems research. Inf. Syst. J. **28**(3), 439–441 (2018)
17. Spinuzzi, C.: Working alone together: coworking as emergent collaborative activity. J. Bus. Tech. Commun. **26**(4), 399–441 (2012)
18. Ruff, N.: Open Source Law, Policy and Practice: Second Edition. (Chapter 19). Oxford University Press (2022)

Posters Track

Where Do Developers Admit their Security-Related Concerns?

Moritz Mock[1]([⊠])[iD], Thomas Forrer[2], and Barbara Russo[1][iD]

[1] Free University Bozen-Bolzano, Bolzano, Italy
{momock,brusso}@unibz.it
[2] R&D Department, Würth Phoenix, Bolzano, Italy
thomas.forrer@wuerth-phoenix.net

Abstract. Developers use different means to document the security concerns of their code. Because of all of these opportunities, they may forget where the information is stored, or others may not be aware of it, and leave it unmaintained for so long that it becomes obsolete, if not useless. In this work, we analyzed different sources of code documentation from four large-scale, real-world, open-source projects in an industrial setting to understand where developers report their security concerns. In particular, we manually inspected 2.559 instances taken from source code comments, commit messages, and issue trackers. Overall, we found that developers prefer to document security concerns in source code comments and issue trackers. We also found that the longer the comments stay unfixed, the more likely they remain unfixed. Thus, to create awareness among developers, we implemented a pipeline to remind them about the introduction or removal of comments pointing to a security problem.

Keywords: Security Indicators · Mining Software Repositories · Continuous Integration/Continuous Development · Pipeline

1 Introduction

Developers use different means to document their activity and store their artefacts. Generally speaking, source code is the preferred one, Krüger and Hebig [6], but when specific tasks are concerned, the opportunities multiply. For instance, the most common places where developers document not-quite-right code that works (technical debt, [3]) is again source code, but also commit messages, issue tracker, and pull requests, [7,11].

Source code comments are also used to store knowledge about security concerns, [2,5]. *Security Indicators* are keywords [2] which are left behind by developers to express their worry connected to security within an application; this worry can be a vulnerability, potentially exploited by a third party. Current studies also combine information from different sources to investigate the same concern. For instance, code and comments were explored to identify both technical debt and code vulnerabilities, [5,9].

L. Marchesi et al. (Eds.): XP 2024 Workshops, LNBIP 524, pp. 189–195, 2025.
https://doi.org/10.1007/978-3-031-72781-8_21

In this work, we aimed to answer the research question: *Where do developers admit their security-related concerns?*, therefore, we investigate the relevance of different sources where developers might express security concerns. The approach follows the idea that SAST/DAST tools, like SonarQube [13], SemGrep [12] or Invicti [14], do not fully leverage textual data in the form of comments, commit messages, and issue trackers; hence we want to explore those sources to identify their usability. We have mined three different sources (commit messages, comments, and issue tracker) from four large-scale projects from the industry with a history of up to 29k commits spanning 20 years. Furthermore, we have manually inspected 2.559 instances from different sources to understand which security indicators and sources are most relevant for developers. We found that developers mostly use source code comments to admit security concerns; further investigations are needed to understand if there is a similar correlation between the severity of code, which is not quite right at the time of introduction, the longer it stays within the code base [1]. Additionally, we observed that those comments are either fixed soon (around ten releases) or they stay (almost) permanently. Therefore, we have developed a CI/CD bot that warns the developers whenever a security indicator is introduced or removed so that they are fully aware of comments that hint towards security concerns that are not captured by a SAST/DAST tool. The replication package can be found here: https://github.com/moritzmock/MiningSecurityIndicators.

2   Methodology

The following section describes some of the characteristics of the mined projects, how we performed the extraction of relevant information from the different sources for the commit messages, source code comments, and issue tracker and how the security indicators were evaluated against the inspected sources and repositories.

Characteristics of the Mined Projects -   Table 1 illustrates the characteristics of the four projects mined in the following section. It should be noted that the two projects are of the same origin, namely GLPI [15]; however, this was considered in the evaluation. Additionally, the number of *years of history, # releases, and # commits* is limited as the project was created at the beginning of 2020. Furthermore, one of the evaluated projects, *icingaweb2-module-slm*, is a project developed completely in-house, whereas the other projects are loaned from open source and specific extensions are elaborated for them.

Commit messages -   We leveraged PyDriller [10], which allowed us to easily access and extract the commit messages for each of the inspected projects. For the commit messages, we have mined all the commits and not only those of the release tags, as we did for the source code comments, else the inspection scope was too limited.

Source Code Comments -   We utilized PyDriller to extract the corresponding commit hash of the release tags, then checked out the repository at the obtained hash. At the given commit hash, we performed an analysis of all the present files,

Table 1. Characteristics of the projects

Project	years of history	# releases	# commits	lines of code
GLPIv3 [15]	20.25	10	20.269	2.473.459
GLPIv4 [15]	4.25	34	195	2.557.746
icingaweb2 [16]	11	379	15.674	1.528.409
icingaweb2-module-slm	4.83	217	2.470	42.557

tracing each file with the corresponding comments in order to gather insights into how long it has been in the software repository and when it has been removed. We decided to inspect each tag rather than the commits to avoid including comments introduced for the short term, e.g., as a remark for the developer where they stopped and need to continue the next time.

Issue Tracker (JIRA/Github) - Some projects are loaned from open source, and others are developed internally. Therefore, two different issue trackers are used across the inspected projects. For JIRA, we used the Python package `jira` [18] in combination with JQL-query (Jira Query Language to obtain all the relevant information. Whereas for GitHub, we used the available REST API [17].

Manual Inspection - The obtained data was analysed based on proportional sampling [4] with a confidence interval of 95% and a marginal error of 5% resulting values. Proportional sampling was selected as a methodology for reducing the overall sample size, which needs to be manually inspected. Resulting in 2.559 instances, 819, 1.076, and 683, respectively, for commit messages, source code comments, and issue trackers. The number of samples was calculated based on each individual source and summed up to final numbers. Additionally, we evaluated if pairs of security indicators occur and if those express a security concern only together or also individually.

3 Results

In the following section, each of the mined sources (commit messages, comments, and issue trackers) are discussed. In the following section, at the paragraph *Manual Inspection*, some general observations are made regarding keywords that individually did not address any security concern but paired with others that were used by developers to address security concerns in source code.

commit Messages - We observed that security indicators used in commit messages are used to address that certain parts of the code are now improved or fixed rather than admitting existing security issues in the code, e.g., "fix search engine for XSS". XSS (Cross-Site Scripting) is a security vulnerability in which a third party injects malicious scripts into a web page viewed by other users. This could potentially allow attackers to hijack user sessions or steal sensitive information. This observation is further supported by a quantitative evaluation of the data: 30% of commits containing a security indicator have an associated issue linked to it, e.g., "Fix minor bug in LDAP aliases #2".

Source cod3e Comments -   We have analyzed the three sources (commit messages, source code comments, and issues tracker) and found that not all 288 security indicators are relevant to security-related issues. E.g., "signature", which was used for documenting how the *digital signature* is handled within the application addressed by comments like: "// signature widget". Resulting in a different semantic for it compared to the originally intended one. Furthermore, we observed that some security indicators are removed after a relatively short time, usually around ten releases, or they stay permanently. Depending on the project *years of history*, see Table 1, we observed a shift of the breaking point up to 200 release tags, which was the case for the project GLPIv3, which is maintained for more than 20 years and 20 thousand commits. Figure 1 illustrates the number of release tags needed such that security indicators are removed after their introduction. *Issue tracker (JIRA/Github)* - From the inspected instances, we observed that the security indicators like "hack", "ldap", and "openssl" are present due to sharing the same name with a PHP package rather than indicating a security concern. Whereas "password" and "username" are used in an example code to underline what the issue was; however, they were not related to a security issue.

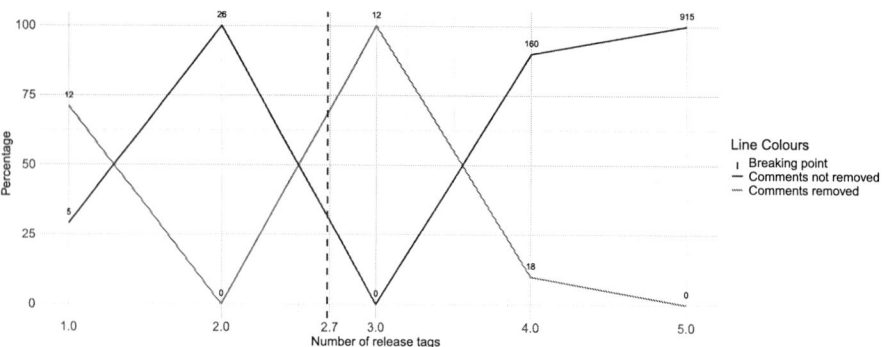

Fig. 1. Percentages of comments that have or have not been removed over release tags for the project GLPI. After the breaking point of 2,7 release tags, the proportion of non-removed comments becomes greater. On top of the line, the absolute values can be found.

Manual Inspection -   Our manual inspection of the different sources (commit message, comment, and issue tracker) classified 98 different security indicators, from which 79 were classified to be relevant. Additionally, we inspected whether security indicators appeared together and performed the inspection of their combination. In a work running in parallel [8], we performed an inspection of comments by three authors independently from each other for a manual classification of security indicators. 68.3% of the keywords are identified in the work running in parallel and in this work as being relevant security indicators. The remaining 31.6% are only identified by this work, which might be due to different sources, programming languages, temporal aspects, or sampling techniques that were leveraged in the two approaches. Inspecting those keywords that were only classified by this as relevant, many of them are related to login, e.g., "two factor", "user account", or "user name", hinting at the project-specific domains of user authentication, especially for GLPI [15].

At this point, we observed that quite general keywords such as "ldap" are used together with "login" or "authentication", which is not really surprising as LDAP (Lightweight Directory Access Protocol) is an authentication protocol. However, due to the connection with other keywords, more attention needs to be brought to seemingly irrelevant ones.

4   Conclusion

Mining various sources demonstrated the potential of combining them to increase the available context. We have manually inspected more than two thousand instances from different sources (commit message, comment, and issue tracker), unveiling that ① not every source has the same quality, i.e., in future work, we need to consider that not all sources provide the same information and richness, and ② not every indicator has a unique semantic meaning, making it harder to detect those keywords which in fact are indicating a security concern. To answer our initial question: *Where do developers admit their security-related concerns?* Our preliminary results indicate that developers use source code comments as the most reliable means. The security indicators applied to the commit messages and issue tracker generate a lot of false positives, hence being a less reliable resource for identifying security admissions.

We plan to expand this work in future work by leveraging deep learning (DL) approaches to automate detection and classification. Besides the challenges in designing a DL approach, building and maintaining trust in such an application is one, if not the major, issue we need to overcome. The DL is planned to be deployed in a CI/CD pipeline to automate the detection of different kinds of issues detached from the development process. Additionally, we plan to investigate the different behaviours of open source and industry developers, especially in a mixed state when practitioners from industry loan projects of open-source and expand them for their needs. Furthermore, how packages and projects are assessed and selected for internal use, i.e., which are the attributes developers consider most important to trust a third-party application.

Acknowledgements. Moritz Mock is partially funded by the National Recovery and Resilience Plan (Piano Nazionale di Ripresa e Resilienza, PNRR - DM 117/2023). The research was carried out during an internship of Moritz Mock at Würth Phoenix, Italy. The work has been funded by the project CyberSecurity Laboratory no. EFRE1039 under the 2023 EFRE/FESR program.

References

1. Bavota, G., Russo, B.: A large-scale empirical study on self-admitted technical debt. In: Proceedings of the 13th International Conference on Mining Software

Repositories, MSR 2016, pp. 315–326. Association for Computing Machinery, New York, NY, USA (2016). https://doi.org/10.1145/2901739.2901742

2. Croft, R., Xie, Y., Zahedi, M., Babar, M.A., Treude, C.: An empirical study of developers' discussions about security challenges of different programming languages. Empir. Softw. Eng. **27**, 1–52 (2022)

3. Cunningham, W.: The wycash portfolio management system. ACM Sigplan Oops Messenger **4**(2), 29–30 (1992)

4. Demšar, J.: Statistical comparisons of classifiers over multiple data sets. J. Mach. Learn. Res. **7**, 1–30 (2006)

5. Ferreyra, N.E.D., Shahin, M., Zahedi, M., Quadri, S., Scandariato, R.: What can self-admitted technical debt tell us about security? a mixed-methods study (2024). https://doi.org/10.48550/arXiv.2401.12768

6. Krüger, J., Hebig, R.: To memorize or to document: a survey of developers' views on knowledge availability. In: Kadgien, R., Jedlitschka, A., Janes, A., Lenarduzzi, V., Li, X. (eds.) Product-Focused Software Process Improvement, pp. 39–56. Springer, Cham (2024). https://doi.org/10.1007/978-3-031-49266-2_3

7. Li, Y., Soliman, M., Avgeriou, P.: Automatic identification of self-admitted technical debt from four different sources. Empir. Softw. Eng. **28**(3), 65 (2023). https://doi.org/10.1007/s10664-023-10297-9

8. Mock, M., Melegati, J., Kretschman, M., Díaz Ferreyra, N.E., Russo, B.: MADE-WIC: Multiple annotated datasets for exploring weaknesses in code. In: work in progress (2024)

9. Russo, B., Camilli, M., Mock, M.: WeakSATD: detecting weak self-admitted technical debt. In: Proceedings of the 19th International Conference on Mining Software Repositories, MSR 2022, pp. 448-453. Association for Computing Machinery, New York, NY, USA (2022). https://doi.org/10.1145/3524842.3528469

10. Spadini, D., Aniche, M., Bacchelli, A.: PyDriller: Python framework for mining software repositories. In: Proceedings of the 2018 26th ACM Joint Meeting on European Software Engineering Conference and Symposium on the Foundations of Software Engineering, ESEC/FSE 2018, pp. 908-911. Association for Computing Machinery, New York, NY, USA (2018). https://doi.org/10.1145/3236024.3264598

11. Zampetti, F., Fucci, G., Serebrenik, A., Di Penta, M.: Self-admitted technical debt practices: a comparison between industry and open-source. Empir. Softw. Eng. **26**(6), 1–32 (2021). https://doi.org/10.1007/s10664-021-10031-3

12. SemGrep. http://semgrep.dev, Accessed May 2024

13. SonarQube. https://www.sonarsource.com/, Accessed May 2024

14. Invicti. https://www.invicti.com, Accessed May 2024

15. GLPI. https://github.com/glpi-project/glpi, Accessed May 2024

16. icingaweb2. https://github.com/Icinga/icingaweb2, Accessed May 2024

17. Github documentation. https://docs.github.com/en/rest/issues/issues, Accessed May 2024

18. Jire python package. https://pypi.org/project/jira/, Aaccessed May 2024

Digital Twin Adapted Agile Software Development Life Cycle

Mariam Jaber(✉)[iD], Abdallah Karakra[iD], Ahmad Alsadeh[iD],
and Adel Taweel[iD]

Department of Computer Science, Birzeit University, Birzeit, Palestine
1215021@student.birzeit.edu, {akarakra,asadeh,ataweel}@birzeit.edu

Abstract. Digital Twin (DT) stands as the premier technology within Industry 4.0 used in multiple sectors. Although there has been considerable recent literature on DT, there has been limited focus on the life cycle methodologies for its development. Lacking a well-defined process can significantly complicate DT development. This paper proposes an augmented Agile Software Development Life Cycle as a methodology for DT development.

Keywords: Digital Twin · Agile · Software Development Life Cycle

1 Introduction

Building an effective DT is a challenging and iterative endeavour [4,5]. Without a clear process for DT development, it can become exceedingly complicated and may result into not addressing sufficiently essential DT specific system features. Therefore, following a software development life cycle (SDLC) methodology for DT development is essential to ensure the successful creation, deployment, and maintenance of such complex systems to operate in critical environments. Several SDLC models were developed to organize and streamline the software creation processes, each tailored for specific project types. Waterfall, Agile, and Rapid Application Development (RAD) models are among the most widely used models in the industry [11]. Adopting the right SDLC model not only streamlines the development process but also significantly increases the likelihood of delivering a successful and quality product. Therefore, organizations must carefully evaluate their project requirements and choose a SDLC model that aligns with their goals and needs to ensure successful software delivery.

The Agile model relies on an iterative and incremental approach, emphasizing collaboration to create software system that meets evolving customer needs in complex domains. This model enables quick adaptation to changes, ensuring the project remains flexible and responsive [3]. In this paper, we will propose an augmented Agile for DT development, given the complex, dynamic, changing and adaptive nature of DT environments, where they are typically deployed to

© The Author(s) 2025
L. Marchesi et al. (Eds.): XP 2024 Workshops, LNBIP 524, pp. 196–202, 2025.
https://doi.org/10.1007/978-3-031-72781-8_22

operate with multitude of diverse and critical systems and technologies. One is more likely to become lost in the implementation of technologies for the DT than to take use of its advantages due to the high cohesiveness of the DT's supporting technologies. Hence, we must consider the manufacturing and environmental context and specific DT characteristics, to accomplish DT capabilities, such as scalability and interoperability [2].

The paper is organized as follows: related work are provided in Sect. 2, Sect. 3 presents the need for augmenting Agile methodologies for DT development. The proposed approach is described in Sect. 4, Sect. 5 validates the sufficiency of the proposed Agile SDLC, and Sect. 6 presents conclusion and future work.

2   Related Work

There are only a few studies, in the literature, that examine the life-cycle path that guides the detailed development of DT systems. This section explores various methodologies documented in the literature for implementing DT in the healthcare sector.

Laybenbacher et al. [6] devised a strategy for constructing a DT of an immune system, and is structured as a four-stage process. Stage 1: defines a specific application and constructs an appropriate generic template model. Stage 2: personalizes the template model to an individual patient. Stage 3: final immune DT testing and uncertainty quantification. Stage 4: collects individual patient data for ongoing improvement of the immune DT. Alternatively, Karakra [4] proposed a methodology for designing a DT of patient pathways in a hospital. The phases of this methodology are the design phase that has two steps (construction and validation), inclusive of transformation and deployment.

Sinner et al. [10], on the other hand, employed a typical process development cycle for their case study on microbial upstream bioprocessing. The paper used standard process development cycle of five phases: early strain and process characterisation, process design, process transfer, monitoring and control, maintenance and continuous improvement. It emphasised that if the DT and underlying models are regularly adjusted to newly available data, DT can integrate with the whole process development cycles. However, for secure DTs, Satyarthi et al. [8], recommended a Secure Software development Life Cycle (SSDLC) methodology, to create and manage secure software. The proposed SSDLC process, based on SDLC, includes configurable catalogue of security controls. It defines several activities: 1) Requirement analysis and description 2) Designing and Deployment 3) Testing and Maintenance 4) Security requirements identification 5) Security Training and Audits 6) End-product evaluation and Configuration 7) Pre-selection of security objectives 8) Exploration of pre-selected ideas 9) Formation of Simulation based prototype and Data Optimization 10) Real-time asset and component management 11) Virtual verification and validation 12) Iteration based virtual testing and finalizes the product.

From the literature, we observed that limited literature work focused on life cycle methodologies for developing DT. Moreover, proposed SDLCs for developing DT are custom-tailored to meet the specific needs of the respective areas in which they were applied. This indicates the necessity for an adapted, systematic methodology for structuring DT development. The Agile model, known for its iterative, update-centric approach, appears particularly suited for DTs due to their need for regular updates to reflect real-world changes. However, there are certain aspects lacking within the various SDLC phases, hence, an augmented Agile SDLC is proposed.

3   Why Augmented Agile SDLC?

Choosing an augmented SDLC for DT over a traditional one is essential due to the nature of DTs. DTs rely on continuous real-time data to function accurately. The standard practices of agile SDLC may not fully address the complexities of integrating and processing real-time data, synchronised from several sources, continuously updating the DT.

While Agile methods provide a solid foundation for adaptability and customer focused development, however they do not explicitly ensure the requirements of DT that includes real-time data integration, interdisciplinary collaboration, diverse resources interoperability and complex analytics. Thus, an augmented approach to the Agile SDLC to fully address these challenges is needed.

4   Augmented Agile SDLC

In contrast to traditional software development, creating DTs demands unique considerations. Beyond the standard Agile SDLC, the integration of real-time data, modeling and simulation, and interaction with physical assets necessitate specialized knowledge and equipment. The Agile SDLC phases have been tailored with additional techniques, technologies, and practices, aligning with the distinctive characteristics of DT.

In this section, we introduce an augmented Agile SDLC as a methodology for DT development. Figure 1 describes the suggested simplified model: each rectangle represents an Agile SDLC stage: 1- Requirements 2- Design 3- Implementation 4- Testing 5- Deployment. In each stage, blue circles represent common steps of traditional software and DT, black circles represent the traditional software steps, and red circles represent DT steps.

4.1   Requirements Stage

In traditional software development, the requirements for each iteration are taken from the product backlog. DT relies on data to address these requirements, with different sources for this data including physical resources such as sensors, devices or other IoT and mechanical IoT instruments, and historical data that has been previously recorded can be incorporated into the model and utilised for additional analysis [1]. Data collected from this stage for DT should be stored either locally or in a cloud [1].

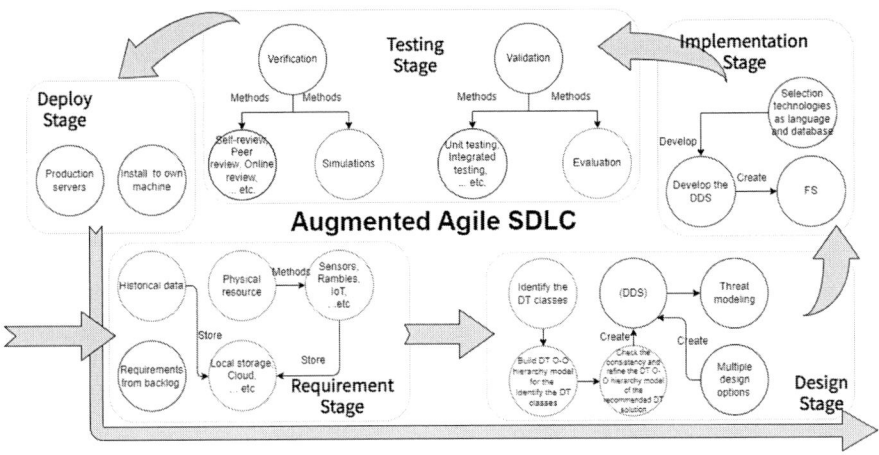

Fig. 1. Agile SDLC simplified model for an iteration.

4.2 Design Stage

In traditional software development, multiple design options for the product architecture are proposed based on the identified requirements. These alternatives are documented within a Design Document Specification (DDS). In DT, the design consists of three steps [7]: (1) identifying the DT classes, (2) incrementally building the DT object-oriented (O-O) hierarchy model for the recommended DT solution, and (3) checking the consistency and refining the DT O-O hierarchy model of the recommended DT solution.

Threat modeling is, also done in the design phase for both DT and the traditional software, defined as a systematic approach used to identify, catalog, and prioritize potential threats, facilitating the development of effective countermeasures against these threats. Once the design for the DT or the traditional software is finalized, Data Flow Diagrams (DFDs) of this design will be created to support threat modeling. A suitable multiple threat modeling tool, such as STRIDE, that aligns with integration into the Secure Development Life Cycle (SSDLC), can be used, making it an integral component of security requirements [9].

4.3 Implementation Stage

The software development process should align with the specifications outlined in the DDS while adhering to established coding standards. Programmers are responsible for creating a Functional Specification (FS) document, which captures all technical-level functions provided by the software. For DT, this phase involves developing the DT models, which may include choosing algorithms and establishing equations. Subsequently, the DT solution is created by producing the software that encompasses the algorithms, equations, inputs, and combines all the components of the DT.

4.4 Testing Stage

The verification and Validation (V&V) process is used for testing purposes [12]. In traditional software development, verification involves self-review, peer-review, online-review, offline-review, and walk through, while validation includes unit testing, integrated testing, system testing, and user acceptance testing.

In DT, verification is employed to verify that the requirements, specifications, and regulations are satisfied, ensuring that DT successfully attains its intended objectives without defects or deficiencies. Formal verification methods, such as reach-ability analysis, model-checking, equivalence-checking, and simulations, are commonly used [12]. Validation evaluates whether DT satisfies the user's needs, primarily at the end of the development process. Typically, historical data is utilized for sensitivity analysis to evaluate the effects of input changes and physical system changes on outputs.

4.5 Deployment Stage

In traditional software development, after receiving a 'Pass' from the testing phase, the product is considered ready for release. The software will either be deployed to production servers or made available for users to install on their machines. In DT, the deployment process for the physical part consists of [2]: (1) preparation for data transmission, (2) provision of an instance of the virtual part of the system, and (3) establishment of a connection between the two parts.

5 Evaluation

To evaluate the adequacy of the proposed augmented Agile SDLC and its additional or modified processes, the model was reviewed by three software engineering experts. These experts were given descriptions of three different healthcare environments within a local small community clinic: the radiology unit, pathology unit, and emergency unit. These departments were selected due to their diverse dynamic behavior, sensitive real-time monitoring, and processing requirements.

The experts were asked to validate the following: 1- The requirements of the selected healthcare environments consistently include the intrinsic features mentioned above. The experts examined the environments against these requirements. 2- The life cycle model contains dedicated processes that produce a system addressing these intrinsic features at various development stages. 3- The life cycle model does not overlook any critical requirements specific to a dynamic complex healthcare environment.

Preliminary results indicate that the proposed augmented Agile SDLC model effectively addresses the identified intrinsic features of the healthcare environments studied, demonstrating its adequacy. However, additional validation is needed to examine larger and more complex healthcare environments.

6   Conclusion

This paper proposes an augmented Agile SDLC methodology for the SDLC of DTs. The Agile SDLC phases have been tailored with additional techniques, technologies, and practices adapted to DTs, addressing the distinctive characteristics and challenges associated with developing DT systems. In future work, we will develop a more complex case study in the healthcare domain, focusing on the emergency department, to validate the proposed model.

References

1. Ariansyah, D., Fernàndez del Amo, I., Erkoyuncu, et al.: Digital twin development: a step by step guideline (2020)
2. Enders, M.: Understanding and Applying Digital Twins - Results of Selected Studies. Ph.D. thesis (2022)
3. Flora, H.K., Chande, S.V.: A systematic study on agile software development methodologies and practices. Int. J. Comput. Sci. Inf. Technol. **5**(3), 3626–3637 (2014)
4. Karakra, A., Fontanili, F., Lamine, E., Lamothe, J.: Hospit'win: a predictive simulation-based digital twin for patients pathways in hospital. In: 2019 IEEE EMBS International Conference on Biomedical & Health Informatics (BHI) (2019)
5. Karakra, A., Fontanili, F., Taweel, A., Lamine, E., Lamothe, J., Barghouthi, H.: Digital twin in healthcare: security threat meta-model. In: 2022 IEEE/ACS 19th International Conference on Computer Systems and Applications (AICCSA), pp. 1–6. IEEE (2022)
6. Laubenbacher, R., Niarakis, A., Helikar, T., An, G., et al: Building digital twins of the human immune system: toward a roadmap. npj Dig. Med. **5**(1), 64 (2022)
7. Qamsane, Y., Moyne, J., et al.: A methodology to develop and implement digital twin solutions for manufacturing systems. IEEE Access **9**, 44247–44265 (2021)
8. Satyarthi, S., Pandey, D., Khan, M.W.: Adaptation of digital twins as a methodology for management and development of secure software systems. NeuroQuantology **19**(7), 300–309 (2021)
9. Shevchenko, N., Chick, T.A., O'Riordan, P., Scanlon, T.P., Woody, C.: Threat modeling: a summary of available methods. Technival report. Carnegie Mellon University Software Engineering Institute Pittsburgh United (2018)
10. Sinner, P., Daume, S., Herwig, C., Kager, J.: Usage of digital twins along a typical process development cycle. In: Digital Twins: Tools and Concepts for Smart Biomanufacturing, pp. 71–96 (2021)
11. Tiky, Y.: Software development life cycle. THe Hongkong University of Science and Technology, Hongkong (2016)
12. Upadhyay, P.: The role of verification and validation in system development life cycle. IOSR J. Comput. Eng. **5**(1), 17–20 (2012)

Drawing Based Game for Teaching Scrum

Krzysztof Marek$^{(\boxtimes)}$ and Kamila Martyniuk-Sienkiewicz

Warsaw University of Technology, 00-661 Warsaw, Poland
`krzysztof.marek@pw.edu.pl`

Abstract. Over the years, the use of gamification in teaching different agile approaches become more popular. Many proposed solutions are
based on moving tasks on physical or virtual boards. Some connect task
realisation with the performance of simple, repetitive manual tasks. The
approach described in this paper utilises the activity of drawing simple
icons on post-its to mimic the active and creative aspect of e.g. software
development. The described game allows for teaching multiple practices
used in Scrum software development connected to software quality and
requirements, including the importance of the Definition of Done, acceptance criteria and continuous improvement based on Sprint Review and
Retrospective. Initial results are promising while working with students
with no or almost no previous understanding of the software development process. Additionally, the game can be easily modified or extended
to help with teaching other aspects of the Scrum software development
process.

Keywords: Gamification · Scrum · Educational games

1 Motivation

When teaching Scrum to university students with little to no previous experience
in commercial software development, we encountered problems while covering
different practices used by Software Development Teams working in Scrum. The
biggest observed issues included: distinguishing between the Definition of Done
and specific requirements in the form of user stories and acceptance criteria,
applying principles of continuous adaptation in practice and overall understanding of how self-organisation and self-management of the Scrum Team works.
Based on those observations, a working theory was established that to build a
better understanding of Scrum students need to experience working in it. Due
to time restrictions of the classes and, in many cases, lack of programming skills
among students, real software development in Scrum wasn't possible. Therefore an idea to create a two-hour workshop showcasing work in Scrum without
programming has been formulated.

2 Related Works

The use of games in education is becoming more and more popular, especially
in the area of computer science. Many studies have shown that the use of gami-

© The Author(s) 2025
L. Marchesi et al. (Eds.): XP 2024 Workshops, LNBIP 524, pp. 203–208, 2025.
https://doi.org/10.1007/978-3-031-72781-8_23

fication in the learning process is a better answer than the traditional teaching process [1]. The use of gamification in the process of teaching agile approaches, especially Scrum and Kanban, has significantly risen in the last ten years. Recent studies on multiple Scrum and Kanban educational games and literature review shop a wide variety of possible games to choose from. Przybylek and Olszewski tested 12 simple games for OpenKanban [2]. However, many games for Scrum mostly focus on simulating task movements on virtual or physical boards, in many cases using popular task tracking tools like Jira or Trello, where task completion is automatic or based on random methods [3–5]. Games that are not a direct translation of work, but methods of consolidating knowledge in the form of tests, are also popular [6,7]. Among the proposed games, we can also find a card game approach, where students learn basic concepts and learn to respond to problems introduced by the opposing team [8].

In the process of gamification of Scrum learning, simpler design tasks are often created, which, by making the task itself easier, allow students to focus on understanding the methodology. One approach uses the Minecraft game, where during a semester-long project, students build a building inside the computer game using Scrum [9]. Other approaches provide some easier manual activity as a parallel to the completion of a real task. Most common examples of such games are Scrum Simulation with LEGO Bricks [10], SCRUMIA [11] or SCRUMIA variation with origami-based tasks [12]. The first has been adopted in professional training courses and uses LEGO bricks to allow for building LEGO houses and cars based on provided user stories. The second takes inspiration from the LEGO game and proposes a cheaper alternative in the form of making paper hats and aeroplanes. Providing a simple form of manual activity/game helps with showing the idea of delivering value to the client at the end of each Sprint. We did not find any games that used drawing as a way to simulate work or value creation. Therefore, the authors decided to build on this idea and explore its possibilities.

3   Game Overview

3.1   Game Requirements and Preparation

During the game, multiple groups of students act as teams, developing icon sketches for a client while working in Scrum. A single team consists of 2 Developers (only persons allowed to draw icons), a single Tester (a person with a list of Acceptance Criteria for each icon) and a Product Owner (the only person who can contact the client). To facilitate different group sizes, the role of Product Owner and Tester can be performed by a single student, making the team size more flexible. The teacher is filling the role of the Scrum Master and client whenever needed. Each team receives the same preselected Sprint Backlog to deliver during the Sprint and tries to deliver as many complete icons as possible. Example Product Backlog Items have been shown in Fig. 1. Each team has 2 stacks of post-its, 2 black markers and 3 different colour markers or crayons at their disposal. At the beginning of the game, the teacher describes the roles and rules. Only one icon can be drawn on a single post-it. Each icon has to fulfil the corresponding acceptance criteria, colour requirements have to be matched, and any changes to colours have to be consulted with the client. The game usually consists of multiple game cycles - Sprints presented in Fig. 2.

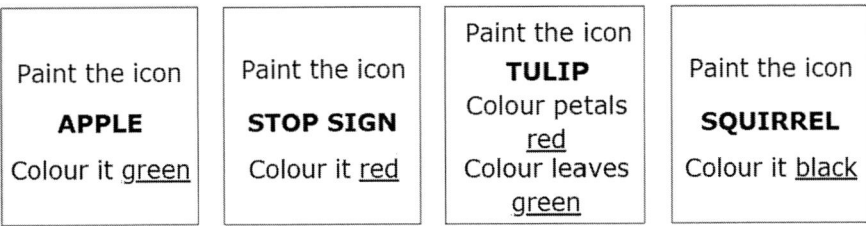

Fig. 1. Single game cycle

3.2 Gameplay

Once the teams are ready, the teacher starts the first game cycle by starting the implementation simulation phase (drawing icons). The simulated implementation lasts only 3 min, leaving as much time for discussions and explanations as possible. After the icon growing has ended, each team posts their ready icons onto the whiteboard. Next, a review with a client (teacher) is performed. Delivered icons are checked for compliance with acceptance criteria and previously undescribed customer expectations. Discarded icons are separated as shown in Fig. 3.

At this time, issues regarding the general quality of icons are discussed, such as how precise the colouring of the icons should be, what the icon orientation is regarding the sticky side of the post-it, and what the expected size of the icon is. After this, an official Definition of Done is created. Next, the teams perform small retrospectives, looking for possible improvements to the process with the teacher's help. Here, aspects such as lack of communication, incomplete requirements, lack of priorities, limited access to colour markers and many others can be discussed. Once new improvements are agreed upon, the game can be restarted, and the game cycle can be repeated. In the new cycle, teams repeat the Sprint with the same backlog and tools but with new and improved policies regarding their work. Results are quickly inspected in another review and displayed next to the initial ones, usually showing significant improvements compared to the first Sprint.

4 Initial Results and Future Work

The described game shows promising results despite being in an early stage of development. The game has been tested with 4 groups of students, each between

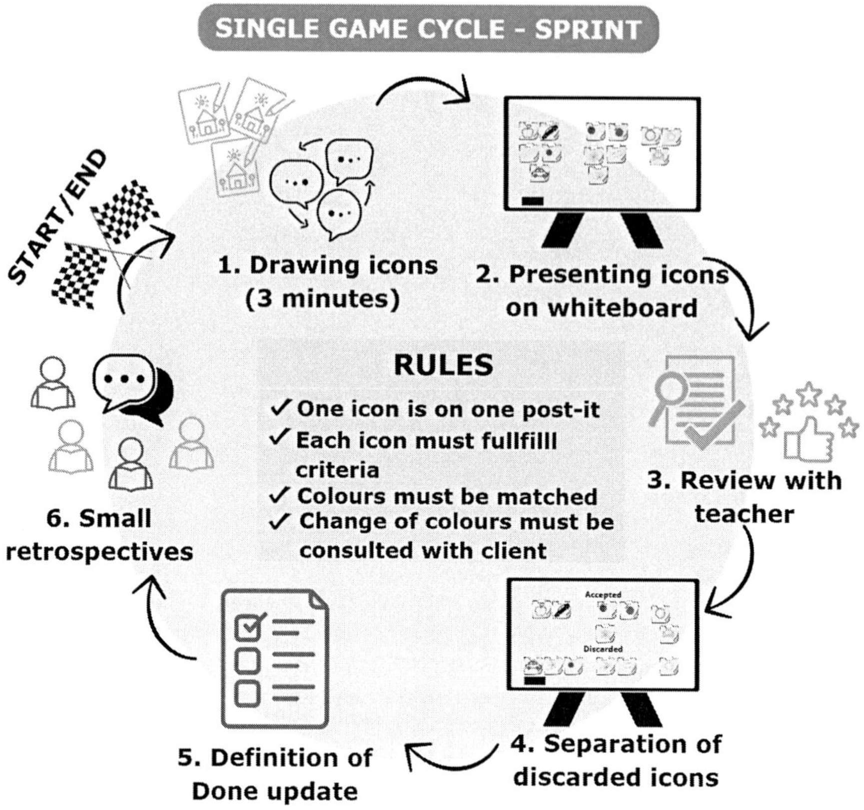
SINGLE GAME CYCLE - SPRINT
START/END
1. Drawing icons (3 minutes)
2. Presenting icons on whiteboard
3. Review with teacher
4. Separation of discarded icons
5. Definition of Done update
6. Small retrospectives
RULES
✓ One icon is on one post-it
✓ Each icon must fullfilll criteria
✓ Colours must be matched
✓ Change of colours must be consulted with client
Accepted
Discarded

Fig. 2. Single game cycle

I
II
III

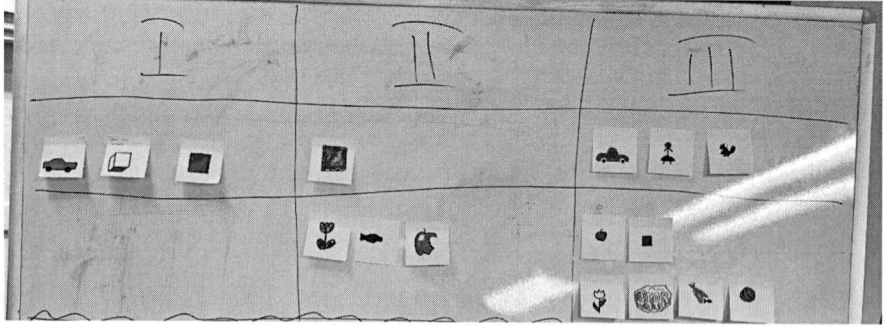

Fig. 3. The icons created after the first Sprint by 3 teams during a single workshop. Accepted icons are in the middle row, and discarded icons are at the bottom row.

11–17 individuals with no or almost no previous understanding of the software development process. After each workshop, students stated that their understanding of Scrum had improved. During the last session, once the authors' initial understanding of the game flow and mechanics was established, students answered a set of advanced questions checking their deep understanding of Scrum practises before and after the workshop. The results displayed in Fig. 4 show significant improvement, especially in the areas connected to acceptance criteria, the Definition of Done and the Sprint Cycle.

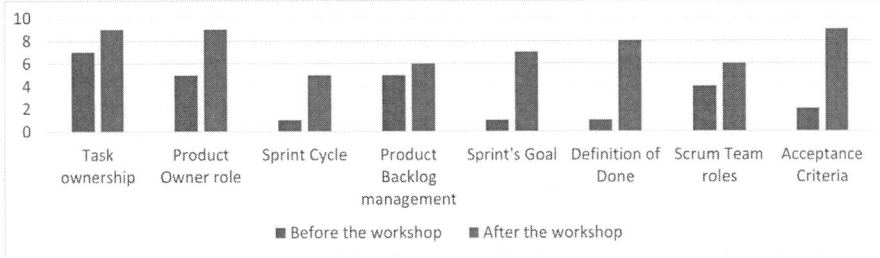

Fig. 4. The number of correct answers in the test given by a group of students (12 individuals) before and after the workshop, respectively.

Drawing icons as a base for simulating work in Scrum brings several advantages. They don't require expensive, branded accessories. Simplified icons are easy to draw and don't require any artistic skills to create. Additionally, the icons can be used as a parallel for creating the graphical user interface. The core of the game is quite simple and allows for multiple modifications. Initial ideas to be explored include introductions of Sprint Planning, where students select Product Backlog Items for the next Sprint based on their experience from the previous one; Backlog Refinement, where students improve the lacking descriptions of Product Backlog Items; item complexity estimation, e.g. drawing a squirrel is much more difficult than a simple square; and execution of multiple Sprints with unfinished icons going over to the next Sprints. This flexibility in adding or removing different parts of the simulation game potentially created an opportunity to personalize the game for each individual group of students based on their difficulties with understanding Scrum, e.g. focusing on the planning and refinement aspects of the Sprint cycle, not the requirements and quality as in the initially described version. Therefore, the game also requires more extensive and methodological validation of its teaching results, focusing on different initial knowledge of Scrum and the impact of different game variances.

Disclosure of Interests. The authors have no competing interests to declare that are relevant to the content of this article.

References

1. De Freitas, S.: Are games effective learning tools? A review of educational games. J. Educ. Technol. Soc. **21**(2), 74–84 (2018)
2. A. Przybylek and M. K. Olszewski: adopting collaborative games into Open Kanban. In: 2016 Federated Conference on Computer Science and Information Systems (FedCSIS), pp. 1539–1543. IEEE (2016)
3. Marques, R., Costa, G., Mira da Silva, M., Gonçalves, D., Gonçalves, P.: A gamification solution for improving Scrum adoption. Empir. Softw. Eng. **25**(4), 2583–2629 (2020)
4. Naik, N., Jenkins, P.: Relax, it's a game: utilising gamification in learning agile scrum software development. In: 2019 IEEE Conference on Games (CoG), pp. 1–4. IEEE (2019)
5. Rodriguez, G., Soria, Á., Campo, M.: Virtual scrum: a teaching aid to introduce undergraduate software engineering students to scrum. Comput. Appl. Eng. Educ. **23**(1), 147–156 (2015)
6. Ciucă, G., Ciupe, A., Orza, B.: Exploring educational scenarios through interactive environments and agile user stories: a gamified assessment case study. In: 2022 International Symposium on Electronics and Telecommunications (ISETC), pp. 1–4. IEEE (2022)
7. John, I., Fertig, T.: Gamification for software engineering students-an experience report. In: 2022 IEEE Global Engineering Education Conference (EDUCON), pp. 1942–1947. IEEE (2022)
8. Fernandes, J. M., Sousa, S. M.: Playscrum-a card game to learn the scrum agile method. In: 2010 Second International Conference on Games and Virtual Worlds for Serious Applications, pp. 52–59. IEEE (2010)
9. Schäfer, U.: Training scrum with gamification: lessons learned after two teaching periods. In: 2017 IEEE Global Engineering Education Conference (EDUCON), pp. 754–761. IEEE (2017)
10. Krivitsky, A.: lego4scrum: A Complete Guide. A Great Way to Teach the Scrum Framework and Agile Thinking. Self-published by Alexey Krivitsky, Kyiv (2017)
11. Von Wangenheim, C.G., Savi, R., Borgatto, A.F.: SCRUMIA - an educational game for teaching SCRUM in computing courses. J. Syst. Softw. **86**(10), 2675–2687 (2013)
12. Sibona, C., Pourreza, S., Hill, S.: Origami: an active learning exercise for scrum project management. J. Inf. Syst. Educ. **29**(2), 105–116 (2018)

Selected Concepts of Leadership in Self-organizing Teams

Jakub Perlak(✉)

AGH University, Krakow, Poland
j.perlak@gmail.com

Abstract. Self-organizing teams are a common way of organizing teamwork in sectors related to modern technologies, especially in programming teams. Agile methods often promote and advocate such teams. One of the problems in this form of team organization is the issue of leadership, and particularly the relationship between vertical leadership - one person, and horizontal leadership - team members. In the literature on the subject, we can find traces of many concepts in such a broad area as the issue of leadership. However, several selected concepts allow us to capture an emerging feature in self-organizing teams which is the taking over of leadership functions by team members. Shared leadership, where the leadership function comes from team members, not from one appointed leader. Distributed leadership is where leadership in the organization is taken over voluntarily by individuals. Balanced leadership, where the vertical leader enables team members to take over leadership functions depending on the situation. The selected concepts presented here allow for a better understanding and research of the nature and phenomenon of leadership in self-organizing teams.

Keywords: Agile Teams · Self-Organized Team · Emergent Leadership

1 Introduction

Self-organizing teams have been becoming a common way of team organization, especially in the case of software development. There is no surprise that the key aspect of Agile methods is work based on self-organizing teams. [2, 3]. Inspired by Agile Manifesto of Software development [1] they are characterized by minimal structure, based on collaboration of the whole team and capability to adapt for changing project requirements [2]. Self-organizing teams is vital topic for research with many open questions [3].

One of challenge of such teams is aspect of leadership [6]. Especially relation between vertical, nominated leader and horizontal leadership among team members [5]. In practice of software development team, particularly those working with Agile methods, the role of the formal leader is not very clear. There is of course recommendation by many frameworks, like the most predominant Scrum how the leadership can look like [7] and usually it is a supportive role.

© The Author(s) 2025
L. Marchesi et al. (Eds.): XP 2024 Workshops, LNBIP 524, pp. 209–215, 2025.
https://doi.org/10.1007/978-3-031-72781-8_24

As leadership play crucial role in every organization, regardless of its type and what aspect it concerns, whole organization, project, or team. The nature of leadership has been examined since very beginning of human's reflection on our interactions and include such topics like the traits of leaders, behavior, and skills, as well as source of power and influence, among many. Scientific approaches to leadership are trying to systemize and provide more rigor in formulating conclusions [10]. Even in management science leadership is not very easy to define and to put in into extreme, there are many definitions of leadership, almost as many as researchers [10].

2 Leadership Concept in Self-organizing Teams

How leadership looks like in self-organizing teams is multilevel phenomena. Staring from the team perspective there is element of sharing responsibilities. Research on teams working with Scrum even suggest element of shared leadership [3]. Despite the roles defined by popular frameworks [6, 7]. If we consider multiteam set-up in organization another concept looks very promising in shading light three is distributed leadership [9]. When we consider formal and nominated leaders another concept helps in explaining the dynamics between the team and leaders which is the balanced leadership [4]. Naturally presented leadership theories are just small fraction from broad landscapes of leadership theories that currently discussed in the literature.

2.1 Shared Leadership – Emergent Phenomena in a Team

Shared leadership is usually described as a team-level emergent phenomenon where one or more team members are taking responsibility for leaders [8]. To better understand the following Table 1, shows its characteristics [8].

Table 1. Shared leadership characteristics

Perspective	Key elements	Opposite situation
Source of power	Influence among team members, horizontally spread by people on the same level of organization hierarchy	Nominated leader only, vertical relations to the team in organization
Level of analysis	Group level where leadership is emerging	Perspective of individual behavior
Scope of influence	Leadership and influence is broadly distributed among team members	Leadership and influence is focused in one person

One wonders what is shared in the concept of shared leadership. In their analysis, Zhu and colleagues [8] cite two approaches, the first is about what leadership style is shared, and the second is about leadership, as a whole. Examples of leadership styles shared within a team in the research include transformational, charismatic, or empowering, in which case, shared leadership becomes a meta-leadership to the dominant style [8]. In the case of a holistic approach, the research does not suggest any specific functions, but most broadly looks at leadership as the aggregate of all leadership activities [8]. Other studies suggests that shared leadership is rarely examined in project-based environment [5] and may bring better understand the team level dynamics which is integral part of any team, including self-organizing one.

2.2 Distributed Leadership – Emergent Leadership in Organization

Distributed leadership was primarily examined in educational context, however its implications become useful in general application in business [9]. The practice of distributed leadership has been relocated in Gronn's famous 2002 article on the level of analysis for such a view of leadership [11]. For the author of the article, distributed leadership is understood holistically, rather than as a simple aggregation of the individual contributions of individuals. Gronn called such holistic and distributed action a concert act, in analogy to a concert and an orchestra [11]. In his analysis, proposed three forms of distributed leadership:

1. Spontaneous collaboration - from time to time, individuals with different skills and knowledge, from different places in the organization and levels of the hierarchy together to use their abilities for the duration of an assignment, after which they return to their previously assigned groups.
2. Intuitive working relationships - this form emerges over time, where at least two members of the organization begin to rely on each other to build relationships, so that leadership permeates the shared relationship.
3. Institutionalized practice - more or less formalized relationships supported by organizational structures.

How distributed differs from shared leadership the Table 2. Describes.

Table 2. Shared leadership vs distributed leadership

Perspective	Shared leadership	Distributed leadership
Source of power	Formal and informal leaders in teams	Formal and informal leaders in organization
Process	Mutual influence among team members	Leadership is created by first leaders and followers through mutual interactions
Shared understanding	Shared cognition and understanding in team	Share cognition and understand is affected by the organization context
Advantage	Team advantage	Synchronized actions in organization
Level	Team	Individual, team, group, organization

So distributed leadership in reality is a term of practice, where the emphasis is mainly on the interactions between leaders and followers [11], rather than a single monolithic definition.

2.3   Balanced Leadership – Interplay Between Leader and Team Members

Third concept presented in this short overview of useful leadership connects in context of self-organizing teams is balanced leadership. The idea behind this concept is finding a balance between vertical and horizontal leadership. The formal leader has an intention to share responsibility when the horizontal leaders are ready and expose it [9]. Attitude, situation, and trust are key factors for enabling balanced leadership in a team [9]. It is temporary situation in a team and change during the project cycle. However, the dynamics of taking reconcilability and sharing in team provides useful framework for research (Fig. 1).

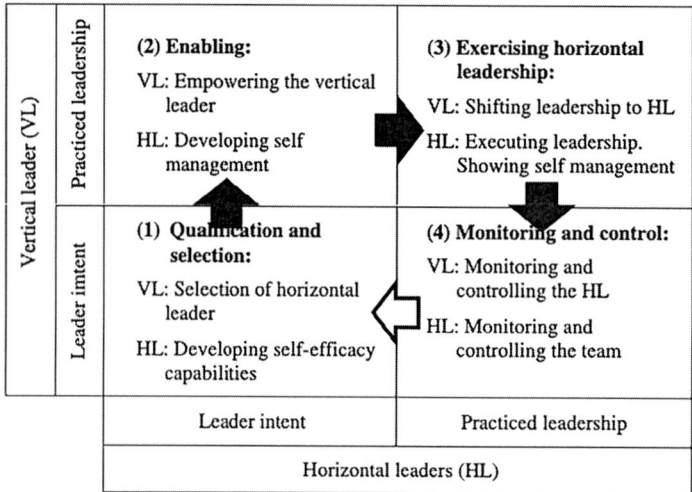

Fig. 1. Balanced leadership according to Müller [4]

The flow of sharing leadership looks as follow, at the beginning there is a need for horizontal leadership in the project. The intentions of both leaders, the vertical and the horizontal, are aligned. The vertical one makes the choice, and the horizontal one expresses his desire and develops his abilities in this direction. Then, as part of the leadership practices, the vertical leader empowers the horizontal leaders, who develop in themselves skills related to self-management. These activities are visible to all members of the project team. Then comes the actual leadership by the horizontal leaders, has been delegated proficiency and responsibility. Eventually, the control and monitoring of the work of the team and the progress of the project, and the control of the work of the leader or horizontal leaders is still in the hands of the vertical leader. After a certain period of time, leadership and responsibility return to the vertical leader [9].

3 Attempt of Synthesis Presented Leadership Concepts Supporting Self-organizing Teams

Scope of leadership in self-organizing teams is very broad. In this very short abstract, there is only a place for most prominent concepts. Leadership has dynamical and interpersonal character and depends on how formal it can be and how it is spread in organization. Visualizing the concepts at Fig. 2. Can be use as helpful tool for examining the leadership in practice of self-organizing teams.

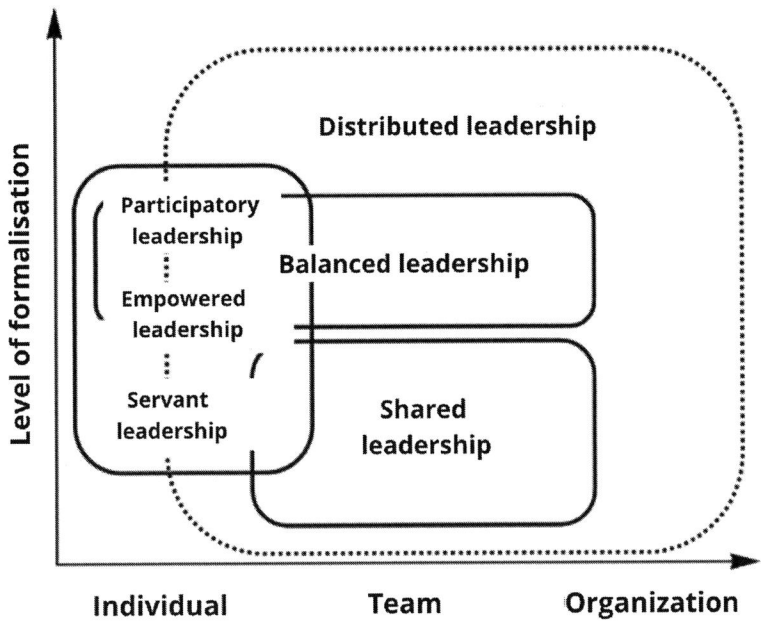

Fig. 2. Synthesis of leadership concepts

More insights how leadership is shaped in self-organizing teams is needed. There are many research ongoing, and one is conducted w by the author of this abstract. Leadership styles and traits of leaders and behaviors such as servant leadership, participative, empowering, or balanced leadership primarily concern formal leaders. Self-management and distributed leadership, as well as shared leadership, are often informal and emerge within a team when the conditions are right.

Leadership in the selected concepts has its different origin and location, following the lead of one can make a compilation of the leadership approaches discussed. They range from formal and internal leadership within the team to external and informal influence on the team. Table 3 presents those situations.

Leadership in self-organizing teams is a deep topic and presented concepts can help articulate what kind of leadership we are discussing and allow for more research with teams using more precise leans for leadership categorization.

Table 3. Source of leadership in the team

Leadership location	Formal leader	Non-formal
Internal to the team	Team leader, Project manager	Shared leadership, emergent leadership
External to the team	Sponsor, Coach	Mentor, Coordinator

Disclosure of Interests. The author has no competing interests to declare that are relevant to the content of this article.

References

1. Highsmith, J., Fowler, M.: The Agile Manifesto. Softw. Develop. Mag. **9**(8), 29–30 (2001)
2. Hoda, R., Murugesan, L.K.: Multi-level agile project management challenges: a self-organizing team perspective. J. Syst. Softw. **117**(July), 245–257 (2016)
3. Moe, N.B., Dingsøyr, T., Røyrvik, E.A.: Putting agile teamwork to the test – an preliminary instrument for empirically assessing and improving agile software development. In: Agile Processes in Software Engineering and Extreme Programming, pp. 114–123. Springer, Berlin Heidelberg (2009)
4. Müller, R., Drouin, N., Sankaran, S.: Balanced Leadership: Making the Best Use of Personal and Team Leadership in Projects. Oxford University Press (2021)
5. Scott-Young, C.M., Georgy, M., Grisinger, A.: Shared leadership in project teams: an integrative multi-level conceptual model and research Agenda. Int. J. Project Manag. **37**(4) (2019). https://doi.org/10.1016/j.ijproman.2019.02.002
6. Srivastava, P., Jain, S.: A leadership framework for distributed self-organized scrum teams. Team Perform. Manag. **23**(5–6), 293–314 (2017)
7. Sutherland, J., Sutherland, J.J.: Scrum: the art of doing twice the work in half the time. Currency (2014)
8. Zhu, J., Liao, Z., Yam, K.C., Johnson, R.E.: Shared leadership: a state-of-the-art review and future research Agenda. J. Organiz. Behav. **39**, 834–853 (2018). https://doi.org/10.1002/job.2296
9. Fitzsimons, D., James, K.T., Denyer, D.: Alternative approaches for studying shared and distributed leadership. Int. J. Manag. Rev. **13**(3), 313–328 (2011)
10. Yukl, G.: Leadership in Organizations, 8th Edition. Pearson (2013)
11. Gronn, P.: Distributed leadership as a unit of analysis. Leadersh. Q. **13**, 423–451 (2002). https://doi.org/10.1016/S1048-9843(02)00120-0

Towards a Double-Edged Sword: Modelling the Impact in Agile Software Development

Michael Neumann[1]([⊠])[ID] and Philipp Diebold[2,3][ID]

[1] University of Applied Sciences Hannover, Ricklinger Stadtweg 120, 30459 Hannover, Germany
michael.neumann@hs-hannover.de
[2] Bagilstein GmbH, Im Niedergarten 10, 55124 Mainz, Germany
philipp.diebold@bagilstein.de
[3] IU Unternational University, Juri-Gagarin-Ring 152, 99084 Erfurt, Germany
philipp.diebold@iu.org

Abstract. Agile methods are state of the art in software development. Companies worldwide apply agile to counter the dynamics of the markets. We know, that various factors like culture influence the successful application of agile methods in practice and that sucess varies from company to company. To counter these problems, we combine two causal models presented in literature: The Agile Practices Impact Model and the Model of Cultural Impact. In this paper, we want to better understand the two facets of factors in agile: Those influencing their application and those impacting the results when applying them. This papers core contribution is the Agile Influence and Impact Model, describing the factors influencing agile elements and the impact on specific characteristics in a systematic manner.

Keywords: Agile Methods · agile practice · impact · influence · causal model

1 Introduction

In the last decades, agile software development has gained a lot of research interest (e.g., [2,10,11]). Today, agile methods are used in a wide variety of contexts (organization, industry, region, ...) with different motivations [14]. Organizations want to improve product quality, increase the speed of delivery of product increments, or optimize predictability. It is therefore not surprising that the question of how to successfully apply agile methods has been investigated [1], which led to an understanding of success factors. On this basis, (causal) models have been defined to systematically describe the influences in the planned or existing application of agile methods (e.g., [3,8]). Two perspectives may be distinguished here: a) The influence on agile practices in relation to their successful application. b) The effects of the application of agile practices on product or

© The Author(s) 2025
L. Marchesi et al. (Eds.): XP 2024 Workshops, LNBIP 524, pp. 216–222, 2025.
https://doi.org/10.1007/978-3-031-72781-8_25

project characteristics. Below, we will focus on two specific models considering these two perspectives. We are aware, that further causal models exist in the SE field (e.g., [5]). However, in this paper we are focusing on agile methods and the possibility to define influences on or by agile methods.

Today, we know that social facets are important for the success when using agile methods as these facets guide the behaviour of people, e.g., how they communicate and act [12,13,15]. Also, aspects with regard to an agile culture are relevant for the successfull use of agile methods [4,7].

To be more precise, specific models were presented explaining the influences of social facets like cultural characteristics on agile methods in a systematic manner in the past. One is the Model of Cultural Impact on Agile Methods (MoCA) [8]. It describes cultural influences on the use of agile methods on a systematic basis. Another model, considering primarily the second perspective is the Agile Practices Impact Model [3] (APIM) aiming to provide a systematic description of the impact of agile practices on specific process improvement goals like e.g. (product) quality, development costs, or time.

However, for the current understanding of the influences and impacts on agile methods the available models, underlying theories and empirical findings do not cover or combine both perspectives. Nevertheless, this knowledge is of high importance as we see the need for a bigger picture supporting researchers and practictioners to find well-suited agile practices for their context considering their specific needs.

This motivated us in a first step to combine our models in order to cover the both mentioned perspectives. Thus, this paper presents the Agile Influence and Impact Model (AIIM) aiming to provide a solution for the explained challenges.

This paper is structured as follows: In Sect. 2, we give a brief introduction of the background, in particular the models we used as a basis for our paper: the APIM, followed by a description of MoCA. The core contribution of this paper is the Agile Influence and Impact Model, which we introduce including a practical example in Sect. 3. Finally, the paper closes with a conclusion in Sect. 4.

2   Background

2.1   Agile Practices Impact Model

The APIM model was created as a basis for an agile capability analysis. The model described the impact of agile practices on the specific impact characteristics, which are detailed as process improvement goals. Even if the model considers the impact on agile practices, it focuses more on the outcome perspective. Thus, the scientific ground for the APIM are agile practices, the impact characteristics and the impact association between them, which is more specified using Influence Factors. The impact between both aspects is defined as binary in terms of a positive or negative impact.

2.2   Model of Cultural Impact on Agile Methods

The MoCA model was defined to provide a systematic description of cultural influences on agile practices. The scientific ground for MoCA are the Cultural and Agile Elements dimensions and the specified impact between them. The cultural dimension consists of specific characteristics based on often used cultural models in Software Engineering. The agile elements dimension was created using the results from a tertiary study aiming to provide an up-to-date list of agile practices [6]. The influence between both dimensions is described as positive or negative, in terms of the application of the agile element with regard to the guideline in which it is defined.

3   The Agile Influence And Impact Model

In this Section, we provide an explanation of the formal structure on a presented meta-model in Fig. 1.

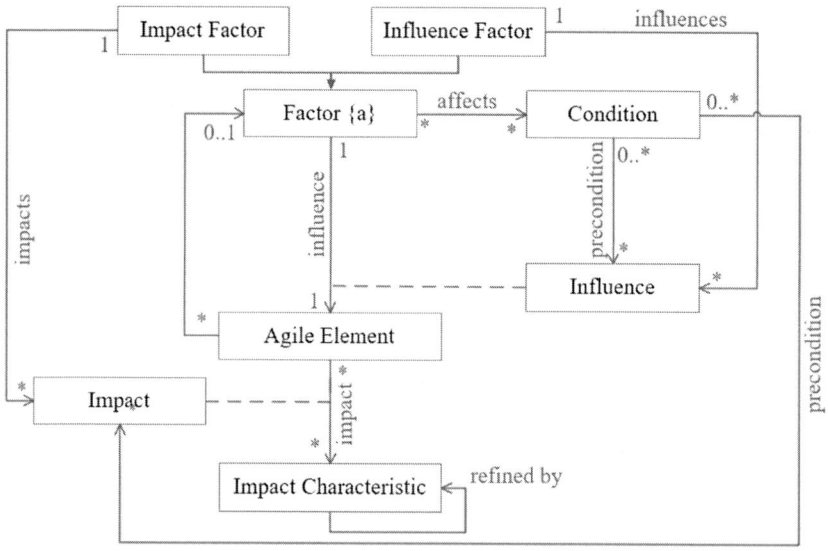

Fig. 1. Agile Influence and Impact meta-model

Similar to the two underlying models, we decide to use Unified Modeling Language (UML) as it fits to the needs explaining the formal structure of the AIIM. Below, we explain the classes and the relationships between them.

An *Agile Element* (using the MoCA wider definition of the elements of agile methods proposed in [9]) is an abstract description of agile activities, roles, and artifacts regardless of their relationship to the different agile methods guidelines.

Also, Agile Activities are abstract agile practices as defined in the paper by Diebold and Zehler [3]. Thus, we consider for the AIIM all the elements of agile elements including specific roles (like Scrum Master or Product Owner), artifacts (such as a Product Backlog), or even agile practices (e.g., Daily Meetings or Retrospectives).

Factor: A Factor can be a specific *Influence Factor* or *Impact Factor*. We decided to use a generalized structure as we wanted clearly differ between Impact Factors and Influence Factors to be able to consider both perspectives of influences on agile practices and impacts of agile practices. A *Condition* may applies as a precondition for a specific *influence* from a *Factor* on one *Agile Element*. This influence is not binary in terms of positive or negative (similar to the impact, which we understand as not binary). We assume that an influence of one Influence Factor (e.g., a cultural value) on an *Agile Element* is defined based on the expected application of the *Agile Element* with respective to the guideline in which this practice is defined. An *Impact* is represented by an Impact Factor on an Impact Characteristic, which are often related to process improvement goals, like Development cost or time [3].

To provide a more practical perspective of the AIIM, we introduce a hypothetical example. A visual represantation of this example is shown in Fig. 2. The example covers three cultural characteristics (as influence factors), three Agile Elements, three Impact Characteristics and the relationship between them. Furthermore, the model covers both two organizational constraints and organizaitonal goals.

Based on the influence, we defined the relationships H1..H3. *H1 (in-depth discussions of questions)* defines a positive influence of a High Uncertainty Avoidance on a Planning Meeting, as we assume in-depth discussions for open aspects (e.g., for requirements) by the team. This would lead to a higher quality of the Planning Meetings outcome, which furthermore should lead to an increased predictability of the teams performance (and plans) and transparency (e.g., of the process). Considering *H2 (open communication (of problems))*, a decreased open communication of problems triggered by a high power distance would affect a Daily Meeting in a negative way, if a manager attends the meetings. This attendance further lead to a decreased transparency, even if the Daily Meeting itself should increase the progress transparency of the team. Both Impact Characteristics Predictability and Transparency would provide a trade off for specific organizational goals. In our example, the Predictability would affect the organizational goal of reducing time to market. Finally, the cultural characteristic of a High Masculinity lead to a decrease of communication of code related problems (*H3: communication of code related problems*), which manifests a negative impact on the Test-Driven Development practice, if a manager attends (or even observe) this activity. The attendance of a manager of Agile Elements could be triggered by the influence of interfaces, e.g., stakeholder which want more in-depth informations. Also, it could be a management decision from a command and control strategy perspective to act in such kind of ways. These organizational constraints are of high importance, as they implicitly trigger such Impact

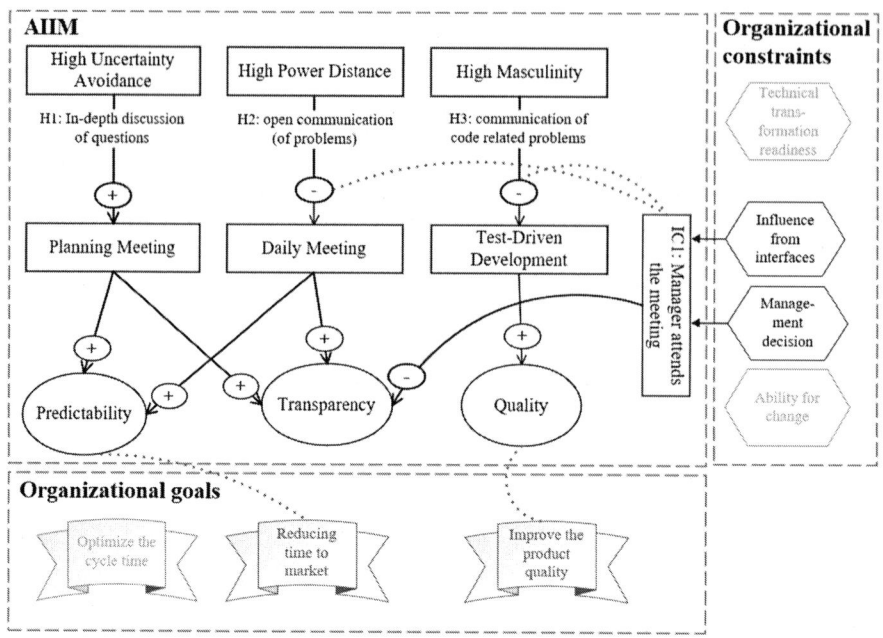

Fig. 2. Example of the AIIM model

Conditions in our model. However, the Test-Driven Development practice lead to a better process and product quality and thus, provide the opportunity to improve the product quality.

The example presented above provide a practical perspective based on three specific influence and impact relationships considering organizational constraints and goals.

4   Conclusion and Future Work

In this paper, we present the Agile Influence and Impact Model (AIIM) aiming to cover both perspectives: The influence on the elements of agile methods and the impact by agile elements on the outcome or output while applying such approaches.

In its current state, the AAIM is a meta-model describing both perspectives of influences and impacts with regard to agile methods. The model was created based on the combination of two existing models: The Agile Practices Impact Model and the Model of Cultural Impact on Agile Methods. To be more precise, we present furthermore a practice-oriented example of the AIIM considering in total three influences on agile elements and three impacts on specific impact characteristics.

We are aware, that the model is in an initial state and we are further planning future work activities. In the next step, we want to define how the model can be applied using examples from our previous models. The vision of the AIIM is to provide a theory which can be applied in real-world settings. Thus, we aim in further step to define an application process for the AIIM to be able to evaluate the new model in practice using empirical data.

References

1. Chow, T., Cao, D.B.: A survey study of critical success factors in agile software projects. J. Syst. Softw. **81**(6), 961–971 (2008)
2. Diebold, P., Dahlem, M.: Agile practices in practice: a mapping study. In: Proceedings of the International Conference on Evaluation and Assessment in Software Engineering (2014). https://doi.org/10.1145/2601248.2601254
3. Diebold, P., Zehler, T.: The agile practices impact model: idea, concept, and application scenario. In: International Conference on Software and System Process, pp. 92–96 (2015). https://doi.org/10.1145/2785592.2785609
4. Kuchel, T., Neumann, M., Diebold, P., Schön, E.M.: Which challenges do exist with agile culture in practice? In: Proceedings of the Symposium on Applied Computing, pp. 1018–1025 (2023). https://doi.org/10.1145/3555776.3578726
5. Lamersdorf, A., Münch, J.: Studying the impact of global software development characteristics on project goals: a causal model. Open Softw. Eng. J. **4**(2), 2–13 (2010). https://doi.org/10.2174/1874107X01004020002
6. Neumann, M.: The integrated list of agile practices - a tertiary study. In: Lean and Agile Software Development, pp. 19–37 (2022). https://doi.org/10.1007/978-3-030-94238-0_2
7. Neumann, M., Kuchel, T., Diebold, P., Schön, E.M.: Agile culture clash: unveiling challenges in cultivating an agile mindset in organizations. Comput. Sci. Inf. Syst. **21**(3), 1013–1031 (2024). https://doi.org/10.2298/CSIS230715029N
8. Neumann, M., Schmid, K., Baumann, L.: Characterizing the impact of culture on agile methods: the moca model. In: Proceedings of the International Conference on Software and System Processes, pp. 81–85 (2023). https://doi.org/10.1109/ICSSP59042.2023.00018
9. Neumann, M.: Towards a taxonomy of agile methods: the tree of agile elements. In: Proceedings of the International Conference in Software Engineering Research and Innovation, pp. 79–87 (2021). https://doi.org/10.1109/CONISOFT52520.2021.00022
10. Przybyłek, A., Albecka, M., Springer, O., Kowalski, W.: Game-based sprint retrospectives: multiple action research. Empir. Softw. Eng. **27**(1) (2021). https://doi.org/10.1007/s10664-021-10043-z
11. Schön, E.M., Thomaschewski, J., Escalona, M.J.: Agile requirements engineering: a systematic literature review. Comput. Stand. Interfaces **49**, 79–91 (2017). https://doi.org/10.1016/j.csi.2016.08.011
12. Schön, E., Escalona Cuaresma, M., Thomaschewski, J.: Agile values and their implementation in practice. Int. J. Interact. Multimedia Artif. Intell. **3**(5), 61–66 (2015)
13. Šmite, D., Gonzalez-Huerta, J., Moe, N.B.: "when in rome, do as the romans do": cultural barriers to being agile in distributed teams. In: Proceedings of the International Conference on Agile Software Development, pp. 145–161 (2020). https://doi.org/10.1007/978-3-030-49392-9_10

14. VersionOne, Collabnet: 17th annual state of agile survey (2023). https://stateofagile.com/

15. Welsch, D., Burk, L., Mötefindt, D., Neumann, M.: Navigating cultural diversity: barriers and benefits in multicultural agile software development teams. In: Proceedings of the Symposium on Applied Computing, pp. 818–825 (2024). https://doi.org/10.1145/3605098.3635988

An Agile Mindset in a VUCA-World

Carolina Appel Bangshøj[1], Tanja Elina Havstorm[2]([⊠]) [iD], and Åsa Algulin[1]

[1] Appel Relations AB, Olaigatan 57, 70361 Örebro, Sweden
`carolina.appel@reba.se, asa@algulin.net`
[2] CERIS –Örebro University School of Business, Fakultetsgatan 1, 70281 Örebro, Sweden
`tanja.havstorm@oru.se`

Abstract. As the world is heading into a new era of software development (SD) an Agile Mindset (AM) has been seen to provide valuable underlying guiding elements to navigate an increasingly interconnected, turbulent, and dynamic business landscape, a VUCA-world. This study investigates the topic of agile methods and an AM through multiple-case studies with IT professionals from four tech companies. The study gathers early-stage research data to better understand what an agile SD team member does on an everyday basis in their work to exercise and achieve an AM, and what factors in the organization are impacting them in being able to do so. VUCA has been utilized as a conceptual background through which the findings – AM means and influences – have been identified, concluding that there is still much to be harnessed and learned about the elements of an AM that can improve project success outcomes.

Keywords: Agile Mindset · Agile Software Development Methods · Project success · Software Development · VUCA

1 Introduction

The field of software development (SD) is undergoing a significant transformation going from the established agile methods that revolutionized the field in the early 2000s [1] to what we now term the "infinite flow" era, often likened to the "wild west" of SD [2]. This shift marks a new phase in SD within the technology industry [3]. Previous research has identified challenges associated with adopting and using agile methodologies, commonly referred to as agile software development (ASD). The identified challenges include a lack of comprehension and rationale underlying adoption and utilization [4], as well as the presence of adverse behaviors that impede the effective application of these methods [5]. Miler and Gaida [6] studied practitioners' opinions on effective teams and the underlying elements of an Agile Mindset (AM). The elements were categorized into four areas: support for business goals, relationships within the team, individual features, and organization of work.

An AM has been seen to provide valuable underlying guiding elements to navigate an increasingly interconnected, turbulent, and dynamic business landscape, a VUCA-world [7]. AM is described through research [7] as an attitude towards 1) Learning spirit,

L. Marchesi et al. (Eds.): XP 2024 Workshops, LNBIP 524, pp. 223–228, 2025.
https://doi.org/10.1007/978-3-031-72781-8_26

2) Collaborative exchange, 3) Empowered self-guidance, and 4) Customer co-creation. These attitudes make up four dimensions that the researchers found to be central in guiding agile IT professionals' ways of thinking and acting encompassing continuous learning and openness, transparent workstyle and knowledge sharing, a high degree of freedom and responsibility, and responding to customer's changing needs [7].

On an organizational level an AM is applicable in three areas (1) Collaboration, (2) Trust, and (3) Continuous improvement [8]. This entails that all results of work to build software are a product of working intensely together, employees being entrusted to make own decisions and taking responsibility for changes and issues arising, and everyone having an open attitude towards each other and feedback [8]. VUCA, originally a military term [9], encompasses Volatility, Uncertainty, Complexity, and Ambiguity. These components characterize the dynamic market landscape that businesses must navigate for success. According to Bennett and Lemoine [10], *Volatility* signifies unstable change, *Uncertainty* involves unclear ramifications of events, *Complexity* refers to interconnected parts forming intricate networks, and *Ambiguity* denotes a lack of understanding of basic rules, making predictions challenging.

Miler and Gaida [6] captured the importance of an AM, to make a team efficient, but does not delve into what team members do to achieve such a mindset. An AM cannot be imposed; it must be grown carefully. Simply implementing ASDMs and practices implies doing agile whereas adopting the culture of values and principles of ASDMs implies being agile [11]. Against this backdrop, and as previous research [7, 11] is concluding that more studies are needed to improve our understanding of an AM, this study aims to answer two research questions: (1) What does a team member in an ASD team do to exercise and achieve an AM? and (2) What factors in the organization impact the team members' ability to exercise their AM in their work on an everyday basis? To address these research questions, this study conducts multiple-case studies with agile IT professionals to gain insight into their perspective on these matters.

2   Method

Our exploratory multiple-case study design [12] involved six in-depth interviews across four diverse tech companies, meticulously selected for a comprehensive understanding, employing snowball sampling strategy to represent various organizational sizes and sectors. Interviewees included experienced IT professionals from ASD teams, both developers and managers with at least four years of leadership experience. Participants P1 and P6 are employed at a mid-sized private company. Participants P3 and P4 work at a large public sector company. P2 is employed at another mid-sized private company, and P5, works at a small private company, details of the participants are presented in Table 1. Data was collected through semi-structured interviews, guided by an interview protocol [13], aiming to uncover insights into participants' attitudes and behaviors within ASD teams daily work environments. The questions asked were framed based on the values outlined in the Agile Manifesto [14] capturing the participants' working contexts, professional experience and which ASDMs they adopted or had developed in their teams and organizations.

Table 1. Details of study participants.

Participant No.	Role description	Year of experience	Organizational size	Sector
P1	Developer in agile teams	>1	Mid	Private
P2	Manager and Agile leader	>7	Mid	Private
P3	Developer in agile teams	>1	Large	Public
P4	Manager and Agile leader	>5	Large	Public
P5	Manager and Developer in agile teams	>7	Small	Private
P6	Manager and Agile leader	>15	Mid	Private

The interpretative research approach [15] facilitated a nuanced exploration, enabling rich and in-depth data collection. Thematic analysis [16] of transcribed interviews identified emergent themes within the dataset, systematically examined in relation to the VUCA framework, illuminating the interplay between team members' AM and the challenges presented by the VUCA components. The emergent themes for the analytic insights came through the six following steps: (1) repeated listening through the transcribed interviews for familiarization, (2) generating initial codes through labeling relevant information, (3) searching for themes, then (4) reviewing themes to refine codes and compound subcategories, (5) defining and naming themes, and lastly (6) writing the report constructing a coherent narrative and presenting the findings. An example of an emerging theme is *Leadership and organizational support* having emerged from the participants responses entailing descriptions that would fall under the following definition: Organizational design and structure allowing the individual team member being flexible and taking on new assignments or roles as the understanding of needs evolve and change, as well as fostering a psychological safe culture in the workplace and within teams.

3   Result

Following our thematic analysis, the study unveiled nine key findings concerning the elements of an AM, covering both its means and influences. These findings directly address our two research questions: Means correspond to research question 1, while Influences pertain to research question 2. Table 2 below provides a comprehensive summary of each thematic element (Means M1-M4 and Influences I5-I9) and their interconnectedness with the VUCA framework. The following text elaborates on the answers to the two research questions.

3.1   What Does a Team Member in an ASD Team Do to Exercise and Achieve an AM?

The study identified four focus areas, i.e., means, (M1-M4 in Table 2) that ASD team does to exercise and achieve an AM. Aligned with expectations the respondents name

Table 2. Overview with identified AM means and influences and relation to VUCA.

Element	Theme No.	Description	V	U	C	A
Means	M1	Customer relationship focus	X	X	X	X
	M2	User centricity		X	X	
	M3	Interdependence within team	X	X	X	X
	M4	Problem-solving orientation	X	X	X	X
Influences	I5	Leadership and organizational support	X	X	X	X
	I6	Development of agile ways of working	X	X	X	X
	I7	Providing spaces	X	X	X	
	I8	Deadlines and sprinting		X	X	
	I9	Non-agile or non-technical user/customer	X		X	X

customers (M1) *Customer relationship focus* and users to be in the center (M2) *User centricity* of what guides their activities and how they build software. For example: *"I was treated as if I was one of the customer's own employees, which was positive for me. I had two workplaces I could go and work at."* [P1] and *"I am driven to work by delivering value, as many of us are, and I would say that the agile way of working allows us to deliver value much faster […] I would say that I would experience my productivity so much worse if I didn't have this continuous release procedure and the feedback loop from the users."* [P4]. Respondents acknowledge that being **interdependent in their teams** (M3) and having a **problem-solving approach** (M4) to work they do not yet know how to solve is of key importance. For example: *"[…]after all, it is a "we" and not an "I". We are a team, we choose our activities together. We choose what we think we can do during this sprint."* [P3] and *"[…] to have the mandate to decide when, where and how I should build something and starting in that order which is technically logical, perhaps not from a user perspective, but to be able to make such decisions, it is important to me."* [P2].

3.2 What Factors in the Organization Impact the Team Members' Ability to Exercise Their AM in Their Work on an Everyday Basis?

The study identified five organizational factors that influence (I5-I9 in Table 2) the team member's ability to exercise their AM on an everyday basis. First is **Leadership and organizational support** (I5), and to being **Provided spaces** (I7) to work collaboratively and speak up being factors that help in coping with demanding and strenuous situations. For example: *"We also talk a lot at the company about providing psychological safety and feedback. To constantly focus on being able to deliver value"* [P6] and *"We'd have meetings from time to time where we discussed how we wanted to work and coordinate"* [P1]. Arbitrary and **Manufactured deadlines** (I8) can increase pressure and stress as well as the lack of understanding of the complexity of SD by a **non-agile or non-technical user/customer** (I9). For example: *"I'm probably not doing it in the best way [working outside of office hours if not being able to meet a deadline]. I have often solved it in* *the evening to catch up. And it's not really like that, or not really, it's absolutely not the way I want my team to work" [P2]* and *"Our work is extraordinarily collaborative, and we're constantly pulling each other into different tasks and different projects to say: I need your opinion, what do you think about this? How have you done this in the past? [...] What's the best way to approach this problem? And I've found in the past that trying to engage non-technical teams in that same process has been difficult. [...] What we actually really would prefer is a collaborative approach to product development to designing all these different aspects together that go into building technology" [P5].*

Also emerging through the analysis are teams' development of tailored **agile ways of working** (I6). A team's development of their own agile ways of working is indicated to depend on the knowledge, maturity, and perspective of what is deemed to fit the specific organization, team, and customer/user needs. Although the values and principles of the Agile Manifesto [14] guided all respondents, they did not express unwavering loyalty to the agile practices and frameworks, and importantly as well as contrary to expectations, would still consider themselves working in an agile way even if/when not following a practice to the letter. For example: *"There are actually different phases one can be in in one's agile way of thinking. When you understand the agile rules, you can start to break them a little. You understand the idea and purpose behind them and then you can start to create your own agile ways of working a little bit. And we push a lot for it. Thanks to my boss, I think we have come a long way. We have worked with so many clients over many years to develop this." [P2].*

Within the results we can see prominent patterns. Table 2 shows that VUCA components are prominent in five out of nine thematic AM elements, indicating a clear application of AM in relation to VUCA. In the remaining four elements, at least two VUCA components are prevalent. This highlights the practical relevance of VUCA in understanding AM, mitigating its theoretical nature. The interaction between AM and VUCA enhances stakeholder resilience and value delivery in software development.

4 Discussion and Conclusion

In today's VUCA-world with businesses working on all angles to maximize their efficiency, it is crucial to explore the mindsets and contexts enabling effective software delivery. A well-developed AM has potential to positively affect SD project success and should therefore not be overlooked. The study builds on the existing body of research in the agile field [7–11, 14] as well as of an AM in relation to the VUCA framework [7]. Connecting what research says and what business does has been of the utmost interest throughout the study and for its future, with the components of VUCA serving as a valuable lens, adding to what previous research has begun to examine [7, 10]. The findings could help organizations better harness ASD team members' performance by improving their understanding of the elements of an AM, how it can be applied in their everyday work, and to study how the deliberate application of it over time can evolve ASD teams' ways of working in a turbulent business landscape. We suggest future research to validate these findings in various contexts and explore when doing agile fails to achieve true agility, as previous studies emphasize the importance of being agile rather than just doing agile [5, 8], as doing agile should not counteract being agile. This study underscores the importance of understanding and effectively using AM elements in ASD teams. The community should retain insights from ASDMs and grasp organizational factors impacting valuable software delivery through agile ways of working.

References

1. Cram, W.A.: Agile development in practice: lessons from the trenches. Inf. Syst. Manag. **36**, 14–22 (2019)
2. Standish Group, CHAOS Report: Beyond Infinity (2020)
3. Digital.ai, 17th Annual State of Agile Report (2023)
4. Havstorm, T.E., Karlsson, F.: Software developers reasoning behind adoption and use of software development methods–a systematic literature review. Int. J. Inf. Syst. Proj. Manag. **11**(2), 47–78 (2023)
5. Havstorm, T.E.: Cargo Cult in Agile Software Development. Örebro University, Örebro (2023)
6. Miler, J., Gaida., P.: On the Agile Mindset of an Effective Team - An Industrial Opinion Survey. 2019. Polish Information Processing Society -- as since 2011
7. Eilers, K., Peters, C., Leimeister, J.M.: Why agile mindset matters. Technol. Forecast. Soc. Chang. **179**, 121650 (2022)
8. van Manen, H., van Vliet, H.: Organization-Wide Agile Expansion Requires an Organization-Wide Agile Mindset. 2014, Springer International Publishing: Cham. pp. 48–62
9. Baran, B.E., Woznyj, H.M.: Managing VUCA: the human dynamics of agility. Organ. Dyn. **50**(2), 100787 (2021)
10. Bennett, N., Lemoine, G.J.: What a difference a word makes: understanding threats to performance in a VUCA world. Bus. Horiz. **57**(3), 311–317 (2014)
11. Klünder, J., Trommer, F., Prenner, N.: How agile coaches create an agile mindset in development teams: insights from an interview study. J. Softw.: Evol. Process **34**(12): p. n/a (2022)
12. Yin, R.K.: Case Study Research: Design and Methods. SAGE (2009)
13. Kvale, S., Brinkmann, S.: InterViews: Learning the Craft of Qualitative Research Interviewing. Sage Publications, Los Angeles (2009)
14. Beck, K., et al.: The Agile Manifesto (2001). https://agilemanifesto.org/
15. Walsham, G.: Doing interpretive research. Eur. J. Inf. Syst. **15**, 320–330 (2006)
16. Braun, V., Clarke, V.: Using thematic analysis in psychology. Qual. Res. Psychol. **3**(2), 77–101 (2006)

The Right Amount of Technical Debt in an Agile Context

Marcus Ciolkowski[1]([✉]) [iD], Philipp Diebold[2,3] [iD], Andrea Janes[4] [iD],
and Valentina Lenarduzzi[5] [iD]

[1] QAware GmbH, Munich, Germany
marcus.ciolkowski@qaware.de
[2] IU International University, Erfurt, Germany
philipp.diebold@iu.org
[3] Bagilstein GmbH, Mainz, Germany
philipp.diebold@bagilstein.de
[4] Free University of Bozen-Bolzano, Bolzano, Italy
ajanes@unibz.it
[5] University of Oulu, Oulu, Finland
valentina.lenarduzzi@oulu.fi

Abstract. Agile and technical debt management should have a symbiotic relationship, as technical debt was conceived as a metaphor (or tool) to balance the benefits of taking shortcuts for early release and user feedback with the responsibility of 'repairing' the effects of these trade-offs. Agile processes provide the necessary flexibility to achieve this balance. However, in reality, feature greed often takes over, making it difficult for development teams to ensure that technical debt is repaid. This paper discusses experiences and best practices to address Technical Debt in an Agile context.

Keywords: Agile · Technical Debt · Risk Management

1 Introduction

In the dynamic world of software development, Agile methodologies have become the common approach for most projects. However, this very emphasis on rapid delivery and customer satisfaction often raises an intriguing paradox: on one hand, Agility values immediate functionality over long-term code quality; this inherently encourages the accrual of Technical Debt (TD) (often called "featuritis") and can lead to a precarious buildup of maintenance challenges and future hurdles. On the other hand, the iterative nature of Agility offers an ideal setting for addressing and mitigating TD, presenting opportunities for continuous refinement and improvement.

This position paper seeks to start discussing the complexities at the intersection of TD accumulation and Agile methodology's capacity for debt resolution. We aim to initiate an exchange that sets the stage for an in-depth research agenda. This will lead to an insightful perspective on determining the optimal

© The Author(s) 2025
L. Marchesi et al. (Eds.): XP 2024 Workshops, LNBIP 524, pp. 229–235, 2025.
https://doi.org/10.1007/978-3-031-72781-8_27

amount of TD for each unique Agile project setting. Recognizing that agility is not a one-size-fits-all solution, we argue that the appropriate balance of TD is intricately linked to the specific Agile practices tailored to the needs of individual companies or projects.

Through this exploration, we aim to contribute a foundational perspective to the ongoing debate, proposing that the future of Agile project success lies in the strategic navigation of TD, tailored to the unique Agile context of each project.

2   Related Work

TD is a well-known metaphor in software engineering that emphasizes the importance of continuous refactoring in iterative development to increase long-term project speed. The metaphor compares TD to borrowing money, where immediate programming with partial comprehension allows for faster code delivery and user feedback. However, like any debt, failure to repay one or more installments can lead to project bankruptcy. TD interest affects maintainability and various software qualities, resulting in increased costs. Cunningham in 1992 [6] suggests refactoring to repay TD by incorporating gained knowledge. The concept has been both narrowed and broadened over time, encompassing deficits in internal quality. Fowler [8] expands TD to deliberate or inadvertent, prudent or reckless actions. The definition has further evolved to include any disliked code, fostering discussions about software quality. Researchers began investigating TD in the early 2000s, with a surge in studies from 2010 to 2015, categorizing and conceptualizing TD. Code debt is the most studied TD type, focusing on issues like code smells and financial aspects. Commercial tools, such as SonarQube, have been developed to identify and estimate TD, contributing to its widespread adoption in the industry [5,11]. The industry quickly adopted the TD metaphor, aligning with Agile concepts, practices, and frameworks that emphasize software quality and continuous refactoring.

In the Agile context, TD holds significant economic and technical implications drawing increased attention from academia and industry. Behutiye et al. [12] identified five key research areas in the context of Agile: managing TD, architecture's relationship with TD, TD know-how in Agile teams, TD in distributed Agile, and TD in rapid fielding development. According to their results, TD in Agile is the consequence of poor software development practices, citing quick delivery and architecture/design issues as frequent causes. Another important aspect that can increase TD is related to the insufficient understanding of system requirements and inadequate test coverage. As for the other development processes [11] the possible negative effects of TD in Agile Software Development can be summarized in reduced productivity, system degradation, or increased maintenance costs.

3   Difficulties in the Combination

Technical Debt (TD) is a concept that has garnered considerable attention within the software engineering community, notably due to its profound implications on project agility and overall management. The term was originally coined by Cunningham in 1992, highlighting a peculiar aspect of Agile development processes: the tendency to initiate development with an incomplete understanding of the problem at hand [6]. This approach, while accelerating the delivery of working code, inherently incurs what is metaphorically referred to as "technical debt"[7].

Cunningham introduced the metaphor of TD to articulate to his managers the necessity of continuous refactoring, especially within the Agile framework that prioritizes iterative development over traditional, waterfall methodologies. The benefit facilitated by such an approach mirrors financial borrowing, where immediate progress is made possible by leveraging a yet-to-be-fully-comprehended problem space. This strategy enables faster delivery of working code, allowing for user feedback to more precisely align with user needs. Nevertheless, akin to financial debt, the accumulation of TD without periodic repayment can severely hamper a project, potentially to the point of "bankruptcy" when the cost of new features and maintenance overshadows the allocated budget [1].

Agile methodologies offer a framework that inherently supports the management of TD through practices such as regular backlog grooming and planning sessions. These practices are designed to ensure that TD is acknowledged and addressed continually, preventing it from spiraling out of control.

Despite the theoretical advantages of Agile methodologies in managing TD, the practical application often reveals a different scenario. The urgency to introduce new features frequently supersedes the inclination to address accumulated debt. This preference is understandable when considering the pressures exerted by project stakeholders, such as deadlines, milestones, and customer demands, which provide a tangible rationale for prioritizing feature development or enhancement.

Conversely, the decision to allocate a budget towards the resolution of technical debt is fraught with ambiguity. Often, debt quantification (both in terms of principal and interest) remains elusive, making it challenging to justify expenditure in this area. The "interest" in TD can manifest in various forms, including increased costs for feature development due to reduced maintainability, higher operational expenses, and usability issues that may deter users or increase their task completion time [5]. The crux of the issue lies in determining the financial impact of a specific debt item: how much does it cost if left unaddressed, and conversely, what savings can be realized upon its resolution?

In conclusion, while Agile methodologies provide a structured approach to managing TD, the practical challenges of quantifying and prioritizing debt repayment necessitate a nuanced understanding and strategy. The balance between advancing feature development and mitigating technical debt is a delicate one, requiring careful consideration to ensure the sustainable progress of software projects.

4 How to Solve That

Balancing is not new but still needed [3]. Here, we talk about balancing features against the payback of debt items. However, the ability to balance requires information about both sides (here, features and debt)

Peter Drucker is often quoted as saying, "You can't manage what you can't measure." In the context of this paper, finding ways to measure technical debt and so to increase its visibility is critical for being able to manage it. To be able to measure TD, previous authors have decomposed it into the classical elements of a loan: principal, the original sum of money borrowed, and interest, the cost of borrowing the principal amount, which is charged by the lender. When paying back a debt, part of each payment goes toward reducing the principal, and part goes toward paying the interest. In terms of code, the principal represents the initial deficiency in the code requiring future correction and the interest in the costs of reduced productivity, system degradation, or increased maintenance costs.

So the question is: How can we make the interest (or hidden cost) of debt items more tangible? That is, how can a team support their product owner to understand and better grasp the consequences of delaying paying back debt? A popular way to measure debt is to use tools that identify, based on previously defined rules, violations that indicate issues that need to be resolved. Using such tools it is difficult to understand whether the identified violation is due to the principal or due to the interest, i.e., because of a shortcut that was taken years ago, today e.g., redundant code is needed.

Another approach is to identify implementation delays, risks, or product (in)stability [2]. This can occur by studying records from issue tracking systems, e.g., to identify tasks that took longer than estimated or to identify recurring problems. Another approach is to analyze the logs of source code management systems like git to identify components that need to be repeatedly fixed. There are two challenges in this approach: first, it is difficult to identify a baseline: it is difficult to understand that something took *longer* than it should. One possible approach to address this challenge is to compare similar user stories or projects to understand that there *are* delays or to use retrospectives to discuss if debt was slowing down past activities.

The second issue in trying to measure TD based on records is that it might be confused with *waste* (in the context of Lean Manufacturing and Lean Software Development [9]): In Lean software development, "waste" refers to any activities or processes that consume resources but do not add value to the customer. Typically, the consideration that is made is as in Fig. 1: one starts identifying all activities that are consuming resources (the inner circle "All activities"). Then, these activities are divided into value-adding (the green part in Fig. 1) and non-value-adding (the yellow part in Fig. 1). Finally, the non-value-adding activities are further divided into necessary (the red part in Fig. 1) and not necessary (the gray part in Fig. 1). An example of necessary, non-value-adding (for the client) activities is "accounting" or "project management". These activities are necessary but the customer does not care how we keep costs under control using accounting.

However, TD and waste manifest themselves in the same way: productivity is low because time is *wasted* in activities that do not provide value, the system is degraded and this leads to a visible *waste of time* when extending it, maintenance costs are high because one has to *waste a lot of time* understanding it when making changes. It is, therefore, necessary to understand if observed problems are because of *debt* (in this case it is necessary to repay the debt) or because of *waste*, in this case, it is necessary to remove (when not necessary) or minimize (when necessary) it.

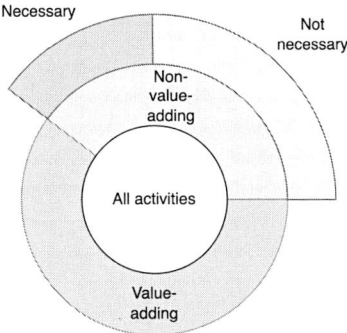

Fig. 1. Division of activities into value-adding, non-value-adding, necessary and not necessary (adapted from [9]).

A last consideration that we want to make is to consider the evolution of TD. The laws of software evolution by Meir Lehman [10] predict that software systems that perform some real-world activity are constantly under pressure for change or become progressively less satisfactory. On one hand, this is the source of the issues with TD: without that pressure, modifications would not be that necessary and debt would be less of an issue; without that pressure, it would not be necessary to constantly add features leading to the mentioned "featuritis".

However, this pressure also includes a possibility: as software is evolving, new necessary features are added but there are also old, not-anymore-needed features that could be removed. Unfortunately, this is not happening (this antipattern is called the lava flow antipattern [4]) because deleting features that have cost a lot of work and time seems counter-intuitive but one has to consider that unused features represent *waste*: they do not add value to the client but cost resources. From a Lean and Agile perspective they should be removed or at least moved to an external application/code base where the obsolete code can be used only in case of need. By removing unnecessary functionality, the code base becomes smaller, refactoring becomes simpler, and paying back debt (if it was not removed already with the unnecessary code) becomes cheaper. In this context, *agility* (in the sense of being able to adapt the code to what is adding value and to remove what is not adding value) reduces the burden of paying back TD and—as a consequence—lowers the impact of TD when it is necessary to make debt. We see it therefore as a requirement to continuously measure how features are used, also after delivery, to understand how features are used, when they are used, or if it is time to remove them.

5 Conclusion

In the future, the rules of the game may change, as the way that systems are developed. With AI coming into play, if a whole system can be generated by AI, the definition and perception of debt will change: in such a scenario the development speed and agility increase. However, generating millions of lines of code using AI that cannot be maintained is not a solution. Using AI itself might be seen as TD if adapting AI-generated code to changed expectations will cost more time than for hand-written code. Here, too, it will be necessary to strike a balance between generated code and handwritten code to keep TD under control.

References

1. Ampatzoglou, A., Ampatzoglou, A., Avgeriou, P., Chatzigeorgiou, A.: A financial approach for managing interest in technical debt. In: Shishkov, B. (ed.) Business Modeling and Software Design, vol. 257, pp. 117–133. Springer, Cham (2016)
2. Avgeriou, P., et al.: Technical debt management: the road ahead for successful software delivery. In: 2023 IEEE/ACM International Conference on Software Engineering: Future of Software Engineering (ICSE-FoSE), pp. 15–30. IEEE, Melbourne, Australia (2023)
3. Boehm, Turner, R.: Balancing Agility and Discipline: A Guide for the Perplexed. Addison-Wesley Longman Publishing Co., Inc., Boston (2003)
4. Brown, W., Malveau, R., McCormick, H., Mowbray, T., Thomas, S.W.: Lava Flow (2017). http://antipatterns.com/lavaflow.htm. Accessed 26 June 2024
5. Ciolkowski, M., Lenarduzzi, V., Martini, A.: 10 years of technical debt research and practice: past, present, and future. IEEE Softw. **38**(06), 24–29 (2021)
6. Cunningham, W.: The WyCash portfolio management system. In: Addendum to the Proceedings on Object-oriented Programming Systems. Languages, and Applications (Addendum) - OOPSLA 1992, pp. 29–30. ACM Press, Vancouver (1992)
7. Fairbanks, G.: Ur-Technical Debt. IEEE Softw. **37**(4), 95–98 (2020)
8. Fowler, M.: Technical Debt (2019). https://www.martinfowler.com/bliki/TechnicalDebt.html. Accessed 26 June 2024
9. Janes, A., Succi, G.: Lean Software Development in Action. Springer, Heidelberg (2014)
10. Lehman, M.M.: Laws of software evolution revisited. In: Montangero, C. (ed.) Software Process Technology, Lecture Notes in Computer Science, vol. 1149, chap. 12, pp. 108–124. Springer, Heidelberg (1996). https://doi.org/10.1007/bfb0017737
11. Lenarduzzi, V., Besker, T., Taibi, D., Martini, A., Arcelli Fontana, F.: A systematic literature review on technical debt prioritization: strategies, processes, factors, and tools. J. Syst. Softw. **171**, 110827 (2021)
12. Nema Behutiye, W., Rodriguez, P., Oivo, M., Tosun, A.: Analyzing the concept of technical debt in the context of agile software development: a systematic literature review. arXiv e-prints arXiv:2401.14882 (2024)

Stories Vs. User Stories: A Terminological Clarification

Xavier Franch[1]([⊠]) [iD], Hans-Jörg Steffe[2], Stan Bühne[3], Lidia López[1] [iD],
and Stefan Sturm[3]

[1] Universitat Politècnica de Catalunya, c/Jordi Girona 1-3, Barcelona 08034, Catalonia, Spain
{xavier.franch,lidia.lopez}@upc.edu
[2] solvistas.com, Linz, Austria
hans-joerg.steffe@outlook.at
[3] International Requirements Engineering Board (IREB) e.v., Karlsruhe, Germany
{Stan.Buehne,Stefan.Sturm}@ireb.org

Abstract. User stories are the main vehicle to describe user needs in Agile projects and Agile project developments. But being this concept universally agreed, we may find that not all work increments have a clear user-centric view. In this paper, we focus on the distinction between user-centric "user stories" and other type of simple narratives, which may be simply called "stories", which can be at the same level of abstraction. We propose a conceptual model in the form of UML diagram, and associated definitions, to clarify this distinction. The model also makes clearer the distinction among (user) story and (user) story template, which is not always kept clear.

Keywords: User Story · Story · Template · Agile methodologies

1 Motivation

User stories lie at the heart of Agile methodologies. They were first introduced at the end of the 90s and were quickly adopted by the upgrowing Agile community, mainly because they are an excellent means for Product Owners to communicate requirements to all stakeholders and developers.

Originally, user stories were conceived as an instrument to express value, as recognized in the IREB glossary: "A description of a need from a user's perspective together with the expected benefit when this need is satisfied" [2]. But on the other side, user stories have been also considered basic management units in Agile projects. For instance, in their glossary, the Agile Alliance states: "In consultation with the customer or product owner, the team divides up the work to be done into functional increments called "user stories".[1]

On the other hand, in spite of the Agile Alliance clearly distinguishing them, we can regularly see some confusion on the concept of the user story with the template used

---

[1] https://www.agilealliance.org/agile101/agile-glossary/.

© The Author(s) 2025
L. Marchesi et al. (Eds.): XP 2024 Workshops, LNBIP 524, pp. 236–241, 2025.
https://doi.org/10.1007/978-3-031-72781-8_28

to write them, typically the "role-feature-reason" originally proposed at Connextra and popularized by Mike Cohn in his seminal book *User Stories Applied: For Agile Software Development* [1] using the keywords "As a- I want to-so that…".

Last but not least, as its name clearly denotes, user stories put the user in the center, i.e. they are user-centric. However, there are certain types of tasks that are difficult to justify from a user perspective, but still needed in order to progress in the project. Lately, we are witnessing how some methodologies and tool providers are recognizing this fact. For instance, the SAFe methodology[2] uses the term Story and distinguishes between User Stories and Enabler Stories, which are stories that "bring visibility to the work items needed to support exploration, architecture, infrastructure, and compliance".

While these ambiguities and contradictions will probably not jeopardize the success of any Agile project, it is also true that it may create some confusion in several contexts, especially related to training. In particular, at the International Requirements Engineering Board (IREB), we have experienced the pernicious effects of this ambiguity both at the level of writing material and provide training to Agile certification candidates.

2 Understanding the Problem

In order to get more insights about this perception, we contacted a number of IREB training providers for the Agile certification. We sent them a short description of the problem and then we asked them whether they find the term "User Story" ambiguous (awareness), to what extent this possible ambiguity affects their training (impact), and what solution do they propose (action). We obtained 10 responses that we summarize below.

- **Awareness**. A slight majority of respondents (6) agreed that the term "User Story" is ambiguous, e.g. "On the one hand user story as a phrase and on the other hand user story as a small backlog item that fits into a sprint". The rest "have never noticed any discussion or problem on this topic".
- **Impact**. From these 6 respondents, most (4) don't experience any problem in their daily business ("Yes, the term is sometimes used differently in practice, but I've never really had any problems with misunderstandings"). Still, the others experienced that "the teams constantly had heated discussions about what they each meant by the terms", and therefore they "have to explain this difference in the training sessions and make it clear which meaning we are talking about".
- **Action**. Here we find even more diversity. Reported actions are:

  - Introducing variants of the term "user story", such as "story" as generic terms, or other subtypes of stories such as "development story" for requirements of technical nature.
  - Adhere to the well-known generic term "backlog item" and then consider a "user story" as a particular type of backlog item.
  - Slightly different than above, leaving the term "user story" as a concept for writing requirements in Agile, but use "backlog item" when it comes to documentation.

---

[2] story/https://scaledagileframework.com/

– Clearly distinguish a user story from the template used to write it ("I think it's a bit of a shame that the term user story is often reduced to the template").

Some respondents mentioned additional nuances or threats:

- Context matters: "the meaning of the term user story almost always results from the context in which you are currently discussing or using the term", meaning that each organization or team may have their own vocabulary.
- A respondent highlighted that "The confusion of terms is even worse with the terms epic, theme, feature, etc.", questioning that we focus on this term only.
- When different terms are considered, we need to be careful because "replacing the term user story would definitely mean moving even further away from a standardized terminology".
- Finally, as yet another respondent commented, "The big tool manufacturers and the people from SAFe have put their own interpretations of the term user story into the world, and thus also contributed a little to the blurring of the term".

3   Proposal

In this section, we present a conceptual model emerging from the insights of the preliminary study reported in Sect. 2. It is expressed in the form of a UML class diagram. We can see that a `Backlog` (of any type; details not needed in this paper) is composed of a number of `Backlog Items`. For simplicity, we are showing only two types of `Backlog Items`: `Epics` to represent high-level concepts, and `Stories` as proposed in this paper. Other concepts, such as features and themes, could be integrated into this hierarchy without impacting the core of our proposal (in fact, we remark that the specialization hierarchy, as others in the model, is qualified as "incomplete"). Besides, we are leaving tasks out of the picture since they are on a lower abstraction level and do not affect the current discussion.

Using Atlassian's words, we can define a `Story` as "one simple narrative".[3] It is not only their granularity what defines them; from a managerial perspective, `Stories` are the fundamental unit from a project management perspective: they are estimated through `storyPoints`, they have `priority`, and when moved to the sprint backlog, they progress through a sequence of `states`.[4] We recognize several types of `Stories` such as `Constraints` (a classical concept in requirements engineering [2] and also proposed to be added to the Agile world by Newkirk and Martin [3]), `Qualities` (modeling the quasi-synonymous terms of quality attribute, quality requirement and non-functional requirement) and then `User Stories`, which can be defined as user-centric stories or more precisely, "functionality that will be valuable to either a user or purchaser of a system or software" [1].

---

[3] https://www.atlassian.com/agile/project-management/epics-stories-themes.

[4] The types of these attributes are left open, since they may vary from project to project, and their value does not affect our proposal.

`Backlog Items` are described following one particular `Template`. Nothing prevents different `Backlog Items` in the same `Backlog` adhering to different `Templates`, even being `Backlog Items` of the same type. The least restrictive `Template` is using just a plain `Natural Language Sentence` to describe the `Backlog Item`, but many others may be proposed. One of them is the `Connextra Template`, including exactly one `Role`, one `Goal` and one `Rationale`.[5] `Connextra Template` can be used for any type of `Backlog Item`, although given the motivation of the work, it can be expected that it will be rarely used for `Stories` that are not `User Stories` (Fig. 1).

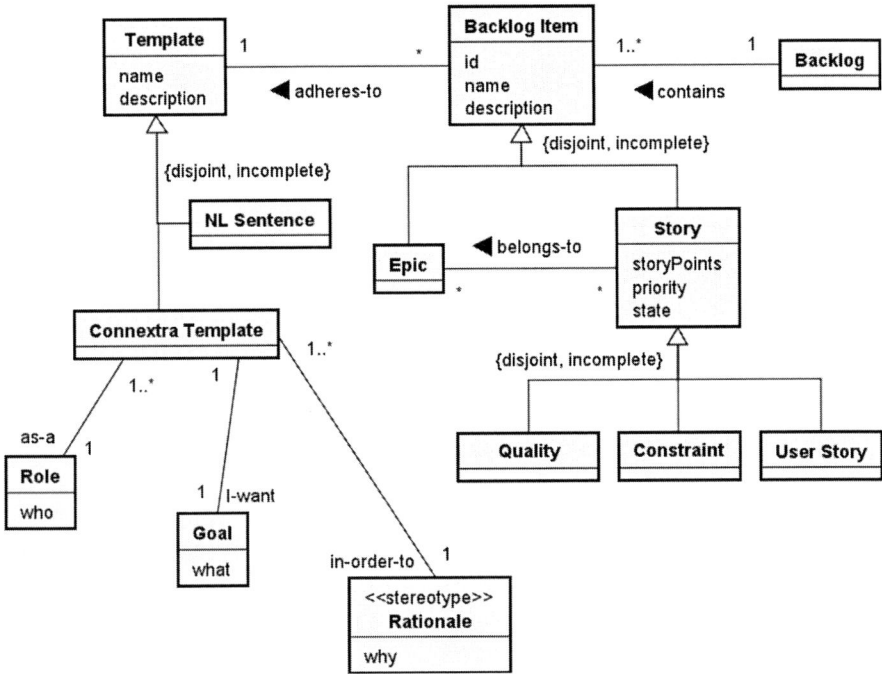

Fig. 1. A conceptual model in the form of class diagram for backlog items and templates.

This conceptual model is then fulfilling a number of competence questions driving this research:

- It introduces the concept of "story" as a simple narrative, being the unit of interest in terms of estimation and prioritization.
- It recognizes the existence of different types of stories, being user stories one of them.
- It decouples the backlog items' semantics from their syntax, which can be expressed using different templates.
- It introduces Connextra template ("as a … I want … in order to …") as one of these formats, but others are possible.

---

[5] Some authors such as Cohn [1] allow User Stories without Rationale. The impact of such change is limited to the multiplicity in the in-order-to role of the class diagram.

- It allows using Connextra template (as any other template) in any type of backlog item.
- It can be extended to host new types of backlog items, stories and templates.
- It can be integrated with the rest of fundamental concepts involved in backlogs and their items, such as tasks, acceptance criteria or backlog types.

We interacted with participants in the 25th International Conference on Agile Software Development (XP 2024)[6] using questionnaires to be responded after the presentation of our poster in the conference, in order to get some preliminary evaluation of our proposal. On the one hand, they provided feedback aligning well with the responses gathered from IREB training providers as reported above, concretely three out of the 7 respondents consider the term "user story" ambiguous. Only one of them declares that this ambiguity causes some problems during their Agile projects. On the other hand, we asked them about the nature of the items in the backlog. Responses were:

- All respondents except one disagreed (five of them strongly) on the statement all the backlog items are user stories.
- We found a divide on the response to our main terminological proposal. To the question "the generic term 'story' could be used to embrace several kinds of backlog items", four respondents partially agreed while three of them completely disagreed.

Last, we wanted to know current practices and possible future directions on the use of templates for user stories (or backlog items in general). At this respect, we learned from our respondents the following:

- Only two of the respondents agreed that all backlog items should be expressed using a concrete template (one of them only partially agreed).
- We got diverse positions regarding the use of the Connextra template. While the two respondents arguing above for using templates, are regular users of the Connextra template always, the rest of respondents disagreed except for one who didn't express any direction.

4   Conclusions

In this paper, we have reflected on the ambiguity of the term "user story" in the Agile development context, and proposed a conceptual model that eventually can be used as reference for Agile development teams. The main message is the need to clearly distinguish different types of "stories", being "user stories" only one of those types. We think that this reference model is necessary because even main players in the Agile world use these terms in a non-consistent way. When talking about stories, Atlassian documentation states "Stories, also called "user stories," are short requirements or requests written from the perspective of an end user" (see footnote 3). At its turn, SAFe defines "stories" as "short descriptions of a small piece of desired functionality written from the user's perspective". These fundamental contradictions are solved by our approach.

We contacted a number of IREB training providers for the Agile certification to have a better understanding of the problem. We collected some insights referent whether

---

[6] https://www.agilealliance.org/xp2024/.

they find the term "User Story" ambiguous (awareness), to what extent this possible ambiguity affects their training (impact), and what solution do they propose (action). Most of them agreed that the term "User Story" is ambiguous, the majority of them don't experience any problem in their daily business. We find more diversity related to the actions to be taken, like using the variants "story" or "backlog item".

We plan to present this proposal in different fora, mainly using the IREB practitioners' network, with particular emphasis on Agile Training Providers recognized by the organization, in order to assess for its adequacy and therefore decide about its adoption in the different Agile-related certification programs proposed by IREB. Also, we would like to enlarge the study embracing other type of backlog items (epics, features, …) and concepts, remarkably quality requirements which are always challenging to represent in the backlog [4].

Acknowledgments. The authors want to acknowledge the effort from the Agile Working Group at IREB.

Disclosure of Interests.   The authors have no competing interests to declare that are relevant to the content of this article.

References

1. Cohn, M.: User Stories Applied: For Agile Software Development. Addison-Wesley (2004)
2. Glinz, M.: Certified Professional for Requirements Engineering: Requirements Engineering Glossary, v. 2.1.0 (2024). https://www.ireb.org/content/downloads/1-cpre-glossary/ireb_cpre_glossary_en_2.1.pdf
3. Newkirk, J., Martin, R.C: Extreme Programming in Practice. Addison-Wesley (2001)
4. , Behutiye, W., Karhapää, P., Costal, C., Oivo, M., Franch, X.: Non-functional requirements documentation in agile software development: challenges and solution proposal. PROFES 515–522 (2017)

LD@Taiga: An Embedded Learning Dashboard for Agile Project Management in Student Teams

Carles Farré[✉] ⓘ, Lidia López ⓘ, Marc Oriol ⓘ, and Xavier Franch ⓘ

Universitat Politècnica de Catalunya, c/Jordi Girona 1-3, Barcelona 08034, Catalonia, Spain
{carles.farre,lidia.lopez,marc.oriol,xavier.franch}@upc.edu

Abstract. We present LD@Taiga, a learning dashboard seamlessly integrated into the Taiga agile project management tool. LD@Taiga provides visualizations of individual and team performance metrics, offering students valuable feedback and aiding their decision-making. A preliminary evaluation revealed enhanced usability compared to a previous version, although there is still room for improvement.

Keywords: Learning Dashboard · Agile Project Management · Agile Project Metrics

1 Introduction

Team-based software development projects serve students as a practical setting to learn about teamwork and project management in near-to real-world scenarios. However, students' experiences may not always align with their expectations, e.g. having to manage uneven contributions from team members, with some team members contributing the bulk of the work [1]. To bridge this gap, we have explored the potential of learning dashboards to assist student teams in software engineering courses [2]. Learning dashboards are visual tools specifically designed to support students and instructors in their learning and teaching activities [3].

In this paper, we introduce our experience with LD@Taiga, a novel tool designed to enhance the dynamics of students' teamwork in agile development projects. Building upon our initial Learning Dashboard (LD) [2], LD@Taiga seamlessly integrates into Taiga's project management tool, thereby facilitating a more intuitive and cohesive workflow for student teams.

The rest of this paper is organized as follows. Section 2 provides the context and background for the development and implementation of LD@Taiga, detailing its predecessor LD, and the initial feedback gathered from its use. Section 3 describes the architecture and implementation of LD@Taiga, including its integration with Taiga and the enhancements made based on previous feedback. This section also presents a preliminary evaluation of LD@Taiga, analyzing usability scores and user feedback. Finally, Sect. 4 concludes the paper with a summary of findings and outlines potential directions for future work, including planned improvements and broader integration strategies.

© The Author(s) 2025
L. Marchesi et al. (Eds.): XP 2024 Workshops, LNBIP 524, pp. 242–248, 2025.
https://doi.org/10.1007/978-3-031-72781-8_29

2   Context

In the 2021/2022 academic year, the Learning Dashboard (LD) [2] was introduced in two subjects: Web Applications and Services (WAS) and Software Engineering Project (SEP). These courses are part of the Bachelor's degree in Informatics Engineering at the Faculty of Informatics of Barcelona, Universitat Politècnica de Catalunya (UPC). The aim was to provide student teams and teachers with a tool that delivers accurate and timely feedback to monitor project progress and support task prioritization and planning. LD is an adaptation of another dashboard, the Q-Rapids Dashboard [4], to the teaching context. To this end, LD integrates data from two software development tools that student teams use: Taiga, a project management tool, and GitHub, a well-known code repository management tool. Different metrics, such as the percentage of tasks completed by each team member, are calculated from these data sources to provide a global view and assessment of the project. LD's user interface is a web application that shows these metrics' current state and historical evolution. A screenshot of the LD's user interface is provided in Fig. 1.

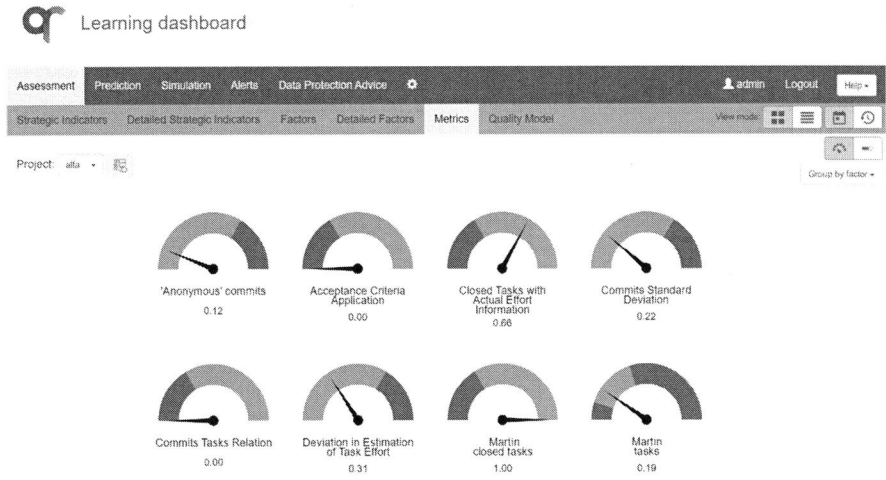

Fig. 1.   Screenshot of the LD

Access to LD was given to roughly half of the teams to have a control group. The feedback they provided through questionnaires and interviews can be summarized as follows [2, 5]:

- Students infer the purpose of the metrics but sometimes have difficulty integrating them as part of their workflow.
- While the LD offers a clear user experience, it lacks the visual appeal and engagement necessary to truly captivate users.
- Most students cite time constraints and inadequate LD training as barriers to regular use, feeling overwhelmed by the prospect of having to learn "yet another tool."

3   LD@Taiga

Based on the LD's feedback, we refined our strategy to achieve the full potential of the LD. Our revised approach centers on two key principles: 1) embedding LD metrics within Taiga, the student teams' project management tool used at UPC, to facilitate a more intuitive and cohesive workflow for student teams; 2) improving the clarity and usability of the metrics' visualizations to facilitate easier interpretation and application.

3.1   Architecture and Implementation

The architecture of LD@Taiga is presented in Fig. 2. Data from *GitHub* and *Taiga* are fed into the *Learning Dashboard* through specialized *Connectors*, which retrieve the required raw data and store it in a structured manner in the *DB repository*. Periodically, the *LD-eval* component evaluates the obtained raw data and computes different metrics related to the project development (e.g. number of commits). The Learning Dashboard provides a RESTful API, named *LD-API*, to get the results. The LD@Taiga extends the *Learning Dashboard* architecture with the *LD@Taiga-back-end* and the *LD@Taiga-Chrome-extension*. The *LD@Taiga-back-end* acts as a bridge between the *LD@Taiga-Chrome-extension* and the *LD-API* whilst storing and managing the required information in the *LD@Taiga-DB,* decoupling it from the core components of the *Learning Dashboard* to facilitate its maintainability. Finally, the *LD@Taiga-Chrome-extension* implements the visualizations embedded within Taiga as a Chrome extension. Further details on the implementation are described in [6].

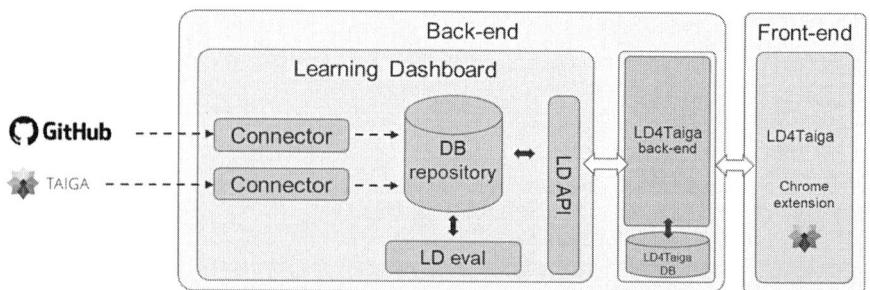

Fig. 2. LD@Taiga Architecture.

The set of metrics evaluated by LD-eval could be configured at the level of the student's team. Table 1 includes the complete set of metrics, and their data sources, configured in the Learning Dashboard for monitoring all teams in the mentioned two courses. In this specific case, the set of metrics is related to the quality of documentation in the project management tool (e.g., acceptance criteria, tasks with Estimated Effort), the quantity of work is assigned to the team members (e.g., tasks), and the quantity of coding (e.g., closed tasks, modified lines). Depending on the process scope, we could have metrics for example related to operations (e.g., number of critical issues/bugs closed).

Table 1. Available metrics in LD@Taiga.

Type	Name	Description	Source
Project	acceptance criteria check	% of user stories that include some acceptance criteria	Taiga
	pattern check	% of user stories following Connextra's template (as a – I want – in order to)	Taiga
	tasks with EE	% of tasks with estimated effort information	Taiga
	closed tasks with AE	% of closed tasks with actual effort information	Taiga
	deviation effort estimation	Deviation in task effort estimation (estimated vs. actual)	Taiga
	unassigned tasks	% of unassigned tasks	Taiga
	tasks sd	Standard deviation of assigned tasks in the team	Taiga
	commits task reference	% of commits that refer to a task id	Taiga GitHub
	commits sd	Standard deviation of commits in the team	GitHub
User	tasks	% of tasks assigned to a specific team member	Taiga
	closed tasks	closed tasks/assigned tasks (per member)	Taiga
	commits	% of commits by a specific member	GitHub
	modified lines	% of modified lines by a specific member	GitHub

Figure 3 shows a partial screenshot of the LD@Taiga integrated into Taiga. Full screenshots are not featured due to space restrictions. On the left, the Taiga platform is displayed. On the right, the LD@Taiga displays a chart related to one concrete project-related metric (closed tasks with AE). LD@Taiga displays the metrics grouped based on whether they pertain to the team (Project Metrics) or to the different members (User Metrics).

The tool provides a filtering feature allowing the visualization of concrete metrics and/or team members. If the visualizations are filtered to see all the metrics for a given team member, the kind of chart used is a spider chart, allowing visualization of all the metrics for the same team member in the same chart (Fig. 4, left). LD@Taiga also includes one option (Metrics Evaluation) to visualize all the user metrics for all the team members in a single spider chart (Fig. 4, right).

3.2 Preliminary Evaluation

LD@Taiga replaced LD in the Fall 2023 term in the same two subjects (WAS and SEP). Again, feedback was collected through online questionnaires and personal interviews

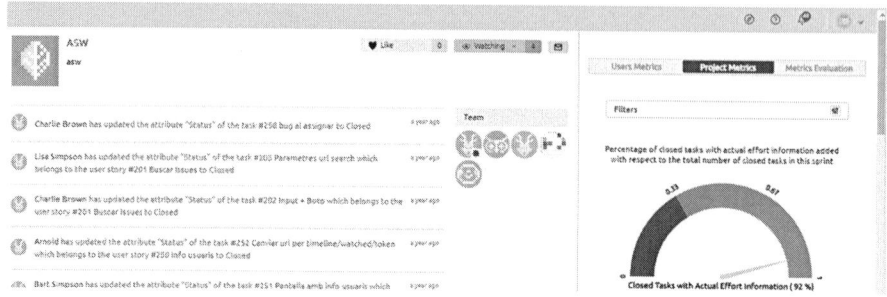

Fig. 3. LD@Taiga visualizations.

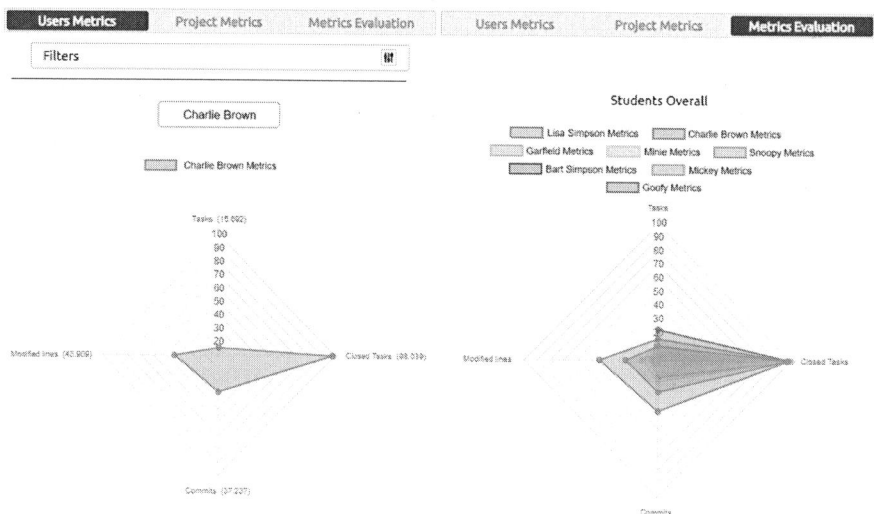

Fig. 4. User metrics visualizations

conducted at the end of the course. This time, questionnaires included 10 questions to analyze the System Usability Scale (SUS), widely applied for assessing usability [7]. The online questionnaires were filled by 10 students from WAS and 22 students from SEP. Personal interviews were conducted subsequently to a subset of 8 students to gather further insights. The feedback is summarized as follows:

- Aggregated SUS scores in WAS and SEP were 64.25 and 61.59, respectively. Considering that scores over 68 (0–100) would be considered above average, the results suggested that, while the acceptance is not bad, there is still significant room for improvement.
- Some students appreciate LD@Taiga's usefulness in tracking large projects and group performance, whereas others view it as a tool to enhance teacher oversight.
- Generally, user metrics (e.g., tasks completed by a developer) are more appreciated than project metrics (e.g., unassigned tasks).

- User experience and usability are generally well-valued, but some issues and feature requests exist. For instance, users complain about having to scroll down to view all metrics, and that some metrics are still hard to understand. Users also want to visualize specific metrics using advanced filters.
- Students reported being overworked and primarily used LD@Taiga for monitoring rather than decision-making.

4   Conclusions and Further Work

By embedding the LD's analytical functionalities within Taiga's versatile project management interface, LD@Taiga aims to improve student engagement, bolster team collaboration and cohesion, and ultimately enhance overall project performance.

Future enhancements of LD@Taiga will focus on refining it based on the early feedback and broadening its functionality. We aim to fine-tune LD@Taiga to address the specific concerns raised in the preliminary evaluation. Additionally, we plan to introduce gamification elements to boost engagement and motivation [8]. Exploring integration with other project management tools, notably Jira, is also on our agenda, although the decision to use Taiga in these courses is out of our control.

Acknowledgements. The Universitat Politècnica de Catalunya funds this project under the call for grants for teaching improvement and innovation projects *Galàxia Aprenentatge 2023*. We sincerely appreciate Gerard Álvarez for implementing LD@Taiga and Adrià Espinola and Albert Miñana for their support in collecting and analyzing students' feedback.

Disclosure of Interests. The authors have no competing interests to declare that are relevant to the content of this article.

References

1. Iacob, C., Daily, S.: Exploring the gap between the student expectations and the reality of teamwork in undergraduate software engineering group projects. J. Syst. Softw. **157**, 110393 (2019)
2. Farré, C., Franch, X., Oriol, M., Volkova, A.: Supporting students in team-based software development projects: an exploratory study. In: RCIS 2023, pp. 568–576 (2023)
3. Verbert, K., et al.: Learning dashboards: an overview and future research opportunities. Pers. Ubiquit. Comput. **18**, 1499–1514 (2014)
4. López, L., et al.: Q-rapids tool prototype: supporting decision-makers in managing quality in rapid software development. In: CAiSE-Forum 2018, pp. 200–208 (2018)
5. Volkova, A.: Specification and design of a dashboard for monitoring the learning process in software projects developed by teams of students. MSc Thesis, Universitat Politècnica de Catalunya (2022). https://upcommons.upc.edu/handle/2117/371383
6. Álvarez, G.: Integració al Taiga d'un sistema per monitoritzar el progrés de Projectes Software d'estudiants. BSc Thesis, Universitat Politècnica de Catalunya (2023). https://upcommons. upc.edu/handle/2117/396284
7. Lewis, J.R.: The System Usability Scale: Past, Present, and Future. Int. J. Hum.–Comput. Interact. **34**(7), 577–590 (2018)

8. Farré, C., López, L., Oriol, M., Espinola, A., Miñana, A., Franch, X.: GLiDE: integrated gamified learning dashboard environment. In: CAiSE Research Projects Exhibition, pp. 34–42 (2024)

XP 25th Anniversary Workshop and Panel Report

XP 25th Anniversary Workshop and Panel Report: Innovating Software Solutions – Past, Present, and Future

Steven D. Fraser[1] and Dennis Mancl[2(✉)]

[1] Innoxec, Santa Clara, CA, USA
sdfraser@acm.org
[2] MSWX Software Experts, Bridgewater, NJ, USA
dmancl@acm.org

Abstract. Software practitioners have adopted many new ways of working over the past 25 years. Change has been driven by a diverse and global community of users, practitioners, researchers, and vernacular programmers. What have we learned over the past 25 years? What skills will software researchers and practitioners need in the future? Will AI or other emerging technologies offer opportunities for greater achievements, or will they become an obstacle to the human touch needed to develop software products? This paper reports on a combined workshop and panel organized and facilitated by Steven Fraser (Innoxec) together with Dennis Mancl (MSWX Software Experts) and Werner Wild (Evolution Consulting). The workshop and panel were part of the 25th Anniversary Track at the XP 2024 conference held in Bolzano, Italy.

Keywords: Software Innovation · Agile · Collaboration

1 Workshop Discussion

More than a dozen participants from Europe and the Americas participated in the workshop. Discussion was structured around software innovation successes, challenges, and the future.

1.1 Successes

The workshop attendees observed improvements in software innovation over the past 25 years. The improvements included the core elements of Agile development practices: automated testing, rapid feedback, accelerated development and delivery at a sustainable pace, plus continuous improvement. Software frameworks and libraries have also made an enormous impact on quality and productivity. The adoption of frameworks combined with software libraries has reduced what Fred Brooks [1] referred to as "accidental complexity." Peopleware [2] issues are now better understood and mitigated – inspiring collaboration through tools and techniques such as pair programming plus new ways of integrating teamwork and customer partnerships into software innovation.

© The Author(s) 2025
L. Marchesi et al. (Eds.): XP 2024 Workshops, LNBIP 524, pp. 251–257, 2025.
https://doi.org/10.1007/978-3-031-72781-8_30

During the workshop discussion, it was noted that the number of *vernacular program-mers* [3] is increasing. These are practical computer users who are not trained/educated as programmers but who craft software to achieve scientific, business, or personal goals. For these developers, "design and coding" is the manipulation of spreadsheets, databases, web authoring systems, or other tools.

1.2   Challenges

The workshop participants brainstormed various challenges associated with past and present software practices. Workshop participants suggested that team members may feel a sense of being overburdened with "busy work" – e.g., meetings or too many Slack channels. Team turnover also creates gaps in "organizational memory." There is a loss of know-how, and companies that rely on "gig economy" models are possibly the worst offenders since staff come and go frequently. In the past, innovation was catalyzed in corporate labs, but today's product innovations are more likely to be sourced from startups. Workshop participants suggested that new communications strategies might help inspire and better spread innovation.

Poor communication creates extra burdens. Teams are confused and can't meet busi-ness goals because of a lack of business awareness. Teams suffer from poor organization and communication gaps due to geography and/or developer-customer relations. Some teams struggle with culture conflicts, while others find that poor collaboration reduces the amount of learning across the team.

"Agile fatigue" seemed to be a common issue. Fatigue may become evident if teams are constantly pushed to adopt the latest tools and practices. Another discussion focused on the extra effort required to manage project iterations when there is a complex and evolving product backlog. Libraries and frameworks help to accelerate development, but when they evolve frequently, rapid change may spawn more disconnects and knowledge gaps.

"Fake Agile" was identified as another challenge. Workshop attendees suggested that some managers may mandate long lists of required tools and practices, even when they are unneeded. However, to be effective, agile development practices need to be customized somewhat for each new project "context." For example, when Scrum Masters and Product Owners are tasked with project management responsibilities, it may reduce their ability to keep their team's development processes lightweight and flexible.

1.3   Plan-Driven Versus Iterative

"Working with business executives" is another challenge faced by development teams. Some leaders choose to give teams more independence, while others prefer to enforce a hierarchical management structure to guide planning and execution. The workshop par-ticipants discussed a troubling trend – development organizations that oscillate between "iterative" and "plan-driven" approaches. It is an understandable dynamic, because each approach has its benefits. Organizations should not be limited to a binary choice of "pure" Agile versus Waterfall development strategies: instead, teams should focus on practices appropriate to specific contexts.

1.4 Addressing Today's Software Product Innovation Challenges

The workshop participants offered observations on future directions for software innovation, but they reached no firm conclusions. The adoption of emergent technologies such as AI or hardware acceleration will likely influence how development practices roles will change as technology evolves. These technologies may reduce the amount of direct human engagement in software design. On the other hand, they may increase the need for humans to focus on testing and configuration management.

To meet today's challenges, software development teams should improve their skills in communication and collaboration: partnering both internally (within their organization) and externally (customers, open-source communities). In today's world, it is important for teams to work with global, virtual, and external open communities. It was also observed that development practices can be truly innovative when they focus on outcomes, not just on the approach or process.

However, collaboration challenges will likely not be solved by the wave of new artificial intelligence tools. AI may miraculously "shrink the work" of developers, but collaboration is a human endeavor.

Dealing with churn and issues of predictability will continue to be a challenge – be it from unstable software libraries, stakeholder interactions, delivery processes, or evolving software practices. In many companies, there is a natural tension between Operations and Development. Ops prefers a stable configuration, and may feel that Dev teams release too frequently. Organizational maturity can reduce churn and improve predictability; education and coaching are also factors. The goal is to build a better business – to enable business stability and growth.

2 Panel Discussion

Panelists included: Alberto Brandolini (an Italy-based IT consultant, the author of *Introducing EventStorming* and the founder of the consulting firm Avanscoperta); Brian Fitzgerald (a software researcher and Principal Investigator at Lero, the Irish Software Research Centre, and a professor at the University of Limerick, where he also served as Vice President Research); Marko Hirsimäki (an Agile Coach at RELEX based in Helsinki, Finland specializing in Agile development and designing applications and architectures), and Diana Larsen (a US based Leadership Agility Advisor and author of *Lead without Blame*; *Agile Retrospectives*; *Liftoff*; and *Five Rules for Accelerated Learning*).

The panel began with a question posed by the workshop: What might follow – ad-hoc, Waterfall, and Agile software development models "post-Agile"?

Brian and Diana observed that Agile software practices emerged as a rebellion against the notion that there was "a single right way to develop software." For most of us in software development roles, software requirements are in flux. Generally, it isn't practical to follow a "rational process."

In his XP2024 keynote, Brian had reinforced this point by referencing the 1985 paper "A Rational Design Process: How and Why to Fake It" [4]. Parnas and Clements explained that developers aspire to design in a rational way: "Most of us like to think of ourselves as rational professionals. However, to many observers, the usual process of designing software appears quite irrational. Programmers often appear to make decisions without having reasons." Their conclusion: "The picture of the software designer deriving his design in a rational, error-free, way from a statement of requirements is quite unrealistic." Projects and teams face process challenges. The paper described the most common knowledge gaps: incomplete and changing requirements, lack of domain experience, complexity, design mistakes, and errors in internal documentation. The authors believed that an "ideal process" is impossible, so they suggested strategies for "faking it."

Diana asserted that we need to constantly update our methods. "The world is changing fast and we need to become learners. We can't just rely on old best practices, old knowledge. We need to be refreshing that all the time."

Marko and Alberto agreed. Marko stated: "My goal is to find better ways to work all the time." Alberto noted that he would frequently change his approach, or he would apply multiple approaches to the same problem. Even though he has a recipe, he tries to solve problems with multiple approaches. "It doesn't work this way, so let's try this other way, and then try this way." But not everyone is so flexible. Alberto complained that some processes aren't staying flexible: "I'm seeing an inertia towards rigidity." He also lamented that Agile suffers from "bad marketing."

The context of software developers today looks a lot different from 25 years ago. Software intensive companies are more focused on cost-cutting and delivering value. Programming languages and tools have evolved considerably since the turn of the century and software practitioners are struggling to keep pace with advances in cloud technology and AI.

Unfortunately, many trainers and coaches reference old and dated principles, practices, tools, and publications that are no longer applicable. Brian called for more flexibility: "All of those [Agile] principles have to be taken in context." Development teams need to use their judgment to decide which parts of their work might require "documents" (for example, to communicate component interface details with third parties). In some cases, a plan-driven approach can work effectively and efficiently because the system's feature set is already known and documented.

Diana explained that many ideas that were incorporated in "Agile" existed for many years prior to 2001 [5]. For example, "customer satisfaction" was part of Total Quality Management of the 1980s. Customer issues will remain important in the future. Diana wanted to know "what will endure" – what are the parts of Agile that will persist beyond the marketing name.

2.1 How to Talk About Agile Principles and Roles Today

The discussion veered in the direction of "how to address the generation gap" between seasoned experts and today's youthful practitioners. One of the audience members, JB Rainsberger, an experienced software consultant from Canada, offered this point of view: "The things that last are either the things we take for granted, or they are the things that we are constantly rediscovering." If we rediscover an idea, it might satisfy a current project need. But shouldn't we have read about this in the literature or learned it in a course?

Learning is hard. We are constantly rediscovering useful ideas and approaches for software development – "because they are important." If young folks are struggling to learn these principles today, we shouldn't be surprised. These ideas were just as difficult 25 years ago for the pioneers of the Agile movement.

JB thought that coaches need to be more positive and supportive. When speaking to today's software teams, rather than "preaching" we should be more engaging. We could say, "We wanted to go back to the arms of Waterfall. We tried it, but it didn't work. You're going to try it, and it probably is not going to work for you either. Welcome to the club! Let's figure out what we can do about that together."

Panel comments suggested that it is time for the younger generation to drive a new software revolution. The next generation should craft the next set of software development principles and practices. It's a mistake to mindlessly adopt dated practices from 25 years ago. Software developers face new development tasks and they are working in new contexts. The panelists explained how new development practices might require new roles, new responsibilities, and different job titles. Role titles can be useful to raise visibility for emerging technologies.

Brian suggested that AI is a new context. "You will have new ceremonies, roles, and artifacts to bring AI into the agile world." Brian said that one obvious role is "training the AI language model." Alberto explained that for today's generative AI systems, "prompt engineer" is an emergent role. (A prompt engineer [6] creates and optimizes the inputs to generative AI systems, possibly with the help of other AI systems.) Alberto suggested that we may also need to remove AI-generated garbage, so "content cleaner" might be another new AI-related role. A content cleaner would clean up the content and code generated by AI.

2.2 Education

Steve (Panel Impresario) asked the audience for their experiences in software education programs to answer the question "how you are educating your students on how to be more innovative," and how to look beyond just coding.

Peggy Gregory from the University of Glasgow made several observations. She explained "Students are still grappling with learning a lot of new technology," and there is considerably more technology than when she was a student. Teaching the development process isn't easy. Glasgow's curriculum requires that most software students participate in a third-year project – working on a team and building systems for real customers. But "learning Agile" is a challenge. "We put them in teams and we give them an Agile coach. But they still behave like students."

"Even after a four-year degree, their real interest is in learning the technology [languages, tools, AI]. They are much less interested in learning all of the other things – things that will become more important to them after they leave, but we can't yet persuade them how important they are."

2.3 AI and Software Development

There were a few comments about AI's potential contributions to software innovation. For example, will AI replace developers?

Brian observed that AI hasn't made it to the undergraduate curriculum yet at the University of Limerick. AI education is mostly directed at graduate students at present. Because we aren't educating average programmers and software engineers in AI, he sees the technology as "a long way from being available." While Brian could see AI as a decision support tool, he wasn't impressed by the software generated by AI.

Diana was concerned that AI might take over her writing: "I want to keep the fun part and have AI do the drudgery part."

2.4 Panel Wrap-Up

Each of the panelists had their own spin on software innovation.

Marko was a forceful advocate for innovation: "I don't want to go back. We need to keep reinventing."

Brian emphasized the need for diversity. We need to expose young people to technology, the experience needs to be fun, with learning from role models.

Diana suggested that new ideas (which may define new roles and career opportunities) will always be emergent. Diana shared own experience in the early 1980s. She decided to connect to the technical world, but not everyone needs to be a coder. Deciding "what software needs to be written" is just as important.

Alberto shared his thoughts about the balance between profitability and sustainability. Alberto viewed profitability as the top goal for many companies. A project might face a choice when building some new features – whether to make the design of that feature more sustainable while reducing the potential profitability. Maybe within the constraint of profitability, we will try to be as sustainable as we can.

3 Summary: Innovating Software Solutions – Past, Present, and Future

Software innovation has evolved greatly over the past 75 years. Advances in technology have improved hardware capabilities in speed, capacity, and connectivity. In parallel, software processes evolved from plan-driven (Waterfall) to those that are more iterative (Agile). Future software innovation must go beyond today's AI and cloud computing frameworks. We must discover new ways for individuals and companies to innovate.

Both the workshop and panel observed that the context for software innovation has changed over the past 25 years. As technologies have evolved, peopleware issues are better understood, and companies are more sensitive to the quarterly drumbeat of the stock market. There was consensus that it is wrong to mindlessly apply dated principles without regard for new contexts and technologies.

"Agile fatigue" and "Fake Agile" are symptoms of a context mismatch between today's reality and some Agile principles based on a "25-year-old Manifesto." In his XP 2021 Keynote talk [7], Steve McConnell argued for updating "Agile" with principles such as continuous testing and limiting work-in-progress. Workshop attendees suggested that "busy work" was becoming more of a problem – and we should look forward to a younger generation of developers and researchers leading a new software technology revolution.

Today's software innovation depends on increased "business awareness" by development teams. Without business awareness, team and company longevity is at risk. Software is now a core part of every system, and more systems have customer-visible requirements, such as security, safety, and responsiveness.

University curriculums are evolving in response to both student interest and company talent needs. Our universities need to be prepared to teach both new technologies (AI, data science tools, vernacular programmer tools) and new post-Agile software development processes. Global innovation accelerates when relevant software practices can be taught and learnt with less effort.

While there were no absolute predictions for the future, both the workshop and panel observed that people issues are critical to software innovation, possibly more important than AI.

References

1. Brooks, F.P.: No silver bullet – essence and accident in software engineering. Computer **20**(4), 10–19 (1987). https://doi.org/10.1109/MC.1987.1663532
2. DeMarco, T., Lister, T.: Peopleware: Productive Projects and Teams, 3rd edn. Addison Wesley, Boston MA (2016)
3. Shaw, M.: Myths and misconceptions: what does it mean to be a programming language, anyhow? Proc. ACM Program. Lang. **4**(HOPL), 234–277 (2020). https://doi.org/10.1145/348 0947
4. Parnas, D.L., Clements, P.C.: A rational design process: how and why to fake it. In: Ehrig, H., Floyd, C., Nivat, M., Thatcher, J. (eds.) Formal Methods and Software Development. TAPSOFT 1985. Lecture Notes in Computer Science, vol. 186. Springer, Berlin, Heidelberg (1985). https://doi.org/10.1007/3-540-15199-0_6
5. Larman, C., Basili, V.R.: Iterative and incremental development: a brief history. Computer **36**(6), 47–56 (2003). https://doi.org/10.1109/MC.2003.1204375
6. Genkina, D.: Don't start a career as an AI prompt engineer. IEEE Spectr. **61**(5), 30–34 (2024). https://doi.org/10.1109/MSPEC.2024.10523015
7. McConnell, S.: 20 Years is enough! It's time to update the agile principles and values. In: XP 2021 Conference (2021). https://www.agilealliance.org/resources/sessions/20-years-is-eno ugh-its-time-to-update-the-agile-principles-and-values/. Accessed on 21 July 2024

Author Index

A

Abrahamsson, Pekka 15
Ahmad, Aakash 15
Algulin, Åsa 223
Alliata, Zorina 110
Alsadeh, Ahmad 196
Awan, Wardah Naeem 53

B

Bala, Saimir 103
Bangshøj, Carolina Appel 223
Barbala, Astri Moksnes 33
Barbala, Astri 90, 123
Berntzen, Marthe 90
Bozagiu, Andreea-Madalina 110
Bühne, Stan 236

C

Chatzipetrou, Panagiota 63
Ciolkowski, Marcus 229
Conboy, Kieran 33
Correia, Filipe F. 130

D

Diebold, Philipp 216, 229
Dillon, Clare 181
Duc, Anh Nguyen 15

E

Emmerhoff, Jostein 33

F

Farré, Carles 242
Filipovic, Marina 141
Floryan, Marcin 33
Forrer, Thomas 189
Franch, Xavier 236, 242
Fraser, Steven D. 251

G

Gilson, Fabian 141
Griva, Anastasia 33

Guerra, Eduardo Martins 130
Gundelsby, Jan Henrik 33

H

Haase, Jennifer 103
Hanssen, Geir Kjetil 83
Havstorm, Tanja Elina 223
Helland, Per Kristian 63

J

Jaatun, Martin Gilje 83
Jaber, Mariam 196
Janes, Andrea 229

K

Karakra, Abdallah 196
Kemell, Kai-Kristian 15
Klotins, Eriks 63

L

Lenarduzzi, Valentina 229
López, Lidia 236, 242
Lund, Camilla Kielland 150

M

Mancl, Dennis 251
Maranhão Junior, João José 130
Marek, Krzysztof 203
Martyniuk-Sienkiewicz, Kamila 203
Melegati, Jorge 24
Mendling, Jan 103
Mock, Moritz 24, 189
Moe, Nils Brede 33, 63, 71, 90

N

Neumann, Michael 216

O

Oriol, Marc 242

P

Perlak, Jakub 169, 209

© The Editor(s) (if applicable) and The Author(s) 2025
L. Marchesi et al. (Eds.): XP 2024 Workshops, LNBIP 524, pp. 259–260, 2025.
https://doi.org/10.1007/978-3-031-72781-8

R
Rasheed, Zeeshan 15
Ribeiro, J. Eduardo Ferreira   161
Rico, Sergio   3
Russo, Barbara   24, 189

S
Sæter, Gyda Elisa   150
Sahling, Kristina   103
Salman, Iflaah   53
Sami, Malik Abdul   15
Semsøy, Susanne   71
Simaremare, Mario   3
Singhal, Tanvi   110
Smite, Darja   63
Steffe, Hans-Jörg   236

Stray, Viktoria   71, 123, 150
Sturm, Stefan   236
Systä, Kari   15

T
Taweel, Adel   196
Tkalich, Anastasiia   63
Triando,   3, 175

U
Ulfsnes, Rasmus   33, 42

W
Waseem, Muhammad   15
Wivestad, Viggo Tellefsen   42, 123